From the Depths of Hell
I Saw Jesus on the Cross

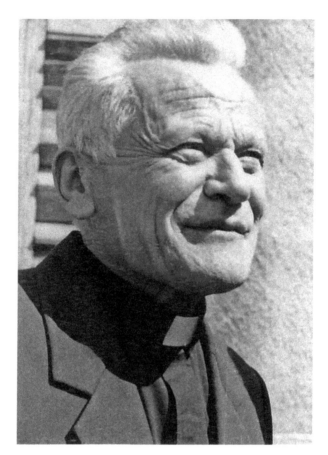

DOM SIMON JUBANI
March 8, 1927–July 12, 2011

DOM SIMON JUBANI

From the Depths of Hell I Saw Jesus on the Cross
A PRIEST IN THE PRISONS OF COMMUNIST ALBANIA

Presentation by
MGR ANGELO MASSAFRA
Metropolitan Archbishop of Shkodër-Pult
Translated from the French by
JOSEPH BAMBERG

AROUCA
PRESS

TABLE OF CONTENTS

PRESENTATION AND ENDORSEMENT

The dissemination of Dom Simon Jubani's testimony of faith, who was a priest in our Archdiocese during his lifetime, offers everyone with good will the possibility to discover or better know the terrible experience under Enver Hoxha's communist dictatorship in Albania. Through the eyes of this priest, who was one of the most affirmed and well-known figures in our country and overseas, the reader will thoroughly understand what these years meant for our country.

But this book is also an occasion to read between the lines of history for the signs of a presence—that of God—who knows how to make good out of the evil that humans commit. Only the eyes of faith allow such a reading of this book.

Dom Simon Jubani was one of many silent guardians of the faith during his 26 years in Albanian communist prisons, where he was sent for the sole reason that he was a priest. He also helped to revive robust religious practices in our country after the dictator's death, even though the climate of terror and fear was still quite strong.

On the thirtieth anniversary of the public return of the practice of the faith with Dom Simon's courageous celebration of the first public Mass at Shkodër on November 4, 1990, after twenty-three years of State-based atheism, it is a joy for me to see this witness published in French.

This result is due to the perseverance and tenacity of our friend Dominique Combette, who personally knew Dom Simon Jubani, greatly helped to travel with him around the world to spread his message and to receive aid for the reconstruction of the churches of his parishes. Our friend Dominique also worked so hard to search and find a translator and an editor.

I sincerely hope that this publication will touch the souls and consciences of the greatest number of people possible so that history does not repeat the atrocities committed in Albania during the dictatorship.

Liberty is fragile and is not acquired once and for all. It is therefore up to each of us to defend it against all fanatical movements and ideologies that search to destroy it.

＋ Angelo Massafra OFM
Metropolitan Archbishop of Shkodër-Pult
Shkodër
September 19, 2020

MOTIVATION TO READ THIS BOOK

The great merit of this very lively work is that it was written not by a journalist or an outside personality who knew Dom Simon Jubani, but by the victim himself. There is no other book of this quality on the subject.

Albania is a country little known abroad. Under the communist regime, it was forbidden to go there except in the framework of agreements and official exchanges between the Governments.

Of all the countries of Eastern Europe that have lived under the Communist yoke, this is the one where the persecution against the Catholic Church has been the most violent. It was led by Enver Hoxha, a brutal and bloodthirsty dictator trained in French universities. Albania was declared the world's first atheist State in 1967. All the churches were destroyed.

In this book, Dom Simon Jubani recounts his life and twenty-six years spent in the communist prisons of Albania. He suffered so many acts of torture that he lost all his teeth. He heroically celebrated the first public Mass in Albania on November 4, 1990, which heralded the fall of the dictatorship the following year.

Dom Simon Jubani was the most famous Albanian priest of his time, both at home and abroad. He was persecuted and thrown into prison under the communist Albanian regime for having celebrated baptisms.

This is what Dom Simon Jubani said in his conferences around the world after he was released in 1990:

> The churches were razed, the clergy slaughtered. As for me, they did not kill me, but wanted to destroy me slowly. I served 26 years in prison; I lived by the miracle of daily prayer to Mary.
>
> Barely out of prison, people came to ask me to celebrate the first public Mass. It was still red terror. The police wanted to shoot me, but seized by the peaceful nature of the crowd, they did not shoot. God conquered and liberated, by my priestly hands, the country from dictatorship.
>
> Today I must continue to carry my heavy cross. I have five parishes, located in the most difficult to reach mountainous areas. I must celebrate Mass in the rain, in dirty cellars, or

on the stairs of ruined buildings. I administer the sacraments, train authentic Christians and gradually undertake the reconstruction of my churches. The Catholic Church attracts because it is the only organized force which defends the people. Conversions from Islam are frequent: it is the first country of the Muslim tradition which begins to convert.

Dominique Combette

ENDORSEMENT FOR THE
ALBANIAN EDITION

This work by Dom Simon Jubani will enrich the authentic bibliography that concerns the tragic period that, in Albanian history, can be compared to Nero's reign. One is reminded of Silvio Pellico's book, *La Noix à la Coque Dure* (Nut with a Hard Shell) which caused more damage to Austria-Hungary than the enemy's army did during the war. If read attentively, Dom Simon's work will produce the same effect. It will prompt older people to think that we need to pardon the criminals without, however, forgetting the crimes. The author, like all priests, knows that forgiveness is impossible when it is accompanied with silence about the responsibility for crimes. Pity should never again be an encouragement for pursuing injustice. Dom Simon's bitter experience serves as a warning to younger readers to tread carefully when dealing with the wolf that changes his coat but not his vice. After reading this book, young and old alike will better understand Enver Hoxha's communism and modern communism in general.

Faced with the current chaos, Dom Simon, who did not accept any compromise when he was in handcuffs, will not accept compromise today. He cannot stay silent. In the words of the prophet's psalm: "I announced the Lord's justice in the great assembly. Behold, I will not close my lips, as you well know" (Ps. 40:10). Dom Simon expresses himself with great courage like he did in prison. To Albania, he dares denounce all the abuses that he witnessed.

Father Daniel Gjeçaj
Shkodër, 2001

Presentation of Albania and of Dom Simon Jubani

A lbania is a very ancient Christian country. It was evangelized by St. Paul in the first decades of the Church. Later, towards the end of the Middle Ages, the Ottoman Turks invaded through the South. Christians were hunted down and forced to leave their ancestral lands for the North. All of Albania except the North became Islamic. Christians could either leave or die. Yet one branch of Catholics found refuge in the Northern mountains, where, in hiding, they kept alive the Catholic faith until today. Albanian Catholics, therefore, have the spirit of resistance. The other branch of Catholic Albanians crossed the Adriatic out of fear of repression and founded Albanian colonies in the South of Italy—Calabria and Puglia—where they have survived until now. As a result, before the arrival of communism after the Second World War, Albania was 70% Muslim (mostly in the center), 20% Orthodox Christian (mostly in the south), and 10% Catholic (mostly in the north).

Among Eastern European countries forced to live under the communist yoke after 1945, Albania experienced *the most direct and violent attacks* on religion. The red dictator, Enver Hoxha (pronounced "Hodja"), was educated in French schools and then at the University of Montpellier. While in France, he was strongly influenced by the radically anti-religious ideas of the French Revolution. He later imprisoned or massacred all of Albania's clergy. In 1967, unhappy that he had failed to eradicate religion, which remained in the hearts of Albanians, and on the recommendation of his Chinese counsellors, Hoxha proclaimed Albania the world's first atheistic State. Religion was totally banned, ecclesiastical organizations suppressed, and churches and mosques destroyed. While all religions were victims of oppression in Albania, the Catholic Church faced the most violent persecutions because it produced the country's intellectual elite. Enver became the new religion, the new divinity on earth, for many. Some believed he was immortal, which caused quite a shock the day he died.

In order to prevent the development of any organization capable of fomenting a counter-revolution either rising from the people or from the intelligentsia, personal cars were also forbidden. Albania was the only Eastern-bloc country to have taken this step. Allowed to fall into disrepair, roads were full of holes during the dictatorship's forty-five years. The old road between Tirana and Shkodër, still in a state of disrepair today, is a "museum." This has restricted Albanians to horses or bicycles.

Among all the imprisoned priests, Dom Simon Jubani was the most well-known overseas. I discovered his will and fearless temperament through articles published about him and through the small book *Albania, Where They Wanted to Kill God* by deacon Didier Rance. This book provoked a strong desire in me to get to know Dom Simon, but communist Albania was closed to almost all foreigners. As I was interested in the architecture of ancient churches, I wrote a report on the dozen ancient Byzantine churches that had not been destroyed. I presented it at the Albanian embassy in France and was selected for a bursary to visit the country in 1986 as part of an exchange of the two Ministries of Foreign Affairs. This was during the time of Hoxha's successor, Ramiz Alia, immediately after the death of Hoxha the dictator. However, staying at the *Dajti Hotel* in Tirana, which was reserved for foreign officials and was under constant camera surveillance, I was not free. I was always accompanied by two Communist Party members who were my chauffeur and guide. This guide would pick me up in the morning and drop me off in the evening. I was even forced to lay a wreath at the tomb of Enver Hoxha. I was not able to visit the North of the country. Due to its rebellious nature, it was closed to foreigners.

The dictatorship fell in 1991. In 1992, when the Albanian State had become practically non-existent, I went to Shkodër (the large Northern city, called also "Shkodra" by the Albanians and "Scutari" by the Italians) for the first time with a car I had rented at Igoumenitsa, Greece. I twice traversed the entirety of Albania from the South to the North and the North to the South without seeing any other cars because they were still banned. I shared the road with the very rare Chinese truck on its last legs. Poor quality gasoline bought in Albania rattled the car's engine. Enthusiastically singing, I drove along the pot-holed road. The road was surrounded by ancient bunkers built by the old dictator Enver, whose name was written in giant letters on mountain peaks. The whole time, I was connected to God through prayer. As I drove, I feared the mechanical or suspension failure of my small car because I had undertaken this risky journey during which I would not meet anyone who could help me.

Finally arriving at Shkodër, I easily located Dom Simon's house because everyone knew him. When I told him that I had come from his much-beloved France specially to meet him, he immediately opened his door, curious about this courageous person. He had been released from prison three years previous, in April, 1989. He knew many people but trusted very few. Little by little, I grew on him and became his great French friend and confidant. He was passionate for the truth and uncompromising. Such a lively and tough nature had helped him endure the twenty-six long years that had worn him down in Albania's communist prisons. This highly intelligent though impatient man had a great heart. He was always provocative and justice-seeking. Forever rebellious against every authority, he did not know how to obey or listen, even though he loved his audience to listen and not contradict him. His sometimes biting words were always passionate. He loved the apostolate of adventure and risk. He would drive up a mountain's rocky torrential riverbed in his Toyota 4x4 to reach his parishes in the mountains in the Mirditë region. These parishes were otherwise inaccessible even via hiking trails.

Later, Dom Simon came to France and I returned to Shkodër many times to visit him. I always went with him on his apostolate of adventure. That helped us get to know each other well. This apostolate was very demanding. Once we had arrived in a valley, the children would spot the Toyota 4x4 and run to greet him and to receive small Bibles and a blessing. Everywhere he went, he expressed his love for his flock, who deeply loved him in return. His greatest chagrin was the arrival of non-Albanian missionaries to the mountain parishes from far-away countries such as Argentina. They came in order to take over from him but they did not know his tragic history or the persecution of the Albanian Church.

In this book, Dom Simon recounts how he survived twenty-six terrible years in prison in communist Albania merely for baptizing parishioners. For one thing, God gave him an athletic build. Moreover, having always dreamed of becoming a monk, his prison became like a monastery of prayer. He recalled his first public Mass after his prison release on November 4, 1990, which took place during the communist period. The Mass venue, a little cemetery chapel, was filled with spies who could have killed him at any moment. Dom Simon's courage reassured the fears of many faithful. This historic Mass was the precise point of departure for all the freedoms that Albania received henceforth. In this sense, Dom Simon is a heroic witness of Jesus in two ways. He is the man of the prisons and also the man chosen by God to give freedom to this country. Nonetheless, at the book's end, Dom Simon gives a caustic yet true remark on the changes that took place in the old European communist bloc after 1989, including in Albania.

As soon as Dom Simon and I crossed paths, we felt so much mutual love for one another. For me, he was the image of one of the most courageous heroes of the faith. This love for him sparked compassion and then the desire to act. To set up a support network for this confessor of the Faith, I first had a small interview with him published in a local journal. I next spoke of his case on the radio in France and in some countries abroad. At his request, I accompanied him on many of his missionary adventures around the world, which I organized. The objective was to spread his message and obtain resources for the reconstruction of his parish churches. This fit into my own life, a large part of which was dedicated to supporting the martyred clergy in East European countries. Out of admiration and love, I also followed St. John Paul II to forty-two countries, from Guatemala to India, including East European countries, those of the Caucasus, and the Islamic countries of the Middle East.

Dom Simon's homilies or conferences often began in this way: "Excuse me, I cannot enunciate very well. They broke all my teeth." As a marvelous orator, he very quickly caught his audience's attention. He was a very effective teacher who, like Jesus, used parables to allow his listeners to retain the most important elements of his talks.

Sometimes communication between us and the audience was difficult because of language issues. In Russia, Dom Simon gave testimony on a parish's radio and held conferences in an auditorium, often attended by students who did not know anything about religion, not even the Our Father. But we always succeeded at getting them to understand. Dom Simon had well deserved to meet good Samaritans on his way.

Dom Simon loved to teach us that the communist terror in Albania was the cruellest of the twentieth century after that of Pol Pot in Cambodia. Yet if this book describes firstly the lies, inhumanity, brutality, and savagery of the communist terror in Albania, it is also a vibrant and powerful witness to the power of regular prayer. It is also a praise to the Church, the Body of Christ. Even if people sometimes try to ignore its message, the Church nonetheless preaches only peace and concord between men using the language of the Truth. Nowadays, the Truth disturbs.

In his conferences, Dom Simon often reminds us that the Church is as solid as a rock and indestructible. He often provides the example of a metal cup. When you drop it, it does not break. He reminds us that the Church is unbreakable like this cup because it has a divine and not human foundation; it is the only structure that has existed since the beginning of time; it was, is, and will be until the end of the world and in the next; on the other hand, all of the organizations founded by humans will in the end disappear from the world. This includes false religions, such as sects.

Dom Simon also loved to talk of television and its frequently destructive power. If it is not used advisedly, it can be devastating. TV harms communication between parents and children. Television does not inform, but spreads propaganda. It forms and conditions its audience members to unconsciously structure their thinking in the cause of the dominant interest, which is often antichristian, perverted, and destructive. Many programs are diabolical. Dom Simon said that television is nothing else but "a mirror to see the devil in color!" In effect, it can be education from the devil.

After twenty-six years of prison, which sometimes led Dom Simon to the verge of depression, what was the source of this exceptional priest's ferocious energy that later allowed him to go on exhausting global tours to spread his testimony, if not God? Dom Simon was a true man of God and of the Cross. Through him, all those he met could see Jesus on the Cross. Dom Simon confirmed my faith and love for the Church. No one will find perfection in this world because it exists only in the next world. We must look to Jesus, not to other people. In this sense *this book is not a page of history, but its message is and will remain current.*

At a time when Western countries, particularly France, face tremendous risk of leaning towards fundamentalist Islam or other forms of modern dictatorship, this book has the merit of showing us what might be awaiting us since the persecutory methods used by communist or Islamic totalitarian regimes are the same.

This book also shows that atheism and the rejection of God are Western concepts, fruits of an ideology that according to reason should not exist. Religion is a natural thing; it is even required in certain countries. Living and proclaiming the rejection of belief in our creator is anachronistic. We should unceasingly seek whatever in this world can connect us to God. And to do that every day we need to create an inner silence and reject the world's noise in order to listen to the Father, who guides us and shows us the path to true happiness. He only comes to us in silence, not in perpetual agitation. The Lord said to us: "Withdraw into your inner chamber in order to pray" and "I am the Way, the Truth, and the Life."

Through the extraordinarily profound witness to faith, I hope that this book attracts many readers, especially the young, and allows them to triumph over their fears and stand up to defend the Church each time it is unjustly attacked.

I also hope that reading this work will give everyone the opportunity to meet Jesus on the Cross and to desire to follow Him. I hope that each reader can contribute to rebuilding the unity of families and, through this, open the way to many priestly vocations, which are a dire need in Western countries. If families strengthen themselves through prayer, Western society will heal and priestly vocations will flourish once again.

Finally, my wish is that this exceptional testimony can strengthen the faith of both the sick and prisoners and give them courage and consolation. I hope the author can give divine value to any kind of suffering.

Dom Simon's interior strength came from his daily prayers to the Virgin Mary. He prayed a lot, sometimes several times a day. Prayer is the only way to eliminate the evil that, permanently living in us, tempts and attacks us. Remember that Mary is always depicted with a serpent at her feet, for she is the only human to have received from God the power to smash this reptile. The more someone wishes to be a saint, the more necessary it is to have recourse to regular prayer to Mary.

Some will undoubtedly see this book as *training for personal spiritual battle*. This is the aspect of Dom Simon's message that is most relevant for today. In the past, we witnessed evil in atheist communism, especially in Albania, but today we see it everywhere in other but equally barbarous, aggressive, and dangerous forms. Influential individuals try to create a "new man" — savage and soulless, without family or spiritual roots. This new man exists independently of everything that made up his history. It is only thanks to the sacrifices of countless authentic witnesses to the faith in Albania, individuals who gave their lives for the kingdom of God, that the country is experiencing a period of freedom today.

Dom Simon passed to the Father on July 12, 2011. He rests in peace in Albania with other persecuted priests in the chapel of the cemetery of Shkodër, where he celebrated his first historic Mass. His brother Dom Lazër, who was poisoned to death, lies in the cemetery outside the chapel with the rest of the family. When Dom Simon died, no one in Albania told me, not even his family or chauffeur. That is how people are regarded in Albania. I do not doubt Dom Simon's feelings for me, as he often expressed these. Nor do I doubt how the Lord himself regards me, as I enthusiastically served Him through Dom Simon. In any case, a person advances along the path of his vocation, and the Lord provides.

Thank you, Dom Simon, for your holy witness to the Faith. Thank you for your life, which you offered and gave in service to the Church. Without you, without priests, the faithful would have no access to the sacraments, which offer us entrance to eternal life. Thank you for your exemplary witness to suffering, including your own, which lasted twenty-six years. You are not far away, up in Heaven. You remain close to us through strong memories and by your teaching. Stay with us and guide us towards what the Lord expects of us.

Versailles, May 13, 2020, on the 103rd anniversary of the first apparitions of Mary at Fatima and in thanksgiving to my patron Saint Dominic.

Dominique Combette

FOREWORD TO THE ALBANIAN EDITION

This book was inspired by a sentiment of rebellion, but also responsibility. It aims for a more objective analysis of the events that took place between 1990 and 2000 in Albania. Those events did nothing but worsen misery, wipe out hope, and suffocate dreams.

When Dom Simon sent me his manuscript, I thought it would simply be a last reading, one that I had promised him for a long time. Focused on my work, I forgot it in a corner until one day I finally decided to open it. Like a collection of pearls, a series of impressions of an extraordinary life lay before me, a memory of someone who had undergone the terrible ordeal of more than thirty years of torture. In these pages, I could see the prison cells, the judges' offices, the torture chambers, the concentration camps, former assemblies all over the world, halls of senators and congressmen, emigration destinations to Europe, America, and Asia, images of heroes, heads of criminals, confessions, meditations, moments of indescribable anger and of joy, tremendous highs that reached ecstasy but also lows. This all came from the perspective of an altar where Dom Simon celebrated his first public Mass after fifty years of persecutions. He had come all the way from the terror of death to the light of liberty, from complete isolation to crisscrossing the world from Japan to the United States. He showed his friends and enemies that Albania is the Golgotha of modern times, the place where Jesus was crucified again and is once again resurrected on the third day.

The book refreshed some of my own most lasting memories. I was not present at the first Mass on November 4, 1990. No one knew who would come, and the Mass was celebrated unplanned and unannounced. I also missed the second Mass seven days later because of a funeral obligation in Tirana. Without that obligation, I would have reflected deeply about whether to go to this Mass or not; at that time, life and death were so close to each other as to make the boundary almost nonexistent. To put it plainly, we had the impression that, in the old cemetery, with its broken crosses, death had made its reappearance through the thousands of tombs that gaped open. We feared being on the receiving end of bloody violence.

At least that is what we Catholics thought. We had always lived in blind terror of blood, between suffering and the cross. I remember the first few days of the return of Jesus and the panic of the entire people, men and women who had bathed in the tears of the perfidy regarding their Creator. Then, I recalled the blessed Christmas midnight of 1990, when thousands of people, standing very close together, warmed up the cold river and obliged the icy north wind to sing a softer song. I had left the house early in the morning in order to find a place as close as possible to the altar, close to my Lord, who had come back to us. I had set the table at home and had promised myself not to close my eyes throughout this long-awaited night. The face of the priest is fixed in my memory, which burns with inspiration. His words are engraved in my memory. They poured out without embarrassment. They astonished all the believers who knew that this priest normally stammered a little. "Do you need a miracle in order to believe? Look, therefore, the miracle is in front of you. Such a night, with Jesus, is it not a miracle? Such a night, with these cypress trees that have turned into Christmas trees. He who, like in the time of the first Christians, was born from the piles of bones in order to give us back life?"

I always remember the moment of the elevation of the Blessed Sacrament. When Dom Simon held the host high, we believers in the crowd went on our knees, as called for by such a solemn act. We were on half-broken plaster and risked falling into the holes of the tombs or in narrow spaces between the tombs. We knelt on little paths that were covered over in the icy mud of November. We were pushed against the cypress and cynara. The only ones left standing were the representatives of the Democratic Party, who had come to make us believe that they too followed Jesus now that He had descended from the Cross and was at the right hand of the Father, from where he would judge the living and the dead. They looked around, stupefied, in front and back of themselves, unable to understand what was happening. When they realized that they were the only ones standing, sticking up like leeks, they felt that they had to get down on their two knees like all the other children of God. At the end of the day, it is better to kneel before God than before an executioner. And in this respect, their knees were not without experience.

As I turned the pages of Dom Simon's biography, I was chagrined by the thought that nowadays history and the truth switch places like night and day; the deformed switches places with the good. This is because the facts continue to be examined from an ideological point of view, projected onto an ideal or, even worse, come from strictly personal points of view. In such an atmosphere, a prophet becomes undesirable and harmful. Then long live cicuta! Did not the Greeks do the same thing with Socrates when their democracy degenerated into demagoguery, atheism, and sophistry? Did not they chase away their greatest thinkers because of the danger to their god, Democracy? Did not they switch around all of the most illustrious people by considering heroes as murderers and murderers as gods? That was in their interest. It is exactly the same today in Albania! Moreover, we are not the first and will not be the last to distort history. Among the millions of pages written on rocks, bricks, tiles, papyrus, parchment, metal, and paper, the truth is rarely mentioned. This is even more true of Albanian writings. There are those who believe in portraying a better image of a dignified Albania to the world. They forget that foreigners are not dopeheads. As for the Albanians, they already tried all the narcotics dispensed by the socialists.

But to return to the main point: I continued to page through the collection of pearls, like one handles rosary beads: white, yellowing, light red, and green pages, new and old pages, pages written on a computer, with a typewriter, or by hand. The pages were multicolored, like the author. I finally came upon the guiding principle that could provide a focus. From reading the first lines, I understood that these reflections came from a powerful force of resistance and from the idea that a person must have the courage to show to these poor people the naked truth, the truth of yesterday, of today, and of that expected in the future. I ended up buried in these pages. They flew past, though the book still had no definite form. I forgot about all my other work and consecrated my whole self to Dom Simon's pearls. I was firmly convinced that Albania was in need of just such bold individuals, who were called idealists and patriots by their sympathizers but fools by their enemies.

The book was made ready without any cost. But when the time came to have it published, we noticed once again that, in Albania, the truth is scathing and that censorship is still a word with meaning. In order to get the book printed, Dom Simon had to start his travels again, like he had done in order to rebuild the churches in the Mirditë region. It goes without saying that he did not ask for support from political parties nor from certain social groups or classes who believe that the pen and the freedom to think can be sold for money or a new armchair. Far from feeling the temptation to compromise, the author succeeded at preserving his work from all sorts of violations and remained its master by getting it into the hands of readers just as he wanted it: As a key for reading Albanian life.

But who will read this book? The author knows very well that this book will be read with great interest by his companions in suffering, those with whom he shared prison cells and deportation camps. This work will be read by all those who feel deceived, denigrated, and ignored by pseudo-democracy and its actors. It will be read by those who want to know the truth about today and tomorrow.

Dom Simon also knows very well who wants to attack him. He will be attacked by those who do not want to see their back-room games brought to daylight, by those who wish to put old criminals on heroes' pedestals, and by former criminals who have turned against each other. They are power-hungry and seek to promote the psychosis that communism is not a criminal ideology, but that it was applied in a criminal manner because it had been put in place by criminals who are already dead. As for the living, ...

The author recognizes all the wounds of the system in which he lived. He does not hesitate to show Albanians that they can either return to the concentration camps where they were or shake off their apathy and free themselves from the psychosis of isolation and take their destiny in their own hands without waiting for the exterior world to come in aid. Throughout history, we have only experienced death from the rest of the world in a thousand ways, from a thousand hands, in a thousand languages.

The author rebels, condemns, and denies. But his rebellion, condemnation, and denial are not enough. Albanians need confession and faith-related propositions. A priest refuses to tell the people that they should complain at the doors of the powerful and that they should beg for alms, as they turn first to eastern culture and then to western. The priest teaches them to knock on the door of heaven, to ask for help from the Lord of Life, who holds in his power the destiny of the powerful and the small. The man, Dom Simon, who triumphed over persecution with the force of He who triumphed over death, with firm conviction and without any hesitation, proposes a civilization that has justified itself for over two thousand years: Christian civilization, the civilization of Love and Life, of Truth and

Justice. "Where must I go, Lord, You who alone have the words of eternal Life?" It is with this affirmation that the author closes his book, a book that is written and published for Albania, and not only for the city of Shkodër. But it was this city that was always the citadel of liberty.

I did nothing other than contemplate a collection of pearls written in lines. I hope that these pearls enrich the poor treasure of contemporary Albanian literature with a book that reveals the simple truth.

Ana Luka
Former contributor to the Albania program of *Vatican News*[1]
Shkodër, August 2001

---

[1] *Vatican News* is the new name of Vatican Radio.

TRANSLATOR'S FOREWORD

Dom Simon Jubani wrote like he seemed to live: from his heart with uncompromising truth. As he repeatedly confesses in this book, he could not help but say what was on his mind, regardless of the consequences. He spoke and lived the truth. Unsurprisingly, *From the Depths of Hell I saw Jesus on the Cross* is filled with outrage, confusion, and relief. His mind worked furiously to put into words his outrage at the Communist crimes he witnessed. Yet his humility and simple service to the truth also leads him to admit confusion. He never claims to fully understand the evil he witnessed, even with his keen sense of history. His relief would come when, on one occasion or another, his or the Catholic laity's suffering would abruptly and inexplicably come to an end, though for how long no one could know.

Such an emotionally charged book presents certain challenges to a translator. How can a translator remain faithful to the irony, humor, depression, resignation, and Christian hope that this most faithful priest and son of the Church conveys? How can one faithfully translate the layers of very nuanced observations that support these emotions? Perhaps on account of this emotional experience, Dom Simon's writing style was not disciplined. He sometimes wrote in long, even flowery phrases full of descriptions with overused or repeated adjectives. Long, meandering paragraphs, sometimes pages long, described the sights, sounds, and smells of prison, his fellow cellmates, the small things — bad breath, body odor, boring and juvenile conversations — as well as the larger, more grim things — hunger, beatings, the isolation cell, murdered prisoners. Then the narrative might switch to short sentence fragments filled with the author's justifiable bursts of anger and sense of injustice and sin. He was perhaps more of a poet than a prose writer in this descriptive immediacy. The chief difficulty as a translator from the French text, itself a translation from the Albanian, was in smoothing out so many ungrammatical expressions and run-on sentences that express not only sadness and solidarity with the Albanian people and gratitude for his foreign supporters, but also rage at the Communists and indifferent Western Governments.

It was a privilege to translate this book. Dom Simon Jubani deserves to be read because he survived the worst that the Communists were able to throw at him short of execution. He survived with his integrity, personality, sense of humor, and faith all intact. He perfectly followed Alexander Solzhenitsyn's command, *live not by lies*. His book testifies to the absurd lengths that the purveyors of lies will go to in their attempt to terrorize and root out those who speak and embody the truth. His book testifies to the spiritual battles faced by many in the twentieth and twenty-first centuries. Dom Simon's religion was not therapeutic and feel-good, but virtuous, heroic, truthful, and masculine, which is to say, the best of Christianity.

Joseph Bamberg

I

Autobiography

I was born in Shkodër on March 5, 1927. My parents, Zef and Çile, both pious Catholics, offered to the Church and the country an intellectual martyr, Dom Lazër Jubani, my brother. He was poisoned with arsenic by the communist police in 1982. At the age of sixteen, called by the Lord, I entered Catholic school in order to become a Jesuit. In March, 1946, the Albanian communists, fearing the rapid loss of power, suppressed, sequestered, or destroyed all the traditional Catholic schools. Those schools taught the entire nation to read and write. I was forced to go to another school, a public lyceum, where I did not really want to be, where students still learn today that a human is a monkey without fur. After that I was transferred to Tirana to take a radiology course.

After having worked at a military hospital in the capital for a while, I was mobilized into the army. Though I wanted so strongly to become a Jesuit, a missionary, and a preacher for the peace of the Gospel, I had to put on a green army uniform, carry a weapon which killed, and go to the country's Southern frontier. I survived civil conflict in Greece where, in 1949, I was put alongside the others, like a herd of sheep, on the first line, to fight with the communists of General Marcos face-to-face against the Athens-based coalition. After suffering in the army for three years, which I remember being as difficult as prison, I returned to the city of Shkodër, where, without losing any more time, I went to see Monsignor Ernest Çoba. I begged him to ordain me a priest. The bishop, a saint and, later, a martyr, counseled me to wait. I had to go back to square one in terms of earning a living by returning to working as a radiologist at the sanatorium in Shkodër. To keep fit, I did the sports that I really loved, calisthenics and football. I quickly made the Vllaznia football team and then the national team, whose coach was the corpulent Soviet Boris Aputin. The salary was 33,000 leks a month, at a time when the best-paid Government workers in Albania made, at most, barely 3000 leks.

Ordained in 1957–58, I was sent to exercise my apostolate in the region of Mirditë. I defended religion and churches that were menaced by atheism. Always "a nut with a hard shell," I devoted myself to a public apostolate because I never liked to do things behind the scenes. But what pleased me did not please the communists. They took me away in handcuffs. This was the beginning of a long and difficult journey which left the Mirditë region with only four priests. I remained on this journey for twenty-six consecutive years, leaving a trail of my blood everywhere. Always an active militant who went face-to-face with torturers and spies in Burrel prison, I finally tasted freedom again on April 13, 1989, along with other members of the clergy, thanks to perestroika. I still owed another fourteen years of my sentence to the Central Committee. In fact, I am not sure that I will not have to pay off the last bit of it. I returned alive to my old house at the foot of the walls of Rrëmaji, in the shadow of cynara and cypress trees. The house was immediately transformed into a church, similar to the houses of the other twenty-seven priests who had been saved from Enver's sword (whose name I would write in lowercase letters if I were not a Catholic priest).

Until their last breath, humans live in moments of light, shadow, darkness, brightness, depths of abysses or heaven's spheres. If ever a painter wanted to depict my life through symbols, he would need to buy an easel filled with black paint. However, he could not forget gold paint because everywhere I breathed, the darkness was dissipated by the illuminating radiance of Holy Communion. Nevertheless, if someone asked me what the darkest day of my life was, I would respond without hesitation: the day that I received the knowledge of the death of my mother, after she had mourned the death of the imprisoned and poisoned Dom Lazër, my younger brother. Much later, I was informed that she would stay silently glued to the window for a long time, looking at the mountains that separated her from her son. She was only sustained by the fact that she believed in God and by loudly proclaiming human rights and liberties. These rights and liberties were tread underfoot by the same masters who still dominate us today, indifferent to healing old wounds. They even think of ways to give us new ones.

How my mother would have been happy if she had been alive on November 4, 1990, to see me in the burned chapel of Rrëmaji's cemetery celebrating the first public Mass before two-to-three hundred of the faithful. At that point, the chapel was sequestered, degraded, and proclaimed a national structure. Now it is lit by the faint glimmer of the prayer candles for the souls in purgatory. On that gloomy, rainy November day, the raindrops splattered and ran like teardrops on the autumn flower petals which were on the tombs. These were no longer the tears of mourning but of joy. These raindrops announced the new era of freedom of belief, which started with the improvised speech of a priest tattered in prisons, opposed by foreigners and his own, around whose neck hung a very old stole, and in whose hands was an old Latin missal. The strangers and supporters contradicted the priest's wounds. The broken thread was renewed!

The week passed by in a flash and led to a great event on November 11, 1990. Again at Rrëmaji chapel and once again in an environment of communist terror, when one did not know what was happening or, more importantly, what could happen, I celebrated the second public Mass. This time I had a well-prepared homily with which to break twenty-three years of living in the catacombs.

After that came both happy and sad days. The liberty which we believed we had won turned to mockery. The political class only provided obscenities in these years. That is why the atmosphere of the first Mass remained fixed in the memory and heart of the people, who had started to wake up. Perhaps that is why they think back to that Mass with profound veneration and tear-filled eyes. It is because of this precious contribution to national life, given by the Lord to me, who am unworthy of such a difficult and dangerous ordeal, that the University of San Francisco granted me the *Doctor honoris causa diploma* in Human Sciences in 1991 with the following words: "Protagonist of a new era in Albania." This was a tribute to the Catholic clergy who were martyred in Albania. The diploma needs to be laid on the tombs of the martyrs of the Church. Sometime after that, in July 1996, the State of Michigan granted me another such diploma with the following words:

> "Initiator of free speech and a free Catholic press, born from the written word on December 20, 1990, close to Christmas. Initiator of activities that opened Albania to the West.
>
> Builder of bridges that link Tirana and the Vatican.
>
> Founder of the first study bursaries and overseas aid.
>
> A priest who, with his words, raised awareness throughout the planet about the suffering and resistance of the Albanian people against communism and about the anarchy caused by this ideology."

The University of San Francisco, California, granted me the Doctor Honoris causa *diploma in Human Sciences in 1991 with the following words: "Protagonist of a new era in Albania." This was a tribute to the Catholic clergy who were martyred in Albania. The diploma needs to be laid on the tombs of the martyrs of the Church.*

Dom Simon Jubani, the first Albanian to be received by Pope John Paul II after perestroika.

I was the first Albanian to be received by Pope John Paul II after perestroika. I also met other individuals such as the king of Belgium, Italian Prime Minister Guilio Andreotti,[1] senators, legislators, and Government ministers.

I was the first simple priest to be invited two times by the American administration in Washington, once by the Russian Parliament, several times by France, Italy, Belgium, Germany, and once by Spain, Israel, Egypt, and Turkey; but I refused visits to China (Hong Kong), Taiwan, Mexico, and Argentina because I believed that my role overseas in defending the rights and freedoms of the Albanian people no longer had any meaning. For the different Government ministries around the world, the last word had been said by Clinton and his wife, and then by the younger Bush. When I was in prison, I believed that the world listened to the martyred more than to the torturers. My experience after being released from prison to the entire world unfortunately changed my opinion.

I continue to happily travel to churches and to non-Christian institutions throughout the world. I put all my strength as a simple soldier of Jesus Christ into the Albanian Catholic Church. Truly, when I spend a few days in holy places around the world, I feel at least ten years younger, whereas upon my return to Albania I feel twenty years older. This is how the last years of my life are — becoming younger or getting older.

I have always preferred a difficult apostolate, in places where atheism has sown the most evil seeds and where, as a result, wickedness, bitterness, ignorance, and crime have grown. I have traveled night and day along winding roads, facing strong winds in Albania's Gjader region, putting my life in danger on several occasions, often tumbling along with my "white wolf," my Toyota, which is as indestructible as its master. With God's help, I founded a large religious, health, cultural, and sport center at Kalivaç, in the Mirditë region, where there are not any roads. I also helped support four religious and two women in their missionary work. This work is the first in the history of this region. I also founded parishes at Spiten and Kaftalli in order to provide support to the less fortunate.

---

1 *Giulio Andreotti* was born on January 14, 1919 in Rome and died there on May 6, 2013. He was a journalist, writer, and Italian Statesman, leader of the Christian Democrats, and an important protagonist in twentieth-century Italian political history.

I have traveled night and day, along winding roads, faced strong winds in Albania's Gjader region, put my life in danger on several occasions, and often tumbled along with my "White Wolf," my Toyota, which is as indestructible as its master.

I do not need to mention the amount of money I raised for the churches in Jubani, Çela, and Hajmel, and for the restoration of the archbishop's quarters and the cathedral in Shkodër, as well as for the purchase of vehicles for the parishes. This goes as well for study bursaries that I was able to provide for more than one-hundred young men and women, for the Catholic intellectuals of tomorrow, and above all for the education of men and women religious. I have constantly knocked on the doors of ambassadors in order to get entry visas, and I have wandered through the streets of the world to develop the talents of unknown or forgotten children.

I am a member of the party of the poor who were massacred and tortured and are victims of yesterday and today. I was born in Shkodër and am growing old in Mirditë. I want to rebuild what was destroyed and what the political class continues to destroy. Since 1990, I have let the whole world know that the Albanians have gone from the frying pan into the fire. And after having read the memoirs of Boutros Ghali, former United Nations secretary general, I agree with his idea on the current role of the United States of America. The antichrist that is the United States today is causing much trouble, blood, anxiety, and tears in Rwanda, the Balkans, Albania, and East Timor.

I finished my university studies in communist prisons, where I continued to learn what they had tried to make me forget when they kicked me out of the Jesuits' seminary. I therefore learned to read and write in Latin, Greek, Italian, French, and English. Those languages were very useful for me. They helped me fill entire pages of newspapers around the world, which made many friends for Albania by keeping the world up to date on the situation in my country. I was given the title of "Prophet."

I have a lot of regrets when I see that the old, pre-war generation, to which I have the honor of belonging, is much more cultivated and has much more of a moral code than the post-war generations. They have pockets full of money, but their souls are half empty. They are poorly educated and have little moral code and even less faith, because they were degraded by the atheism and pragmatism brought from the Yalta Conference in February 1945. Albania's younger generations were degraded by television, brothels, drugs, and nightclubs. All of these are empty of value. It is the most terrible misery that the human soul has known.

I am in very good health and, although toothless, "I eat a communist every day." If I had all my teeth, "I would be able to eat ten a day." Thus, nourished in such a fitting way by those who had broken all my teeth, I now use all of my physical and spiritual energy to heal the wounds caused by war, particularly the Second World War.

I give thanks with all my heart to the missionaries, men and women, who have answered the call of the Holy See to rebuild Albania's churches, especially the Italians and their Christian culture. They represent a baptized land. And I thank the traditional Church in Europe, as it has the task of transmitting all its riches to the Albanian people. I also thank the Kosovars, who have come to cultivate the vines of Jesus that were destroyed in Albania. On the one hand, they can do more than others because they know the Albanian language; on the other hand, their culture leaves much to be desired. Perhaps we need culture much more than bread, because culture is the source of liberty.

The Church in the West is supported by the offerings of the faithful, and it is impossible for me to avoid criticizing Albanians, Catholic and non-Catholic, who claim everything from the Church, as if it were a profitable multinational corporation. In fact, thanks to the freedom to travel and to emigrate, Albania's economic situation has notably improved in comparison with the Hoxha era which had driven people to misery and even the precipice. But unfortunately, a plutocracy has taken root in Albania based on shady business dealings. This plutocracy is doomed to worse failure than the one experienced by the plutocracy of the old regime that had prompted the installation of the communist regime.

In order to keep my freedom of opinion, I did not accept any financial offers. I can prove this by revealing a conversation I had in November 1990 with Sali Berisha. He had been sent by the communist Central Committee of Tirana to convince me to make a public appeal in the church to vote for the Democratic Party. Many have been fooled, but not Dom Simon, who almost died in prison and who had developed a faculty for detecting the scent of blood that is emitted by the communists, even when they alter their name and appearance and speak of peace and progress.

I am not a man of meetings, but of the altar, of church bells, candles, Masses, and ecumenical dialogue. I will remain until my death an indignant son of historic, martyred, democratic, and unbowed Shkodër. I humbly accept all judgements of Shkodër!

2

Call to the Religious Life

T he real path of my life began in 1943, when the Lord called me to become a Jesuit. As usual, I talked over the idea with my best friend, *Tonin Harapi*, with whom I tended to share all joys and sorrows. We discussed consecrating our whole lives to Jesus. And so, one beautiful day, we bid farewell to our families and departed. I went to the apostolic school to become a Jesuit while Tonin went to the Pontifical Seminary to become a diocesan priest. I was immediately seized by the spiritual, cultural, and — I can say this in all truth — paternal atmosphere in which new recruits to the Society of Jesus were formed. For the good of our spirits, each afternoon we took a walk around the city, while Thursdays and Sundays we went for a walk in the morning too. I completed my studies at the classical lyceum in 1944, the same year that the communists seized power. They styled themselves "The Army of National Liberation." We were all curious about the sense of the word "liberation." Among the meanings that interested us was "to liberate oneself from an evil that one has committed in order to be good." Was that the meaning of what had taken place? Only time would tell!

The Church, which was the first to have created a space for studying the communist virus that first appeared in Russia in 1917, had prepared us to easily discern communism. We had been informed of the civil wars instigated by communism around the world. We had read books and watched films on the French Revolution, the persecution of the Church in Mexico, Father Miguel Pro, the Spanish Civil War in 1936, and the wealthy Spanish who spent all they had to fight evil. We had heard of the activities of Huan Marces. We had read the book entitled *G. P. U.*, which revealed all the atrocities of the Russian secret police against dissidents, the former aristocracy, the nouveaux riches, and the Russian intelligentsia.

The building which housed the classical lyceum also hosted the inter diocesan seminary. This latter included the devout and renowned seminarian *Mark Çuni* and other theologians. Unknown to their superiors, these theologians had printed the first anti-communist tract that was distributed not only at Shkodër, but throughout the country.

Not long after the distribution of this tract there appeared long lists of those first to be executed by firing squad. The first were killed in Shkodër public space, witnessed by terrorized locals. Thus began without due process the execution of the best of the country, who were firm and rebellious adversaries of the communists. Thus began the terror, on the order of the Serbs, who wanted to incite a civil war. In order to further terrorize the city of Shkodër, which was martyred for democracy and long remained dissident, the executed were not immediately buried in the walled cemetery at Zalli i Kirit. Openly flouting all norms of natural morals, the communists organized macabre farces with the cadavers, which were covered in horrible bullet wounds. Our house's location near the cemetery permitted my family and I to be the first to hear the rattle of death coming from Zalli i Kirit. How could we stay safe and sound and not run to see what had happened and who had been the martyr of the "liberators'" bullets? I cannot help but shake with all of my being each time I recall these scenes and I cannot help but repeat a thousand times the same question: "Is it possible to call those who imposed communism on us human beings? Those such as the barbarian hordes who went North from the South in order to put the intelligentsia and the wisest of our men before the firing squad at a time when the entire world defended the learned and the wise?"

They came and did not know when to leave. Shkodër and its five great mountains lost their inner serenity and the peace in their souls. The only things that were understood were the names of the dead, the hanged, and the strangled whose heads had been pushed through the holes of toilets, names such as Dom Aleksander Sirdani de Bogue and Dom Pjeter Çuni de Rrjodhi. Those were the ideals of the "liberators," who did not fight for freedom but for money and positions. Politicians of the past and the present have such ideals.

And thus began, in addition to the executions, the pillaging of the gold of the business class and even of those who had supported Enver Hoxha's partisans. At that time, they received their just rewards. Those who refused to hand over their gold ended up in the prisons of the secret service with their entire family, or worse. Husband and wife were thrown in prison, leaving babies in the cradle without mother or father. I recall a young woman whom they imprisoned immediately after she had given birth because her husband refused to hand in his gold. The police brought her baby three times a day for feeding because, they claimed, "communists are just. They do not imprison an innocent baby with a guilty mother!" Yet what happened with all that gold, swiped by the "liberators?"

Shkodër began to "progress" at an incredible pace. Instead of one small prison, it had fifteen big ones! Those who succeeded in fleeing to the West kissed the foreign soil but kept close to their hearts a fistful of Albanian soil, which was bathed in innocent blood. Throughout the Russian satellites, communism was spread by Russian tanks. In Albania, however, communism was the work of the Albanians themselves, even before communism came to Yugoslavia, where the Albanians then flocked to crown the victory of Bolshevism. Three thousand Kosovars, adversaries of Tito, fled to Albania, seeking Hoxha's protection, hoping that he would guarantee them safety. But "our hero" sent them to the Yugoslav secret service, which immediately executed them. Later, Hoxha supported the Kosovars with words and weapons in order to fight the Serbs. Hoxha thus became the cause of an even greater repression of the Kosovars. Nevertheless, these latter retained their sympathy for Hoxha without ever showing any solidarity for the Albanians who were suffering under his communism. One of the most annoying consequences of this odd sympathy, for which all sorts of reasons can be found except patriotism, was the attack on the Gheg language. Gheg was the language of most of the Catholic clergy and laity. A large percentage of these were executed. Buried with them was all the Catholic work they did. Shameful for a country that considers itself European!

After three years of study at the apostolic school, and after three interventions by Hoxha's "liberators," we were kicked out and left without even a pen and paper. Everything was confiscated or became the property of communist institutions. Shkodër libraries, which were the best in the country and had been created with passion and a concern for culture, saw the same fate. Books of inestimable value were sold in the city's stores for cardboard. Whatever survived was sent to Tirana and Belgrade and sold for common cardboard because Western libraries only cared about Marxist works. Shkodër libraries thereby shared the fate of Alexandria's famous library in simply disappearing.

3

A Zoo That Is Called Albania

On November 29, 1944, a system of slavery was established in Albania which transformed the country into a zoo. With the Soviet Union preparing to send barbed wire to surround the zoo, thousands of Albanians fled. That should have helped the civilized world see how communism signifies terror and misery. In fact, communism was brought into our land with the jingle of rubles, which filled the pockets of Miladin Popovic, Dusan Mugosha, and the Southern Albanians. It would make not only the Balkans explode, but a third of the world. To what extent did anyone listen to the Albanians who had fled? Today, which of their countrymen knows the stories, supported by terrible and incontestable facts, of those who had sacrificed so much in order to leave if they could? Nobody made an effort to read or publish them, or to learn anything from them! The yoke under which we lived for fifty years speaks for itself. And we would have lived in such a way for five hundred years if great changes had not taken place elsewhere.

The trauma that Albanians encountered at the hands of their fellow countrymen was worse than that caused by the Turkish occupation in the fifteenth century. At that time, those who did not want to submit to the Ottomans could get on a boat and cross the Adriatic to live a normal life in Italy and elsewhere in Europe and the world. They thus helped to enrich the world's civilization and culture with their work. In contrast, on the land of their descendants, the darkness of ignorance grew thicker and thicker. Those who could not save themselves from the communists by crossing the sea sought refuge in the mountains of Dukagjin, Malësi and Madhe, Mirditë, Pukë, and Lezhë. They saved the region, its habits and customs, and its European identity. Those who sought the mountains had it harder than those who fled the country. In the mountains, they made untold sacrifices, living in holes and caves. Little by little, they were able to build cabins high in the mountains, on precipices. They lived like mountain eagles so that they could be safe from the enemy. And so, on the mountain ridges, only one flag flew and was never supplanted. This earned them the respect of the locals. Someone said or wrote recently that these people who fled were nothing but wild mountain folk, who were coarsely clothed, lacked knowledge of Government or self-Government, and lived like wolves or eagles. Withdrawing to the mountain peaks in order to save their lives and refusing any collaboration with the country's occupiers, they seemed to have no place in politics, which is still true for them today.

At that time, it was an honor and a joy to betray your country and its language, customs, and, above all, its religion, and even to collaborate with your wife's and sister's rapists who now lived comfortably in your house — to accept all of that in order to have a place in the Government and to work according to the wishes and interests of the occupier. Apparently, it was those occupiers who knew how to govern. Unaware of any wrongdoing, they had trampled underfoot those who had learned at the school of the eagles how to defend liberty. As long as the country is governed in this way, our officials who have roots in the terrible Turkish years will follow their masters and continue to put into action the lessons of communism, which were worse for the country than the Ottoman occupation.

Encircling Albania with an iron curtain, the communists totally succeeded in blocking the way of their enemies, those who would have wanted to cross the sea in order to find their relatives who had left long ago. People therefore fled the mountains and climbed up to where the Turks had never been able to go because they had failed to develop the mountaineering spirit. It is a spirit that is candid and honest in its simplicity. Yet an Albanian could treat another Albanian worse than the Turks had by committing fratricide and genocide, eradicating faith and religion, and installing in its place unprecedented corruption. This psychological trauma will remain in the Albanian soul for centuries. Lamentably, ten years after the fall of communism, nothing has been done to remedy this state of affairs.

And the terrible influence of television needs to be added to this. In order to forget the trauma brought about by their brothers, Albanians would live only on bread just so they could buy a television in order to entertain themselves and forget. It was a kind of nightly intoxication enabled through self-denial. We risked prison if we watched foreign channels. In the end, what communism had failed to do, television did by creating a type of Albanian who can only find his equal in the zoo.

We therefore have a joke. An Albanian visits the biggest zoo in a European capital. He asks if they have any work for him. They respond that they do, if he wants it. The Albanian cannot believe his ears. There is indeed work, but what kind of work is it? He is ready to clean, to feed, to take care of animals. No, it is not that kind of work. Others are already doing those jobs. What he needs to do is to put on a costume, enter the cage, and play the role of a gorilla, which the zoo lacks. The high cost of buying and feeding a gorilla has prompted that solution. Until now, no one has accepted the job, even though communism tries to convince us that we are the descendants of monkeys.

The Albanian feels happy. It will not be difficult to play this role. Has he not done the same in his own country, which has been turned into a zoo? He accepts the job, and soon finds himself in the cage, doing a better job than a real gorilla. His cage is therefore always surrounded by children and even adults. Some think that he should be awarded for being an exemplary gorilla. One day, while moving like a gorilla, jumping from right to left and making faces, he slips and, falling hard, ends up in the lion's cage. With all his strength, forgetting all animal and human languages aside from his mother language, he yells in Albanian: "Heeeelp! Heeeelp!" Wide-eyed in panic, and totally frightened at the lion's approach, he hears a voice coming from the bowels of the wild beast: "Shut up, you idiot. Do you want us both to be fired and lose this paradise?" It is another Albanian who later informs him that all the zoo animals are Albanians. They all call the place "the communist paradise" because they can earn a livelihood without suffering.

How can I say that Albanians learned nothing from the school of communism? The experience made them capable of playing the role of every animal, domestic or wild. But regarding the role of humans, it may take a while.

Naturally, the Catholic Church could not accept being closed behind barbed wire in the Albanian communist zoo with the wild animals who were the masterpieces of communism. The communists knew very well that the men of the Church distinguished themselves by their courage in opposing the evils that popped out of the soil of hell like mushrooms after a rain. Therefore, when the Soviet blow came, we were already well-prepared to face things: Anti-communist crusades had begun in 1917. However, despite prayer, sacrifice, and the blood of the martyrs, despite the role of the press, despite academic conferences, we were in no place to stem the plague. We had to take up the cross and climb our Golgotha. The Lord expressed enough esteem in us that we would walk the same path that he had made out for his divine Son, charged as well with the cross.

4

In Tirana in 1947

The new "liberators" declared: "Communism cannot be built in Albania in the presence of all of these Catholic institutions." A year after the closure of Catholic schools in 1946, I went to Tirana for a course in medical radiology. I still had all my teeth and hair — my black hair! I went from the school of Jesus to the school of the devil. I could not have temptation. For the first time, I was in a school at which young men and young women attended. And for the first time, I saw in the practical work of the course men and women entirely nude! Additionally, the dance professor came three times a week to teach us the tango, the waltz, the rumba! What more can I say? The day that a group of young ladies from the correctional institute came was the last straw. The communist regime wanted to re-train these prostitutes, who were, it claimed, vestiges of the old regime. Yet they were far fewer than the numbers left by the communists! There were about thirty in all of Albania when I was at the school. As for the male prostitutes, they were in such a horrible condition that no one recognized them as men nor dared condemn them.

I could not have avoided all these temptations except for the small hospital chapel that had, fortunately, not yet been shut down. The chapel was a hospital for my soul, which was beginning to show the first signs of sickness. The religious sisters, who were angels dressed in white, still did their work in the long hallways of this house of pain, though I did not know most of them. The cross at the front of their uniforms made the communists uneasy. The latter looked forward to the end of the year, when these religious nurses would be replaced by five hundred graduating Albanian nurses. The sisters had asked permission to attend the Mass each day, so it was held daily for them at the hospital chapel. Naturally, I attended as well to receive the Eucharist, which helped to counter the unbridled passions and instincts which eat at and lower the human to the animal level. I received Communion and I read under the assumption that only religion and culture could save me from the chaos into which Tirana had fallen, a movement from West to East, from goodness to evil, from light into deep darkness.

5

The Martyr Archbishop Ernest Çoba

The great martyr, Monsignor Ernest Çoba, was the most optimistic and inspired man that I knew in this period of terror. His affable smile and gentle words had healed thousands of human hearts, even when he was surrounded by the omnipresent agents of the Government's information service. Monsignor Çoba became a significant historical figure in the Albanian Catholic Church as much by his saintly life as by his heroic resistance to the dictatorship.

Right during the middle of the Government's terror, in May 1958, Çoba organized the celebration for the centenary of the construction of Shkodër cathedral with a grandiose and totally unique type of exposition. Immediately after, Party members sent from Tirana took steps to get rid of all the documents at a time when it was a question of life and death. Those documents testified to the splendor of the work of the Catholic Church in the service of the nation. The day of the commemoration was delayed several times by the prelate because the secret service organized picnics, demonstrations, and various other gatherings on the same date and hour. This obliged all levels of society to participate. After several delays, the prelate finally won out. One beautiful Sunday, the communist State was forced to leave the people in peace. This was a people that had been crushed under the burdens that the new masters endlessly added, including on Sundays. The authorities wanted to box in the entire population to better control and torture it, and to shift attention away from attempts to overthrow the Government.

For Catholics, persecution became routine, stimulating, and encouraging to the life of faith. Believers felt like the first Christians! I remember even today that right in the middle of the persecution, buses arrived in front of the cathedral from Tirana and Durres filled with people in their Sunday best. They had come to participate in this unforgettable and encouraging ceremony which gave everyone so much enthusiasm. But unfortunately, this event was used by the Communist Party Central Committee to proclaim to the world: "As you can see, we are a democratic country, and the Church is free to exercise its activities." It played this comedy routine whenever necessary.

In the meantime, the Church grew increasingly weak due to deportations, imprisonments, and assassinations of priests, who were sent pitilessly to the execution post as Vatican spies. However, on this unforgettable day, the whole Church — all the faithful — were present. The secret service spies who kept an eye on the celebration had their hands full counting the five thousand people who had come to fill the cathedral, not counting the faithful of Arra e Madhe, Gjuhadoli, and Ballabane. It was this flock that the wise Monsignor Çoba directed. The faithful, full of devotion and admiration, moved in silence as they took in the beautiful works within the cathedral. They stopped in particular in front of two columns on which had been painted images from the Old and New Testaments. The churchgoers were struck above all by the painting of the Tower of Babel by one of my friends, Ismail Lulani. He also included his own portrait in the painting's jumble and confusion, which, from that point on, was the symbol of our Albania.

All around the cathedral's exterior, thousands of documents and portraits that told the story of the foundation and history of the structure were shown. A painting with the theme, "The laying of the cathedral's foundation stone," was also on display. This masterpiece had been started by the well-known painter Simon Rrota, but his work was interrupted when he was given notice by Sadik Rama to appear before the executive committee. The masterpiece was finished by Father Leon Kabashi and Dom Injac Dema. This symbolic work accomplished by three artists shows the tormented evolution of our religious art. The painting, though it had been damaged by humidity, ended up in the caves of the Museum of Atheism and became public once again at the time that the wounded saints were released from prison. After that, I kept the painting in my house for a time before giving it to the archbishop. It was put on display in a more modest setting in the cathedral's presbytery after restoration.

In 1958, the secret service believed they had successfully convinced the faithful who were under the direction of Monsignor Çoba to no longer go to church, but to follow Enver's nonsense. When May arrived, the month of the Blessed Virgin Mary, Monsignor Çoba made Dom Tish Lisna preacher. Due to his talents, his preaching electrified the entire city of Shkodër and led to a fivefold increase in Mass attendance compared to the previous year. This greatly worried the Communist Party because it could no longer attract people with their Marxist discourse. After this, the communist agencies were strongly criticized by the dictator, who was unpleasantly surprised by the courage of the Catholics and likewise thrown into a panic. There is no greater coward than a tyrant who creates enemies from his murders of the left and the right. The more evil he commits, the more anxiety and worry he feels because he knows, as history shows, that vengeance follows the crime.

Reprisals were organized in Tirana by the centralized dictatorship. Shkodër the martyr, Shkodër the democrat, had to be punished. It was declared at Party meetings that Catholic attendance at church signified that Catholics were incorrigible. It was necessary for Catholics to understand that such things would provoke violence because bringing disorder to the ranks was not permitted. It was reported at one of these meetings that more than twenty thousand churchgoers in Shkodër had participated in Monsignor Çoba's appeal to participate in the commemoration of the cathedral, and that they had all worn their Sunday best and were smiling and in a wonderful mood, acting as if Marxism did not exist. Forty priests, ardently yet moderately, preached throughout the day. They transfixed the audience, which then forgot, momentarily, about the dictatorship. While this report was being read, an attendee interrupted and said, "and what if these twenty thousand civilians suddenly decided to attack the Interior Ministry, the Executive committee, and the Party committee? Then what would happen? They would take power from us!" Another fervent Marxist added: "How did it come about that they do not know that after this long transition period, after long lines of people waiting for a small loaf of dry bread and many living in filth, we will provide an unprecedented bounty?"

It was not a question of explaining things to people. These Catholics had to be punished. First of all, Monsignor Çoba, their leader, had to be condemned. But there had to be a reason for the arrest in order not to offend world opinion, which spoke nonstop of the long lists of those who were shot, and which emphasized that communist guns had targeted the Catholic Church. It did not take long for the handcuffs, prepared long before in Tirana, to tighten around the wrists of the saintly archbishop. He would face torture, but he was determined to follow the Crucified One as closely as possible.

6

"Ghegs and Tosks Are One Nation: Separation Does Not Make Sense!"[1]

I t was not a Tosk who said that, but a Gheg, a Catholic priest, Dom Ndre Mjeda. I gave this chapter the above title so that everyone can clearly understand that Ghegs have never felt any sort of bitterness against Tosks. Quite the opposite! They would not even think about denigrating Tosk country and its people, which is just as Albanian as the Albanians in the North. Tosks are brothers who share the same blood and suffering. However, I cannot ignore certain bitter, stubborn, and oft-discussed historical facts, which indicate that the dictator and Government planned to get rid of the Gheg people — their language, identity, and thought. This is why no one today dares to defend the identity of the North, which were once mountains full of fields and flowers but are now shattered pieces knit together. The most monstrous communist crimes took place in the North but were certainly not committed by Northerners or by honest Southerners. Southerners also lived under the communist menace, although this menace weighed most heavily on Catholics, who were the main target of the communists.

Hearing the cries every day of Catholics who were trampled underfoot, who were betrayed, killed, deported, and dishonored, and whose houses were burned to the ground, *Tuk Jakova*[2], a simple carpenter, became a symbol of resistance in the North. He sacrificed himself for his Gheg people. As a Catholic, he identified with his

---

1 *Ghegs* and *Tosks* are the two ethnic groups that make up the population of Albania. The former are located in the North and the latter in the South of the country, in Tosk country.

2 *Tuk Jakova* (1914–1959) — Albanian politician. He was President of the Constituent Assembly, Finance Minister, and Vice-Prime Minister twice in the People's Socialist Republic of Albania. In 1941, he represented the Communist Party of Shkodër at the first constitutive conference of the Workers Party of Albania. In 1950, however, he started to oppose Party Secretary Enver Hoxha. The latter accused him of complicity with the Catholic Church. In 1955, he was stripped of his position of Prime Minister and then condemned to twenty-five years in prison.

co-religionists and took on the scorn that was directed at them. He had total solidarity with them and with all Northerners. He dared to say directly to the dictator, in both Gheg and Tosk, what he was doing in the North. Thus, the dictator made him disappear.

Gheg culture thereby lost its sole defender in the Government. This culture remained a widow, without a husband, like *Vaso Pasha*[3] said. The dictator Hoxha was not satisfied with killing, pillaging, and burning down Gheg culture. He also attacked the language. I know that many will get angry when they read this. They will repeat the old lines of division which reappear every time our enemies need them. Even today Gheg culture is caught between the sickles of its assassins on the one side and their servants, the phony academics, on the other. Some of these clever hawkers who unfurl their flags every day in the heart of Europe repeat their usual refrain against the Ghegs by targeting me in particular: "Look at the senile old guy who wants to spread a few old stories!" Yes, dear reader, the old guy expressed himself, and will express himself again, until Gheg culture has found again its honor and has all its rights recognized, starting with the language that it was cut off from but nevertheless still uses.

It is the same thing with the works of the glorious sons of this land, *Ernest Koliqi*[4] and *Martin Camaj*[5], who proved that the Gheg language that had been shot down at Zalli i Kirit happily survived in other regions. Therefore, you do not need to go to Munich to pretend to honor a son of the North. I have hope that one day we will have a faithful son of the Gheg to tell the truth of the tragedy of these regions and correct the distorted history reports on Albania. However, as I had no fear while facing the most inhuman tortures in prison, so I do not fear the hissing of a few snakes who accuse me of dividing the country's unity, which had taken many centuries to build. I also support the country's unity, but I consider it a little

---

3 *Vaso Pasha* (1825–1892) — Catholic man of letters and politician who was born in Shkodër. He held high administrative positions in the Ottoman Empire and was named Governor of Lebanon in 1882 by the Sultan. He died in Beirut in 1892. He never forgot his country and fought for Albanian identity.

4 *Ernest Koliqi* (born in Shkodër, 1903; died in Rome, 1975) — Teacher, poet, novelist, essayist, translator, journalist, playwright, and Minister of Education in the Vërlaci Government under the Italian occupation of 1939 to 1941.

5 *Martin Camaj* (1925–1992) — An Albanian writer who emigrated to Italy and then to Bavaria, where he died.

differently, as a union between brothers and friends where everyone feels at home with his own language and identity! Why was the Tosk dialect imposed on the entire North, including Kosovo? We need to declare and accept the truth once and for all. That imposition played a central role in the war between the Red East and the Catholic West. As we Catholics have always been connected to the West, a huge war was imposed on us. The balalaika and the mountain *lahuta*[6] faced off on the battlefield. Regarding this, *Father Gjergj Fishta*[7], well before the communism of the Slavs menaced our lands, announced that our neighbor the red devil was sharpening his claws in order to pitilessly plunder the Nord of Albania—not only its body, but its soul too!

The poor Ghegs found themselves between two enemies, the Slavs and those Albanians who had sold out to the Slavs. Things got so bad that Gheg culture was close to dying out, with all its writers, their way of thinking, its religion and its culture. It was so threatened because its culture was always linked to Western culture. This is an undeniable fact, despite the efforts to mask the truth behind slogans of a self-declared though sterile patriotism and a union that is based on crimes that have never been punished. When history's tribunal denounces and condemns the crimes committed against the Ghegs for the last century, we will have the moment of Albanian unification, which will be a beautiful and stable union. But at present that all seems distant, even unattainable, because the genetic code—the genes and the chromosomes—was profoundly shaken by atheism, terror, permanent tension, crushing work, and

---

6   The *lahouta*, lahoute, or lute of the mountains, a popular monocord musical instrument that is played with a bow and that accompanies the *chansons de geste* of rhapsodists of the North of Albania.

7   *Father Gjergj Fishta* (1871–1940)—Franciscan priest. He was a religious, political, and literary personality of Albania's North. He worked to affirm the North's identity. His masterpiece, *The Luth of the High Mountains* (Lahuta e Malcis) is a patriotic epic of 17,000 verses that has been called the Albanian *Iliad* or the Bible of the Albanian knights. Mostly composed between 1902 and 1909, this masterpiece was published in its definitive form in 1937 after thirty-five years of work. He was the deputy for Shkodër in the Albanian Parliament and was its Vice-President. His public speaking talents, as much in the ecclesiastical as in the political sphere, aided his participation in Balkan Conferences of Athens (1930), Sofia (1931), and Bucharest (1932). He then withdrew from public life to totally consecrate himself to his religious life and to writing.

idiotic television shows. This has gotten to the point that if you state the truth, everyone will turn against you and attack you with irrational reasons to the point that you can no longer explain yourself. Blind as they are, they will be ready to cut out both your eyes in order to fight as equals! Or they will try to lead you into the black hole of their reasoning, where no light of reason or truth exists.

While I was behind bars, I keenly followed this question of unity, which was an integral part of my suffering. I was always up to date on the situation, perhaps more so than those on the outside who were always busied with the nonstop nonsense invented by the regime. Those people had neither the time nor the desire to follow publications. However, there was an abundance of publications, starting with the press and including the attempt to write *A History of Albania*, whose title hides a great lie. It was the same with the press. We had a common saying: "In Albanian newspapers, only the name of the newspaper is true. The weather section for today and tomorrow is half true. The rest, my friend, is nothing but lies!" Yet, whatever it was, anyone who could read between the lines of the communist press could find interesting information by considering it from the opposite point of view of the official version. A reading of the many variations of the supposed *A History of Albania* is quite interesting. It was continuously altered, even though the events had taken place centuries before. It was edited and re-edited to safeguard it from Western influences and, above all, to purge it of any trace of the undeniable participation of the Catholic clergy and important figures from the North in the principal events of Albania's history.

However, the Tirana clique resembled an ostrich with its head in the sand and butt in the air. This was the case with *Fan Noli*.[8] In publishing his work, Hoxha's press portrayed him as a Russian agent until the last moments of his life. Worse, the papers portrayed him as a man for whom religion was nothing but a way to enrich himself. One need only read his parody of the Bible to be convinced that *Teofan Mavromati*[9]

---

8 *Fan Noli* (1882–1965) — Orthodox bishop and Albanian Statesman. He was Regent and Prime Minister of Albania in 1924. After the Second World War, he maintained contacts with the tyrant Enver Hoxja and pushed the American Government to recognize the new regime in Tirana. Nicknamed the "Red Bishop" from then on, he nevertheless distanced himself from the regime throughout the years.

9 *Teofan Mavromati* — It seems that this is another name for Fan Noli.

had a great God-given talent and intelligence, and that he had used these for God's service. This therefore created a Nolian paradox, which is not so rare in Albania's history and literature. This combination, which leads to the image of "stupid Ghegs," is nothing but the capacity to light a candle for the Lord and another, of grease, for the devil. We refused to light the candles at the altar of the dictator, even though it would have been easy.

This great learned and renowned writer, endowed with obviously positive qualities, wore a black cassock and a large cross on his chest in which a healthy heart beat. Yet he said the Mass all his life at the devil's altar by making himself an evil servant of the Kremlin's empire. He thereby opposed the West as well as the Ghegs and their culture, just like every servant of the devil did in the past and still does today. This great writer insulted the Ghegs by calling them backwards for the sole reason that they were anti-communists. In the meantime, while needing to defend Gheg culture, our mouths were sewn shut by the thread of both foreigners and our own people, who received the support of Enver's press. This proved to us that the Orthodox archbishop had received a great deal of money from the Kremlin, from *Ahmet Zogu*[10], and from Enver Hoxha. That is why he zealously and gleefully defended the dictator internationally, as his influence there surpassed even that of the Kosovars.

The same communist press reported that *Ismail Qemali*[11] had worked under heavy foreign influence. The media claimed he had made a speech that remained largely unknown because it was never published, and that after this great event, which was significant for the core of Albania, he vanished from the political scene. While Hoxha covered over the glory of Ismail Qemali, who had been

---

10   *Ahmet Zogu* (name at birth: Ahmet Muhtar Bej Zogolli): October 8, 1895–April 9, 1961. Albanian politician. Twice Prime Minister of the Republic from January 31, 1925, and then King of the Albanians from September 1, 1928 under the name Zog I (or Zogu), after having replaced the first Albanian Republic by the Albanian Realm. His reign came to an end on April 8, 1939 with the Italian invasion.

11   *Ismail Qemali* (born January 16, 1844 at Vlorë and died January 24, 1919 at Perouse) — He was one of the principal figures of the Albanian national movement and founder of the modern Albanian State. On November 28, 1912 at Vlorë he proclaimed the independence of Albania and formed a provisional Government, with himself as President. On February 6, 1914, the Conference of the Ambassadors named Prince William of Wied head of State.

oriented towards the sultans, the leader denigrated *Faik Konica*[12], merely because Konica sacrificed his life for a European, Western, and unquestionably Catholic Albania, as he had been educated at Shkodër by the Jesuits. These men provided him with an education that gave him every opportunity to shine like a star in the most famous schools of the world. Conversely, we can see today that communism has done nothing in the West for the last fifty years other than create an army of slaves and prostitutes.

Until 1944 Albanians thought in a Western way and followed its civilization. But in that year, they received the order, "Follow us! March towards the backward East!" This brought us all sorts of complications and difficulties. It brought us to the most backward and lost places and right to the bosom of the Chinese. But one day, our Chinese friends abandoned because they were ashamed of being associated with a zoo led by a monkey. In the meantime, the vital contribution of the Catholic schools of the North weakened daily. The atheist schools deprived the human being of all his values and transformed him into a species directed solely by instinct. This is still the case today.

The instant that a slight wind of liberty was felt, it was natural for Gheg culture, a fortress of democracy and progress over the course of centuries, to become the center of the earthquake marking the end of the half-century domination of the hammer of slavery and the sickle of death. In addition to the toppling of monuments and statues to Hoxha and Stalin, the most symbolic signal of the renewal of the cut thread of tradition was the appearance of the rebellious journal *Hylli i Drites*.[13] I had seen its last issue. It treated both the cross and the pen with dignity. I worked that it would see another day, that it would rise from its ashes and be transformed and remade just like the phoenix. It was clear to the Government that free spirits like *Father Zef Pllumi*[14]

---

12 *Faik Bej Konica* (March 15, 1875–December 15, 1942 in Washington) — He was a propagandist of national identity, a learned historian and expert of the Albanian language, an editor, publicist, and Albanian diplomat, an excellent essayist and perfect stylist, a founder of theoretical and practical literary critique in Albania, and a public activist with an orientation towards the Occident. He brought a new model to the Albanian mentality.

13 *Hylli i Drites* — *The Star of Light.*

14 *Father Zef Pllumi* (1924–2007) — Albanian Franciscan, imprisoned between 1946 and 1948, and then from 1967 to 1989. His book, *Live to Witness*, was published in French in 2015. It is the testimony of a man who considered it his

and *Aurel Plasari*[15], who was the sole true convert in soul and spirit, lifted the soul of the people and spread the flame with their torches, which received light from the Star that is the Source of light. Those supporting the Government tried with all their might to blow out this Star in order to extinguish the light. But can a human being blow out a star? I personally think that the Star is hiding somewhere, behind the fog, and that it will reappear when springtime arrives.

What is most annoying, and a consequence of Albania's supposed democracy, is that Gheg culture is identified with Tropojë.[16] This is very odd. This shows the eagerness of the seat of power to renounce the values of other centers of Gheg culture such as Shkodër, which would illuminate the rest of the map if it had the chance. People forget that Shkodër has sat majestically for over four thousand years at the foot of the Tarabosh, Maranaj, and Cukali mountains and is served by three rivers and a lake, which also cradles the towns of Teuta, Barleca, Beçikeme, and Fishta. Yet you can also find Judas, because *Ramiz Alia*[17] himself came from this same cradle of Shkodër.

What still surprises me even more today is that, when we can fix many of these grave errors of history, the allergy to the Truth supports the enemies of Catholicism and the enemies of the North. These enemies have a strange desire, unjustified before God and the nation, to obstinately pursue this path of lies. It leads me to believe that in the effort to cement their crimes forever, the pseudo scientists and other writers of the dictatorship have come to believe their own lies as the truth. And so this is how they present things to the young generations with no one contradicting them. Nowadays it would take someone like Gjergj Fishta to *put these people at the tail of his*

---

task to denounce the years of blood and terror that thousands of Albanians faced during the communist period. Between 1945 and 1990, Albania could be known only through reports that captivated the French public. Zef Pllumi's contribution is unique because it rewrote national history and was the work of rehabilitation that concerned the lies perpetuated by the dictatorship.

15 *Aurel Plasari* (born 1956, Tirana)—Professor, researcher, writer, and translator.

16 *Tropojë* is a municipality in the district of Tropojë, in the North of Albania, near the frontier with Kosovo.

17 *Ramiz Tafë Alia* (October 18, 1924 – October 7, 2011)—He was the second and last communist leader of Albania, from 1985 to 1991, and head of State from 1982 to 1992. He was designated as successor by Enver Hoxha and took power after the death of the latter. Alia died of a pulmonary illness on October 7, 2011 at Tirana at 86 years of age.

lahute.[18] This is why the eagle of Albania is no longer capable of flying. It cannot take to the sky with only one wing. The other has been cut off and broken into a thousand pieces by its own children!

I hope that these lines therefore remain like an apology — or an epitaph — of Gheg culture in its agony. These lines are dedicated to Gheg culture by its faithful son who was destroyed in prisons. In those prisons, first the law of the Tosk spies and then of the Gheg spies reigned, and all of that in an atmosphere of endless reprisals.

---

18 An expression that could be written, "to pay with their heads".

7

Reprisals

Retaliation began even before the arrest of Monsignor Ernest Çoba against a few shepherds of his flock. The guilt of *Dom Ejell Kovaçi*[1] was cooked up. His second arrest was based on heavy accusations, which were the fruit of diabolical phantasmagoria and which aimed to discredit the entire Catholic clergy. He was accused of incest and murder of a parishioner. The accusers believed that the admission of such accusations, prompted by the application of iron and fire to a living body, would definitively distance all faithful from the Church. The montage of such scenes was the work of the artist of crime and torture, *Hilmi Seiti*[2], aided by his faithful dog, *Gac Mazi*.[3] They began by psychologically preparing the city of Shkodër for the impending disaster. People in the coffee houses would say, "You will begin to realize the truth that only the Catholic clergy would commit such ugly crimes when you hear of the criminal process."

Aiming to kill two birds with one stone, the Central Committee was convinced that this conspiracy would lead to the collapse of the clergy and of the Catholic faith. But it was all in vain! No one, not Albanians nor the rest of the world, believed this awful defamation. Knowing that the secret service had already selected a target, everyone was clearly aware that the start of this tragicomedy was very near. Who could say that in Albanian literature the drama genre has little changed over the years? What do you call the genre of a living farce played by real people that then turns to tragedy with the assassination of all the actors, both the criminals and the victims? Perhaps it is an unwritten history that reports the retaliation of Albanian against Albanian. When Tirana endeavored to persuade the world of the

---

1   *Dom Ejell Kovaçi* (1920–1958) — A priest condemned to death on November 13, 1958 and shot. No record of the execution has been found.

2   *Hilmi Seiti* — General and artisan of communist terror for ten years at Shkodër.

3   *Gac Mazi* — Albania's ambassador to Moscow. At the beginning of the 1960s, he was tasked with relaying a message from Enver Hoxha to President Ho Chi Minh. In the message, Hoxha mentioned an eventual visit of the Vietnamese leader to Tirana and complained of the critics of communist Governments against Albania and the Labor Party.

monstrosities of the Catholic clergy via the radio, foreign radio stations asked, "How far will those without faith and law fall?"

Then came the sad year of 1967, when the Central Committee tried to accomplish the impossible and convince world opinion that the clergy members themselves, not Hoxha, had closed churches and mosques due to their conviction that the future belonged to communism, not religion. Then, at the summit of Golgotha, toward which the clergy had been climbing for several years, carrying the heavy cross of persecution on their torture deformed backs, three new crosses were introduced! An unprecedented terror reigned throughout the land.

The communists had done the impossible and persuaded certain muezzins (or "hodjas") and priests to publicly burn their religious clothing, to shave their beards (for those who had not already done so), and to publicly announce, in unity with the Party, that religion had always been the opium of the people. Some Orthodox priests and hodjas also informally recanted their religious beliefs during receptions which were put on by the first secretaries of the Party and which were pompously called "People's Assemblies." But the Catholic clergy, which had always obeyed God, took the unanimous decision despite the closed churches and danger of being killed, to bring Jesus to the people wherever it was being called. The Catholics were proud of this attitude of their pastors. The sheep had resisted the wolves. More furious than ever, the wolves began to howl in chorus that they had suppressed religious organizations for being useless, for the fall-off in church attendance, and other such nonsense. Also, with the objective of gaining the submission of Catholics, a court process took place in the autumn of 1967 in the church of the Stigmatine Sisters of Gjuhadol. There, *Dom Zef Bici* and *Dom Mark Dushi*[4] were sentenced to death. Other clergy received heavy prison sentences.

My brother Dom Lazër Jubani was also the victim of retaliation. He was accused by close members of our family, who should have defended him. A dose of arsenic was given to him on July 10, 1982 by a spy of many years, Mr. Marleci, who was an agricultural worker like my brother. The poison, which was injected into tomatoes by the secret service, did its job, and Dom Lazër gave up his soul after

---

4 *Dom Zef Bici* and *Dom Mark Dushi* — Both priests were martyrs of the Revolution who were assassinated on May 3 or 10, 1968 beside the grave that they were forced to dig.

a tragic agony. No one looked after him when he was hospitalized. The doctors had been ordered by the secret service not to treat him. The order was carried out to the letter. Who was the doctor who went so far as to take him off the medical drip?

My brother Dom Lazër Jubani was also the victim of retaliation. He was accused by close members of our family, who should have defended him. No one looked after him when he was hospitalized.

What kind of a doctor who still today boasts of exercising a humanitarian service would go so far as to speed up the death of this believer in order to save his own life? Only God, who looks down from Heaven and writes down everything, knows! However, seeing Dom Lazër at the mercy of his destiny, family members brought him back home in his last moments so that he could at least die surrounded by his own. He died on July 29, 1982.

Retaliation and resistance! There were five mountains that had protected European identity—Puka, Malcija e Madhe, Dukagjini, Malcija de Lezhë, and Mirditë, the last in the region being the one that resisted most strongly against communism and therefore naturally suffered the harshest retaliation. Even though Hoxha boasted on November 29, 1944 that he had taken total control of all of Albania, he would still not be able to get *Mirditë* to submit until 1953.[5]

Until that year, the mountains and forests of Mirditë were full of Mirditors, weapons in hand and led by the *Gjonmarkaj* family, which lost two of its sons, Sander and Marc, in the fight. These two had caused a lot of problems for the Central Committee because they had called for a general uprising against Bolshevism. Mirditë revolted again when communist detachments, who had been tasked with the region's submission, committed crimes which no pen would dare describe nor any language recount. Only the lawless and the unprincipled could commit such heinous acts. It suffices to recall the long list of men and women from Mirditë who were violently undressed by lieutenant Hodo Habibi, who dishonored dozens of young daughters and women of Mirditë and shot one hundred men for not taking up arms with the Government.

He was one of those rare abominable criminals who quickly paid for his own crimes, as he was taken and hanged at *Hajmel*[6] by those who were able to escape his criminal hands. As the rope tightened around his neck, and his punishers were about to remove the stepladder, the great man of Laberie began to totally soak his pants, releasing the type of "aroma" that was part and parcel of the Albanian communists' exploits in history. After this last achievement, this awful criminal, who spent his last moments covered in his own unbearable stink, was proclaimed the People's Hero by the authorities! In this way, Mirditë, which figures in the Byzantine and Turkish chronicles as a symbol of resistance, became once again a symbol of resistance in the communist chronicles.

The Central Committee killed many by hanging after unheard of and repeated torturing. It then continued its retaliation and repression against Mirditë via organized incidents. It spread its poison because of its fear of another insurrection. In 1949, the communists assassinated *Bardhok Biba*[7] and spread the news that he had been killed by the

---

5   The region of *Mirditë* in Albania under the communist regime is comparable to the Vendee in France during the French Revolution in the sense that resistance to the new masters lasted much longer there.

6   *Hajmel* — Village in the county of Shkodër.

7   *Bardhok Biba* — Militant of the Albanian Communist Party and deputy.

commandos of *Gjon Marka Gjoni*.[8] This latter was still on the loose at that time, which served as a pretext for assassinating the remaining influential locals of the as-yet unsubmitted Mirditë.

The sultan had done the same thing at Manastir with the leaders of Albanian insurgents. They had each received an individual invitation, and once they had all been found, the Sultan had them bound. Seven were hanged from oak trees. Fifteen had their hands tied with iron thread near a large hole. They each fell in, one after the other, after having received a bullet to the head, some already dead, others not yet. Without waiting for them to die, they were covered with earth. Lamentable cries of the men of Mirditë could be heard. They did not ask for forgiveness. They knew whose hands they had fallen into! They begged for the death blow, the last shot, so that the earth would not suffocate them. Their cries made even the trees of the forest tremble where the others had been hanged, while the criminals danced the *labe*[9] around the pit, accompanied by the macabre cries from the earth. They were the most dreadful cries ever heard in the mountain, there where, as so often discussed, custom requires an absolute respect for a dead man. That is what Albanians are capable of doing to each other. When they could no longer hang them or bury them alive, they changed the method and process. They destroyed and buried them in an even worse way than in the dreadful days that marked the fall of the last bastion of anticommunism.

Under the communist regime, terror and repression were worse in the mountains and the villages than in the cities because mountain dwellers and villagers held onto religion more strongly than city folk. These latter, for one reason or another, kept their religious beliefs secretly in their hearts, perhaps because they had no opportunity or courage to openly display it. They therefore lived double lives, with two souls and two faces. Or they openly opposed religious beliefs and became adversaries of religion. In order to prove to the communist regime that they had been converted to this ideology, they were responsible for considerable damage against the Church. I saw it with my own eyes and felt it with my own hands in the mountains of Mirditë.

As a Shkodran, I was able to make comparisons. I not only saw simple believers, but also clergymen who had developed questioning

---

8   *Gjon Marka Gjoni* — Anti-communist leader and founder of the Independent Block.
9   The *labe* is a dance from the South of Albania.

and unacceptable attitudes due to the terror which had consumed their entire bodies right down to the bone marrow. Among those I knew was *Dom Lec Sahatçija*[10], who had replaced Monsignor Gjin, curé of Mirditë. The former had replaced a bishop and hero of religion who had been shot. But because of his own feeling of terror, he was transformed into a wandering curé. He went from one house to another to baptize, administer the other sacraments, and bless marriages and homes. He lived in the greatest misery in Gëziq. Later, he moved, ending up at Shen Mi. But on Sundays, out of fear, he never celebrated the Mass where he was supposed to with the faithful to whom he had been entrusted. On the contrary, he would go to Shkodër's cathedral because at Mirditë the communists had threatened to kill him.

In order to separate the people from the Church, the communists came up with all sorts of stuff. The unfortunate people, for instance, were forced to spend all of Sunday busy doing futile tasks which did not help the health of body or spirit. Even though they were pursued every moment, the people continued to attend church on Sundays at Gëziq and Shen Mi. Because they never found the curé at the altar or otherwise fulfilling his duties, they began to say that Dom Lec had become crazy with fear. But poor Dom Lec, with the tiny bit of courage still found in some part of his heart, fulfilled his religious duties in his house after the churches were closed. Of course, that did not last long, as he was quickly arrested. In prison, he got what he had always feared. He was cruelly tortured to the point that he did not survive. But I remember that he had good relationships with the "constitutional priests" (a term from the French Revolution that I will explain below): Dom Prend Qefalia, Dom Nikollë Luli, Dom Gjergj Vata, and Dom Luigi Kola. However, he never visited them. This was not because he lacked a feeling of sympathy or friendship for them, but because he distrusted them. Being constitutional priests, they had easy access to the Government.

I recall an interesting episode. I had invited Dom Prend Qefalia to give a panegyric for the patron saint of the parish of Shen Gjergj (St. George). He got to the halfway point of his discourse without mentioning God or Jesus; instead, he spoke nonstop about the Government. As I was assisting him at the Mass, I could not control

10 *Dom Lec Sahatçija* — Beatified at Shkodër among 38 martyrs of communism in Albania, on November 5, 2016.

myself. Fearing that the discourse would end as it had begun, I stopped it abruptly from the altar, before the faithful. They were speechless both by the discourse and by the fact that it had been interrupted. I informed Dom Prend that this was not the place to sing the praises of the Government, but that it was necessary to mention the merits of St. George, given the reason for the ceremony. Because nothing like this had ever happened before, the whole region of Mirditë heard about it, and I got a reputation for being fanatically anti-communist. That was not such a great thing at that time, but I have to say that I ardently rejoiced. At the end of the day, in the middle of all the lies, I had dared to speak a truth from the altar at a time when total confusion had been sown in the spirits of the poor faithful of Mirditë and Shen Gjergj because of the crowd of devils that we call the Government.

Retaliation was and is used to maintain the status quo. If someone fled to the West, family members could expect to be interned, deported, imprisoned, laid off from their work, transferred, and even killed. These repressive measures would depend on the behavior of the individual who had fled. Sometimes, having departed due to his anti-communism, the individual would become an agent of the Albanian secret service, which would mean his family would be left alone. But there were many cases where someone was sent abroad to work as a spy for the secret service, and his family would be deported in order to reduce suspicion.

8

Exemplary Models

There were also people who, with God's help, opposed the communist dictatorship's disfiguring of human nature. These people, who came from all levels of society, will remain models for Albanians for all time. At the head of the line, doubtlessly, were several churchmen who suffered with dignity. They did not display the slightest sign of worry in the prisons and concentration camps but held up with a truly evangelical patience. At the top of the list, I will always place Dom Injac Gjoka. He is deserving of commemoration. He is the image of God, a saint. And it is true that very little was and is said about him. A saint like Dom Injac was not able to think badly about anyone. He even considered persecution to be an important part of his religious life and rejoiced in his suffering. He was happy because he felt closer to Jesus Christ on the way to Calvary. The Crucified One was not simply a man but God himself. The more Dom Injac suffered, the more spiritual he felt and the more convinced he was that he was following the teachings of the Gospel. He was found guilty, though he was innocent. Was not Jesus condemned in the same way before him? Dom Injac was threatened with a bullet to the head, which was so little for him compared to the suffering of crucifixion. Dom Injac would have been very happy if his torturers had thought of crucifying him. He could not have hoped for a better death. That was this martyr of religion. He gave testimony about Christ during his court process with an unequaled heroism. After the verdict, this courtroom declaration brought another sublime testimony, that of his blood.

During this period of terror, when no one felt secure but lived with the anxiety of becoming the victim of a stray bullet that would take us to the next world, Dom Injac and I met each other one day at someone else's home. It was the day of his patron saint, which was an excellent occasion to meet and exchange a few words between friends. He mentioned an accountant who had been arrested a few days earlier. We each added our two cents. Some people said that everyone steals. Another said that stealing from the Government was not really stealing; rather, it was charity because the Government stole more from the citizens than they did from it. Others said that, in fact, stealing from the Government was charity, but that you could not steal to the point at which you would get noticed. A luxurious lifestyle in the midst of poverty would be noticed.

When everyone had shared their thoughts on the matter, and the room returned to silence, Dom Injac, who was hosting the gathering, started talking in a way that was well-suited to him as a man of the Church and also as a man of recognized holiness. In fact, his words stupefied his guests: "I feel sorry for the man. He was not able to do his accounts and had made some errors in calculation!" We did not know whether to laugh or cry after such an unexpected and, for us, unimaginable conclusion. Happily, we knew him well enough to understand what he meant. A saint such as he could not think badly of anyone because he knew and lived sanctity to the letter. It never occurred to him to comment on the Lord's words, "Be as simple as doves and as wise as snakes!" Christ left us with this expression so that we would not be as naive as pigeons, who do not know how to defend themselves, but to be as wise as snakes. If attacked, snakes know very well how to defend themselves by slithering into a little hole where no one can follow them. Dear reader, have you already entered a den of snakes? Do you want to follow a snake into its hole, where it lives with its family? Even a saint has to be prudent. Dom Injac, an uncommon saint, was not like those who reflect the Albanian proverb which goes, "Whether you like it or not, even the best are able to mislead seven times a day." Dom Injac never cheated; he could not deceive because he was totally spiritual. That is why we were all seized by insane laughter when we heard him say that with such disarming simplicity.

It was the same with Mother Teresa. I remember in 1922 when she called me down from Kalivaç, where I was living at the time, to see her in Tirana. I had been the first Albanian priest to meet her in Rome in 1991. In order to go from Kalivaç to Tirana and back again, you need one day — a very nice day — because the bumpy, potholed road jerks your car around to the point of making you fly. Once I arrived, I had to wait a long time because Mother Teresa was busy. When she finally had time for me, she asked me a very simple question that she could easily have communicated to me via courier if she had had no one to send to the mountains. I returned to Kalivaç, exhausted and with the thought that saints only live from the Holy Spirit and have no practical sense. Yes, dear reader, I, who do not come close to sainthood, sinned in thinking that, because she had called me. She should have at least offered to pay for the trip, even if I would not have accepted the money. I think it is very good to be a saint, but I also think that humans have to bend a little, either because of people's trickery and pettiness or in order not to look like an idiot when it comes to practical things. Dear reader, to be a saint among saints is not easy.

9

Espionage

Enver Hoxha would not have been able to exercise his tyranny, which is unequaled in modern history, without the service of an uncountable multitude of spies — remarkable spies. He trained them how to be administrators to the point that naive people are surprised even today to see the degree to which they are masters at their craft. Terror facilitates hate in everyone, but, even more, it engenders fear and horror. And it was this panicky fear that pushed many Albanians to become spies. Most people went to the department of Interior Affairs in their district. Nevertheless, some absolutely refused to be a part of this agency, even if the road leading them there was covered in gold. When such people neared the awful building, they crossed the street in order to avoid getting too close to the door that symbolized torture and death. In contrast, those who crossed the threshold of the building, as if they were entering their home, faced misfortune. They were already chastised. They were marked forever with the stain of the criminals.

It is not due to bravery that others did not go there. Rather, if they had shown up, they would have been suspected of being agents of American imperialism looking for a way to achieve power from within the country. However, these two categories of people were called upon when they were at home, in the middle of their own business, unaware of what was waiting for them. Those who did not accept it right away would be forced to accept it after they had been handcuffed and carted off to prison. In this case, instead of being a rat in their house, they were a rat in a prison.

Until 1989, those who agreed to become spies were given amnesty and released from prison. But the amnesty and prison release did not allow them to escape the fact that they had signed the declaration of collaboration with the secret service. They would never be free of this signature for the rest of their lives. It would weigh on them until their graves. And the spies continue their work until today. They are present in every niche of Albanian society from the Government to the Church. They are even better ensconced overseas, where they continue to assure the mission of the guardians of the fortress that they themselves had built. Albanians are wrong to think that they have freed themselves of these people because these spies have gone to the free world. Not even their shadow will escape these spies. Albanians therefore need to pay attention! They cannot believe or say that these spies can no longer harm them. The spies are capable of doing things to you that would never occur to you. If they want to avoid suffering, Albanians need to pay attention to what I am about to say.

10

Psychological Arrests

Atheists act as if they do not believe. They go so far as to state that matter is first, and ideas are second. That does not surprise me. It could not be otherwise because they speak before they reflect. They commit the crime and then realize that they erred. That is why so many people were pardoned by the communists after having been hanged, shot, or savagely tortured to death. After some reflection, the communists mocked the families of these dead, of those who had disappeared without a trace, by erecting a monument as compensation — a monument with a rope around the neck.

Personally, I was arrested dozens of times and always at critical moments or dates. It was a method that aimed to make an impression on the victim, the family, and the social milieu because, always and everywhere, dictators never cease to increase the number of their enemies. It was like that in the past, and it is the same today with every country of the world caught in the web of the American spider, which stays in the middle of the web, ready to pounce on any non-compliant country. I recall my third arrest quite well. It took place only three days before I would complete my ten-year sentence. I was at that time filled with joy because I believed that my suffering in the prisons was coming to an end and that I could finally return home. Just when I was enjoying this beautiful dream, I was summoned. "I am saved!" I said to myself as I rushed to freedom!

No, dear reader. I was sent from the common area to a cell that smelled of mould and humidity. I had nothing to cover myself with. I did not even have a straw mattress, which would have protected me against the cold cement. Prison rats, which were nicer than the spies, judges, and police, kept me company. Instead of family hugs and joy, I was insulted. I had to put up with the dirt and stink of the prison blanket, which caused an unbearable nausea. But when the humidity got into my bones, I quickly forgot the stink and the bugs which moved peacefully across the wrinkles of the blanket. I covered myself as best I could with this blanket of lice. However, a man who believes is strong. At the point where his forces are spent, he knows that the hand of the Lord will protect him from evil because

45

the Lord knows that the believer has faith in Him. Whenever I felt a deep sense of depression and hopelessness coming on, I would begin to pray, and the depression would disappear.

Another time, I was arrested on Christmas Day. That time, I thought that the depression was going to crush me. But God was closer to me than ever. He transformed my prison into the Grotto in Bethlehem and gave me the grace to celebrate Holy Mass there. And just like the Grotto of two thousand years ago, the prison cell was filled with His light because I was there precisely because of Him. He came among us once more on that icy night — on the straw, just like me — shivering, just like me — in the company of animals! Whenever God was present, it was as if the prison was no longer a part of this world, this prison which was for me a true hell. Thus, my head was filled with many ideas. Had I jotted them down at once, I could have produced a marvelous though unedited book. But where I was, people only wrote with their blood.

For people like me, it was easier to psychologically face arrest. Many others, even friends of the Party all the way up the leadership ranks, were thrown into prison at the most disconcerting moments, such as just two or three days before going overseas. The more attached someone was to the Party, the more disconcerting was the arrest because the arrest would morally destroy the person, leave him depressed, and physically and spiritually harm him. When he found himself in front of the judge, he had to submit unconditionally, which would make him look inhuman. His personality, dignity, and gravity were all destroyed. Only his imagination was left. It would function in a unique way, inventing all sorts of nonexistent conspiracies and plots which menaced the Party while simultaneously recognizing that the Party had the legitimate right to counter these actions, that is, the right to fill the prisons and cemeteries.

At first, priests were tortured to death or until they confessed. The poor torturers assumed that the priest was the first to learn the crimes which were commonly committed everywhere. They did not know that the man of the altar is the last to be interested in this sort of thing, that soon after he hears them in confession and tries to find a solution, he immediately forgets them, even if he meets the penitent in the street. He only rethinks them before the Lord, from whom we can hide nothing. However, we priests can adapt to everything, whether to comfort and convenience or to privations of the most urgent necessity.

This is the case, for example, in the absence of toilets and the need to satisfy bodily needs, like hens in a henhouse. Or in the need to sleep close to people who suffer from all sorts of illnesses, and whose bad breath ceaselessly assaults your nose and mouth until at last you fall asleep. And then, in your sleep, you feel another knocking into you in the haunting anguish of prison nights.

In Handcuffs

In the twilight of March 30, 1963, the Police were alarmed that I could no longer be found in Mirditë when they came looking to put me in handcuffs. They had to mobilize an entire network to find my location, as if I had fled to who knows where. I was peacefully enjoying *Dardhë* Pukë[1], where I had gone to celebrate Mass. They found me and, in the light of the day, tied my two hands with rusty iron that served as handcuffs. Imagine my profound humiliation! Not because I was innocent, but because the handcuffs had been put on me by the most radical antireligious Albanians. Those same people today cry crocodile tears over the lives of more than one-hundred thousand Albanians who died at their own hands. For them, I was nothing but a simple, ordinary criminal.

The wolves had put me in handcuffs and had closed the churches in fifteen villages in Mirditë and its environs which by the grace of God, I was able to reopen later. This photo shows the reconstruction of Korthpulë church in Mirditë region (1999).

---

1   *Dardhë* is a village of the commune of Blerim in the district of Pukë, Albania.

The Department of the Interior's *Gaz*[2], into which I had been forcefully thrown, sped down the road. The mountains and the plains faded before my eyes, and I had the impression that I would never see them again. I was invaded by a deep sadness, but suddenly, like a consolation, the words of Jesus came to mind: "I send you out like sheep among the wolves," and, above all, "The gates of hell will never prevail against my Church." The wolves had put me in irons and had closed fifteen village churches in Mirditë. In effect, He who had founded the Church and who does not need the permission of the wolves came to my aid twenty-six years later, on November 4, 1990, when I was supported by fifty thousand faithful of Shkodër. He gave the first sign of his triumph against the pack of wolves.

But at the moment of my arrest, that future day was still a long way off, like a dream, while the Gaz flew along the road towards the torturers. In handcuffs, I tried to give myself courage by recalling the words of the Master, for whom I wore the handcuffs: "Rejoice! Rejoice! For your sadness will change into joy!"; "Do not fear those who can kill the body, but be on your guard against those who want to kill your soul." Who was the criminal and who was the victim? After we had been in the car for at least four hours, they threw me into a cell in the prison at *Lezhë*.[3] I did not realize where I was until I felt throughout my whole being the prison's glacial cold. The handcuffs had been taken off and I had been thrown onto the filthy prison planks.

I felt relieved, like someone who had gotten to the coast after having fought against the waves while trying to save his life. The prison cell seemed to me like a monk's cell. I was almost happy to be there. Instead of living with the permanent anguish of being imprisoned or deported, I now lived with the anguish of waiting. Everything had been accomplished: I was crucified! The great prison, outside of my cell, had its chagrins and its physical and psychological illnesses caused by the Officer of the Department of the Police, Bardhok Ndue Prendi, who prowled the countryside of *Kashnjet*[4] with two dogs. He terrorized the penniless, poorly dressed, and starving peasants who

---

2 *Gaz*—a brand of Soviet cars. The Gaz factory was at Nizhny Novgorod (rebaptized Gorki by the Soviets). In Russian, GAZ stands for Gorkovsky Avtomobilny Zavod. It was founded in 1932 with American help. It is the second most productive car factory in Russia by car units produced.

3 *Lezhë*—Located in the Northwest of Albania, it is the hub of the district of the same name.

4 *Kashnjet*—Village in the district of Lezhë.

were also forced to serve him at table with all they had. As a priest, I baptized more than two hundred babies every year, but one hundred of them died annually due to malnutrition. Mirditë suffered under the most savage persecution because, until 1953, it had been resisting communism. That is why Hoxha spilled more blood there than in the other regions of Albania. He sought to displace Mirditors from their territories in order to thin out the North in the case that they did not want to submit to the regime. But one day they were forced to submit, leaving, however, Mirditë without many Mirditors. I cannot confirm their return to where I had last seen them before the start of my own suffering.

But now Mirditë was outside, and I was inside prison. And I remembered that, in occupying myself with Mirditë's problems, I had neglected my own soul. Overwhelmed as I was with the problems of others, I had forgotten that I had to be filled with grace and the virtues. I understood that I was almost empty, and that if I continued a bit further on this path, I would collapse like so many others. I therefore considered my arrest as a sign from above. It goes without saying that the expression "from above" has nothing to do with the Government.

In fact, when I was arrested, I was a mediocre curé with a horizon as large as a sewing needle. When I was released from prison twenty-six years later, a huge window had opened in front of me, from which I could see the whole world with my free eyes. I had been delivered of all prejudices. My eyes had been purified by physical tortures, which had immensely deepened my spiritual wealth. I needed to be shut in prisons in order to realize that I had built the churches of Mirditë while feeling full of terror for Hoxha. I had built living churches, but I had forgotten to nourish my own soul. Everything inside of me had started to rust and age. I had come to understand that if I failed to live consciously, several souls would certainly end up in hell. Suffering can inundate the spirit and, thereby freeing us of interim values that are in fact mostly anti-values, closely connect us to eternal values.

Dear reader, do not think that it was easy being a Catholic curé in my days, when "the nut with a hard shell," as I was, employed in my preaching the same vocabulary as I use today. I had remained the same free man, the kind of person that the Communist Party hated the most, the same Party that, because of its hatred for me, had sequestered all the items of my churches that were situated in the mountains of Mirditë on the paths of the mountain goats. I had to climb by foot because I could not possibly own a mule. With religious services being so numerous, I had to walk, sweating all over, the paths of these poor mountains from the location of my mission. My presbytery had been taken over by the village infirmary. The nurse, Maliq Sokol Djala, had transformed it into a center of corruption and a public house. It was directed by a man who was not a man and whom, if I was not a Catholic priest, I would endow with a number of nasty labels.

At any moment, they would haul me before their "synagogues," as the gospel says, in order to terrorize me and to get me away from my churches. I would have to walk for sixteen hours on foot in order to present myself to the summoning authorities. Once I arrived, exhausted, I would be on the receiving end of the most barbarous threats solely because I celebrated Mass Sundays and weekdays. They told me that the Mass impeded people from working, that I owned a radio set without the necessary authorization, and that they were going to place restrictions on me. They did not delay in forcing themselves into my home and confiscating the small set, which had been my only way of communicating with the external world. They feared that I would contact the Pope in Rome. They accused me of destroying medicinal plants because I had invited the faithful to come to church on Palm Sunday with palm branches. One day, out of the blue, a peasant came to church with a foal that he wanted to offer to the master of the house. The communists took it by force and kept it for themselves. They did the same thing with all the nationalized goods that they had stolen!

Every Sunday I had the chief of the Police department or chief of the locale as a guest in the church courtyard. They certainly did not come to attend the Mass. They came to intimidate and stop people from attending. These churchgoers had stopped going to the endless communist meetings, but they never missed the Mass. The Police came to hinder me in my work. They yelled in the church courtyard, "The people do not need your lies. They are our business!" I never worried about these undesirable friends or their yelling because the people were with me. The faithful did the impossible in aiding the Church despite their terrible poverty. The State failed to support its own institutions. However, the faithful supported the churches while also looking after their families. Schools and cultural centers, however, looked like hen houses.

Because they failed to stop people from attending Mass through certain ways, they renewed their accusations at Party gatherings and in newspapers. The first Secretary of the Party committee accused me of baptizing babies by force and of devoting myself to committing violence on the population. They then attacked me in newspapers, particularly in *Zeri i Popullit*.[5] It was the prelude to my arrest! The communists trembled when they saw the pictures of Jesus in the poor mountains. Those were the only moral and cultural markings that opposed the traces left in their consciences by the immoral, thieving, leeching, and demagogic state. Everything was permitted for Party members. Their principal work consisted of doing nothing but pursuing pleasure and beautiful women and drinking and eating wherever and however they wanted. They enjoyed absolute liberty within the limits defined by the Party, while the poor, nonmembers of the Party, had lost all freedom. The poor had only had work and no rights, as they had been returned to a system of slavery. Tell me how a priest could remain indifferent to such a situation? Faced with this state of things, I only had recourse to the words of Jesus: "Race of serpents, hypocrites, who resemble white sepulchres on the outside, but stink of a cadaver on the interior."

I had a pistol pressed against my neck to shut me up. When they realized that I had no intention of shutting up, they put me in handcuffs and put me through all sorts of anguish about being arrested. Henceforth, in prison, I no longer had anything to fear. The Government had declared war on me with iron and fire. The scene of the combat was a tragicomedy, with Dom Simon playing one role and the Government the other. Naturally, the Government thought it would quickly win the battle with me. But they had forgotten that behind the shoulders of "Mister" was another much larger and more powerful "MISTER" against whom no one could contend. Realizing that there was nothing that they could stick on me, they decided to send me far away from the scene as undesirable. And so the page of the drama of the Hoxha regime was turned, and the setting was now the decor of the prison. The people whom the Government wanted to deprive of human value were backstage. But from time to time, some were able to make an entrance.

* * *

5 *Zeri i Popullit — The People's Voice.*

All these thoughts came to my mind, and I began to return to earth when I was thrown onto the rough boards of the prison cell, which was just underneath the office of the Chief of Police, Azem Kerxhalliu. I do not intend to describe my suffering and pain, which is not interesting to anyone. I hope that my testimony is not in vain. It is the testimony of a man who has seen with his own eyes and touched with his own hands what one calls "historical truth." It is for the reader to decide who is the victim and who the criminal.

Kerxhalliu was at the top, and Dom Simon at the bottom, the Chief of Police in his office and the priest in his cell. In his office, above the head of Dom Simon, the Chief of Police exercised an unprecedented terror on all the residents of Lezhë. He wanted them all on their knees. Guilt or innocence had no importance. Guilt is quickly invented if necessary. Every day this docile servant of the tyrant of Tirana summoned twenty or thirty rebellious people to his office to educate them. Then, the dance of the devil commenced over the head of Dom Simon. Heavy steps, then nervous steps which creaked under the boots' nails, terrifying screams from which, as they took on a higher pitch, could be clearly distinguished: "I will get you fired right now! I will put you under arrest! I will shoot you now!"

A few days later, after I had become familiar with the tortures of the cell and with Spiro Tate, the spy who had upset me, my anguish started to wane. I was saved. I was much happier than the poor people who, on the outside, expected at any moment to be jobless, arrested, or shot — in short, to be educated. At the time, I was already jobless and behind bars. Only my execution remained. But Calvary's long path stood between arrest and execution! It required a very long time, and at the moment I have little left to say about the slaps, punches, kicks, and knocks against the walls and floor that I received every time I encountered the examining magistrates: Shkelzen, Bajraktari, and their four colleagues.

Later, after what we believed to be the fall of communism, poor Mark Dema told me that my "educator" had found refuge in Rome with Ines Angjeli Murzaku, daughter-in-law of his nephew, daughter of a famous atheist and dean of the faculty of Marxism. At that time, she preached the gospel for Radio Vatican while studying at the Gregorian University. However, after completing his studies at the Urbaniana University and seventeen years in political prison, Dema, who was a fervent and cultured Catholic, had asked for the job before she did. Curiously, they preferred to hire the young daughter of communism. It was in her house that comrade Shkelzen had lived like a king for six months. This was paid for by the Vatican while he negotiated with the Italian Government over the sale of communist secrets because, dear reader, he was not foolish like other Albanians. While torturing us, he had learned well that this world is give-and-take. That is why the great nephews and nieces of my massacred prison colleagues slept under bridges in the civilized world. The only secret that they could have negotiated was our martyrdom, which apparently did not serve anyone except the Lord in Heaven!

After having tortured me as was normal and realizing that this route was not moving things ahead, they turned to softer methods. I was summoned by a Deputy Police chief, who scolded me as he pretended to show me compassion in seeing me in handcuffs and with a broken jaw. "If you were not part of the reactionary clergy," he told me with hypocritical regret, "at the moment you could be pursuing your occupation of radiologist with Doctor Lito. What pushed you, my friend, to become a priest?" I responded: "To defend Jesus!" He became quiet and took me back to prison again.

Four months with the examining magistrates was enough to create a slave psychosis. In Albania, terror prepared generations of slaves. Only death could cure such an ailment. Death came from lengthy torture via electric courants, ice baths, breaking of bones, the amputation of arms and legs, cigarette burns, eye puncturing, wedging nails in tongues, and all at the table of the examining magistrates — an elegant symbol of freedom of speech, a collection worthy of a museum, a collection of all the most dreadful tortures ever used by humanity. I owe it to the truth to state that when I was arrested, some of these tortures were no longer in use. Perhaps that is due to the fact that certain slaves had become so cowardly that slaps, punches, kicks, poking, and spitting were later sufficient. It was the prologue to what then was called democracy!

I went before the tribunal on August 4, 1964. The room was full to the rafters. Family members and friends, ever more angry at a regime that they had never loved, sat in the first rows. Imagine how great their anger became when I was condemned in this courtroom to ten years of hard labor for being an enemy of the Serbian, Russian, and Chinese communist regimes, which is to say the allies of Hoxha, without which he could not hold power.

Moreover, I had begun to give my opinion on the first two of these allies at a time when the Government also said nothing less, both on television and in the newspapers. The Government was even harsher than I was because it had much more information than I did. My fault was to get ahead of the Government, informing it that we next had to break with the Chinese. "Just wait," I said. "They will start to say bad things about the Chinese." My words came true while I was on trial. I left in handcuffs, which I would wear for ten more years. I put myself into a worse situation with the confession before the examining magistrate. I told him that the first person who had to be condemned for agitation and propaganda had to be Enver Hoxha himself, who was connected body and soul with Stalin. In 1960, Hoxha condemned Stalin in his famous article, "The Cult of the Individual," which appeared in the journal *Zeri i Populit, The Voice of the People*. In reality, the paper only published Hoxha's voice. The poor magistrates had learned at the faculty of law, "Keep typing. You will succeed at creating something by typing." Amazed and wide-eyed, apparently, they fell back on whatever they had learned during their studies.

In the work camps, I refused to work, insisting that I was a prisoner of conscience and that I therefore did not have to do forced work. I told others to do the same. Why did the regime boast about the work accomplishments of slaves who had been reduced to skeletons? But since work is a part of human nature, having nothing to do is the worst condemnation. That is why, to unwind, calm our nerves, and interrupt the monotony of prison, we often did work. Or we would purposely break a foot or an arm only so that we could take it easy for a while in the hospital, where we had our own bed. In the camp, however, we slept like pigs.

We called the totally closed-up and windowless vehicle that took us to the hospital the Meat Machine. The dictator feared the light, and therefore windows. And he was right. The enemy becomes more dangerous when he is like a sausage, feet and fists tied up, even with broken arms or legs, and guarded by bayonets. Because then there was the risk that someone would hear our yells through the truck's windows and call for an insurrection to overturn the regime. Those on the outside, more fearful than we prisoners, would kick off the counter revolution, even while trembling with terror! A double-sided tragicomedy of slavery!

When they realized that the only thing that pleased me was to spit venom against the supposed popular power, which had transformed Albania into a blossoming garden by embellishing the prisons and the deportation camps; by people gnawed at by hunger, by terror, by horror, by tuberculosis, cancer, heart disease, STDs; by military service and constant government assemblies; by so-called voluntary work service; by novel forms of torture; by finding the quickest way to dumb down the human being, they thought they would reeducate me in concentration camps. But when they saw that I was incorrigible, they transferred me to the prison in Burrel, where I presented myself as the curé of the prison. After all, every prison needed to have a religious service.

The director of the prison, always a Tosk because the Government had absolutely no confidence in Ghegs, even less in a Gheg who would betray himself by becoming communist, stared speechlessly at me, because he thought that Ghegs called the miller the "curé." He therefore thought that I was a miller and, since they had thrown me in prison, a capitalist miller. But when I told him that I was a man of the Church, he responded, "What are you telling me? We buried religion a long time ago because it had not solved any problems. Only communism can solve problems. The future belongs to it." "You are mistaken, sir," I replied. "You have not buried religion, and you cannot. Christianity is an ancient religion, two thousand years old. It has encountered every obstacle, every persecution, every polemic, every opposition, even those more violent than yours. That is why it has acquired an eternal immunity. It became a global religion because it was the principal contributor to the building of the current civilization, even the culture of human values, whereas your communism is not even fifty years old and you are in the middle of devouring one another. It is a nice monastery, but you lack monks and will never find them."

Though he was a communist, the director tried hard to conceal the pleasure that he felt in hearing my response. He wanted to add something, but his throat seemed to tighten, and he said nothing. He recalled that he was not living with his family and that he had to take full responsibility for his position. He also told a few prison officers, "Do not put him in a cell with others. Put him in the isolation cell for thirty days. He is a huge danger to society!" I was therefore put into isolation, with the humid concrete as sleeping quarters and the filthy and constricting walls as my friends. Naturally, I lived on nothing but bread and water.

The service officer opened the window every day and asked me if I was ready to come out and start to work. And every time I told him that it was not necessary to tire myself out because it was work that machines could do, and I did not want the machines to be unemployed. That would set off the officer, and I would be left to live my prison life. But God does not let anyone, not even the most ferocious dictator, commit evil perfectly. And therefore, a liberal officer, when taking us to the toilets, would let us sneak off a little to the place that had our own stuff. Then we would go back to our isolation cells with a few precious things — a piece of bread or a blanket to protect us from the humidity of the flooring, which aged our bones and made us as pale as living cadavers without flesh or blood but full of health problems.

But I, the eternal dissenter, defied communism. Thanks to my iron health, the fruit of a morally sound and athletic life, my body transformed bread and water into vitamins, carbohydrates, and minerals that always kept me in good form. But I also enjoyed good health because I did not lack another nourishment, which is the most important: prayer. No one could take that away from me. Thanks to prayer, I was safe and sound and could leave the isolation cell, where thousands of innocent people had died. When I spoke to the Lord, I felt stronger, invincible. When my bodily strength left me, heavenly powers took over, drawn from God. It is natural. When we talk with a good and educated man, we regain our strength and retain for a long time our spiritual power with which God also nourishes our soul. Imagine how great this spiritual force is when it comes from God, the Blessed Virgin, the angels and the saints who supported me. This force comes to a greater degree when we can communicate with Jesus Christ himself and take him into our poor hearts. He is the source and author of everything: life, civilization, and, above all, eternity. Those who do not know this consolation are so unfortunate.

Day and night passed by in such a way, between suffering and hope, in communist prisons. I could leave for the work camp, that is, go from one death to another. In the camps of forced work, where I would pass ten years of "reeducation," I nearly forgot all the suffering of the instruction because that suffering was taken over by new suffering. I felt very bad in this conglomeration of every sort of Albanian, from every region and religion, united only in our common suffering. We were all in the same boat, under permanent and heavy terror exerted by the Government on prisoners, on crazy prisoners who lived one on top of the other.

We were divided into three categories: the reeducated, the non-reeducated, and the non-retraining. The first category enjoyed the privilege of working in offices. The others got to work in mines, where brass and pyrite were extracted and where the work was so harsh that many prisoners purposely hurt themselves in order to escape that hell. And then you can imagine other, unwished for accidents that occurred every day. Accidents also happened in the great prison called Albania. And I am not talking about what took place in the depths of the underground mine tunnels. No one cared about security regulations to protect workers' lives. It was hoped, rather, that they would die as quickly as possible. In the camp, I was always considered to be the warped individual who harmed the quality of the work because not only did I not work, but I told others to do like me. We were deader than the dead!

I therefore found myself in disastrous living conditions, in which I could lose not only teeth and hair, but also my head. I was inundated by ideas and thoughts. Thanks to my accessible and candid nature, I openly expressed them in the prison. I was not content to express them only orally. I also had the idea to write them down and send them directly to the tyrant in Tirana. He never tired of breaking my knees and arms as a result. Prison guards would break all of me, allowing me to achieve the most beautiful and oldest dream I had, one that they would never have imagined at that time: My name would be written on the long list of Catholic martyrs. I therefore began to send a long series of letters which eventually came to over one thousand pages. I said everything. I wrote that the Communist Party was nothing but a bunch of immoral thieves who had sold out to the Serbs, then the Russians, and then the Chinese, who were the ones who always made the law for Albania. I wrote that Central Committee members of the Party had nothing better to do than kill and dishonor people and to imprison and deport the innocent. One day when they finished with the poor, they would do the same with their own people. I wrote, and I waited impatiently for my execution. But instead of killing me, they poisoned my brother, Dom Lazër

Jubani. They knew that it was the best revenge: Leave me alive, in a more deplorable state, with wounds even worse than physical ones, wounds of my soul.

My writing, which directly and openly affirmed the truth, made more and more enemies for me, from government workers to other prisoners. It reminds me of what aristocrats used to say: "*Molti nemici, molto onore, ma anche molto terrore!*" ("Many enemies, much honor, but also much terror!"). Most of those who had focused the dictatorship's hatred for the Catholic Church on me were, in many respects, completely unprepared for me. They could never understand what it meant to be "a Catholic priest," and would often stare at me, wide-eyed, as if I had come from the moon. One of them even told me that clergymen were nothing but abandoned infants, found in the street, without family and deprived of feelings, and who therefore became priests. I was asked all sorts of questions from every corner of the prison, even from the director. The principal one was, "*Why do not Catholic priests get married?*"

How could I explain this to people who would not ever be able to grasp it anyway? Tell them the truth or get them to laugh a little? I thought of approaching this situation with humor, knowing beforehand that the truth would not please them. I told them that when God created the world, he made a muezzin, an Orthodox priest, a Catholic priest, and three women. The Orthodox priest took one, and the muezzin the other two. The Catholic priest, without a wife, complained to God, who replied: "Go and ask the muezzin to rent one to you." I responded like that, certain that they would not understand me if I explained to them that Jesus had also been celibate, while most Catholic priests up to the 11th century could be married men. Such a situation caused a problem for the Church due to wifely influence. Every married man knows that he cannot do anything without asking his wife's opinion.

But the priest is married first to the Church, and things would not work out if he was controlled by his wife. Marriage would also divide the priest in two, half for his family and half for the Church, which would not leave enough time for him to support his growth and even less to cultivate the virtues. The Church would be totally different now without this. Thus, Pope Gregory VII Hildebrand, who sat on the throne of St. Peter in the eleventh century, took the decision that the Latin Catholic Church would no longer ordain married men in the Latin rite. From that time onwards, those who set out on this difficult path really had to think a lot before committing to the priesthood. A Latin rite priest must promise to never marry so that he can devote himself entirely to God and to his neighbor. And there, in a few words, is the long and complicated history of what is known about celibacy in the Latin Church.[6]

But let us return to the prison. In prison, like everywhere else, terrorists and gangsters quickly became spies in order to escape the heaviest sentences. They sold themselves for a few coins without worrying about becoming the tools that the secret police exploited against honest people. They usually presented themselves as philo-soviets. They loudly proclaimed their "ideas," while many honest people, knowing their obligation, were constrained to listen to their nonsense. One of them, who had no family support, took care of the sewing of prison uniforms in order to earn something to eat. One day I gave him something to stitch. We prisoners ironically called the ugly cotton jacket which protected us from the cold "Stalin's covering." When he had finished the work, I asked him: "How would you like to be paid? As in the Soviet Union, because that is where your heart is, or as in the USA?" He quickly replied, "As in the USA," because, being a fine connoisseur of the voluntary work that he was in the middle of doing, he knew he would otherwise end up with a handful of ants.

---

6   On the subject of the celibacy of priests in the Latin rite, the reader will find a more precise explanation in C. Cochini, S. J., *The Apostolic Origins of Priestly Celibacy*, which was a thesis defended in 1969 and published in 1981 as a new edition (Ad Solem) in 2006. This thesis was recently taken up again by Cardinal Brandmüller. An outline written by Father Cochini himself is available at www.clerus.org/clerus/dati/2002-04/05-6/Celib_sac.htm. (French editor's note).

12

Torture

I do not know if anyone has studied the history of torture from the beginnings of civilization. Be that as it may, that would be a history rich in variety and, above all, rich in pain. I also do not know if anyone has written a history of torture in Albania's communist prisons. That contribution to the history of torture in the world culminates in the crucifixion of God in person. I will make my contribution in retracing what I felt and was submitted to.

Some typical tortures, without much variation, included the sawing of hands and feet (without anesthetic, obviously), the expansion of the body with a pump, hanging by feet or from the branch of a tree in the middle of winter under the whip of a glacial wind until complete bodily paralysis. That last torture was even used in the work camps when someone did not do the required work. And then there was the compression of parts of the body with iron that sank into the flesh. Blood would flow, and the resulting serious wounds would quickly become gangrenous. There was also physically hard and prolonged work, isolation in tiny, refrigerated cells, and whipping that led to hospitalization.

One of the most odious tortures was the removal of a mustache with pliers. It was odious not so much for the physical pain, which was not a little, but for the moral pain from this terrible dishonor. It seems that the communists had picked up this torture, like many others, from the east, and used it each time they wanted to humiliate someone by leaving him in a laughable state. A man whose mustache had been removed could not enter his own home except to go to his tomb! It was terrible to see these men of the mountains go into their cells with beautiful mustaches and go out, all bloodied in the spot where a little earlier the symbol of the man of the mountains had been! Poor guys!

I knew more than one companion in misery who ended up with hollow shoulders and bones clearly visible because the skin had been burnt with boiled eggs that had just been taken out of boiling water. Others had backs full of holes from the nails that had been pushed in during interrogation, or scars from lit cigarettes pressed on their skin. More imaginatively, there was the torture with a sack: The prisoner was put inside a sack. So that he would not be bored and lonely, he was closed up with two or three cats. Then the torturers would begin to hit the sack, sometimes hitting the man, sometimes the cats. The scared cats would fiercely claw at the body of the man or bite him all over.

There was one interrogation during which the prisoner was placed in a casket, his hands and feet tied. He was tortured to the point at which it was doubtful he would get out alive. At the high point of the torture, the man's teeth were pulled out so that he would not bite his tongue and so that he could no longer confess to his crimes or those of others. And people are shocked to see me without teeth! I tell them that I can no longer stand teeth in my mouth. I am afraid that I will bite my own tongue, above all now that it is free in a certain manner, and then I would not be able to recount what I went through.

Often during an interrogation, victims were transformed into living candelabra. Pine needles were pushed under their fingernails and were then lit on fire. Then the flames burned onto the flesh of the burning fingers. And then there was the torture of sleeplessness. The victim was stopped from sleeping for entire weeks. To keep him awake, he was thrown into a room filled with water up to his knees. There was also the water drop torture. The victim was set in position, hands and feet tied, and then a drop of water would hit him at a steady rate on the forehead: drip, drip, drip, drip. It was really hell, and it had one goal: make it so that the prisoners could breathe with the lungs of Hoxha, see with his eyes, hear with his ears, speak with his tongue, and lose all personal identity, everything that distinguishes one person from another! There was no other issue. We had to do as Hoxha, who himself never breathed with his own lungs nor spoke with his own mouth but with that of Stalin, of Tito, or of Mao Zedong. Sometimes he spoke with the tongue of the living and sometimes with the tongue of the dead until no tongue remained. And his successor would have to collect all the cut-out tongues and seek a way to supposedly speak freely, in order to create the illusion that democracy had arrived! It is the cut-off tongues of yesterday that speak today!

In the beginning, these tortures were carried out on the bodies of the most dangerous and rebellious prisoners. Then these actions were used on their own comrades, who one by one ended up in prison. I can mention Party directors, Hoxha's comrades, such as Kadri Hazbiu, Beqir Balluku, and a few other communists who had not conformed to the Central Committee's orders. When the interrogation meeting of the comrades would come to an end, the comrades went in front of the tribunal totally destroyed. It was normal. From the communist paradise where they had lived, they fell into the precipice of hell, where the people they had directed lived. It was justice that they suffered in the same way as the others.

But Party comrades were made to suffer more than the other prisoners. Obviously, the tribunal would condemn them to death. But before being shot, the torturers would receive the order to cut off noses and ears and adorn bodies with knife cuts and other such ornaments, so that the former communists would go to the tomb as the chief enemies of savage tribes, which, by the way, they had been. At that time, we would hear horrifying shrieks that even today, when I recall them, give me goosebumps. After the cries, we would hear the dry sound of the iron doors opening. It was the prelude to the execution, to salvation, to liberty. The man without a nose, ears, legs, or arms felt happy, mutilated as he was, to be led to his execution.

When I visited *Moscow*, my guide showed me around the Department of Internal Affairs, which was situated in the center of the city and resembled a giant serpent.[1] In the dark depths of this building, which had such a sad reputation, were caves where Penkovski, Beria, and numerous other comrades of Stalin went through the same ordeal as Albania's unfortunate Party members. "Our glorious leader" had learned a lot from the great butcher Stalin. In those kinds of places, a person can only last through recourse to prayer. Otherwise, he can do nothing but blaspheme.

---

1   The author is alluding to the immense building, *Lubyanka Square*, which was KGB headquarters and prison for dissidents and opponents of the USSR.

Dom Simon in Moscow in front of Lenin's Mausoleum. (1997)

Dom Simon in Russia at the spot where Father Alexander Men, an Orthodox priest, was executed by the KGB.

Dom Simon in Russia at the tomb of Father Alexander Men

Dom Simon in Russia accompanied by his good friend Dominique Combette, author of the Preface and Afterword of this book. (1997)

I do not rejoice at the death of anyone, as that is against the religion to which I adhere with all the force of my soul. But it is natural for me to feel greater compassion for those who have suffered like me and my friends than for the dictator, even though I pray in the same manner for the former and the latter. I recall those who shared the same fate: Sulçe Begu, savagely tortured, and Dom Lazër Shanto. Both were dragged to the tomb, as their arms and legs had been sawed off. Dom Leke Sirdani and Dom Pjeter Çuni were drowned in a septic tank after their intestines had been inflated by a compressor used to inflate tires. I pray just as much for those led to the pit to be shot, but who were brought back to the prison and invited to reflect and sign in confession to all sorts of slander. Others were brought many times to the edge of a tomb. They were psychologically destroyed, having been simultaneously alive and dead many times, when in fact people only die once definitively. They fell for the trap and signed. After successfully obtaining the signatures of these dead, the examining magistrate was rewarded by the Interior Ministry because he had saved the regime from a certain counter-revolutionary danger!

There were also among us people who had come to Albania from the free world in order to appreciate the marvelous reality so strongly boasted by the communist regime. When it came to spreading the quixotic slogan, "the ideas of the Workers' Party are the future of the world," this regime did not hesitate to open its wallet, which was filled with the blood and sweat of the people. When these visitors from the free world saw with their eyes the reality in Albania, they started to talk a little too much, given that they were not used to watching their words. And so, as was appropriate, in order to taste the advantages and superiority of communism over bloody capitalism, they also ended up in prison with us. Less habituated than we were to facing the awful treatment, they would hang themselves with drapes close to the prison windows. Or, even worse, believing that they could have recourse to forms of resistance which were normal in the free world, they would die from their hunger strikes. "You do not want to eat anything? Great. You can save the Government some money by not eating this filthy, worm-infested bread!"

The fact was that we were all in some way on a permanent and involuntary hunger strike. The hunger was so terrible and throbbing that we all had the impression that a great big dog had entered into our guts and was eating our intestines at its ease, unhindered by anyone. It was an unprecedented torture, which obsessed prisoners to the point that they would hide a dead comrade in order to get an extra portion. The daily portion was so tiny that most prisoners only had a mouthful, which left nothing for dinner or the next morning. Then the dog would recommence stirring our guts, and another would die, which meant an additional portion the next day. Hunger would often force prisoners to eat the vomit of a sick comrade whose stomach could no longer tolerate anything. *Hunger even pushed us to eat the body of a dead prisoner.* When the guards came to get the body, they would notice that an arm or a leg was missing. The evidence could lead one to suppose that the numerous rats living all around us, as if keeping us company, had eaten it.

Another torture was linked to our natural urges. We were all put tight together in one small room on top of one another, living together, men, women, and children, boys and girls. And we had to meet our bodily needs, right there, in the presence of everybody. That remains engraved in my spirit as one of the worst tortures because it was the most odious and most unspeakable.

I came to understand that a man lying prostrate sees himself more as an animal than he really is. Perhaps his hands seem to him more like feet when he is stretched out on the earth. Bunched one against the other and in the absence of the opposite sex, with other beasts abandoned to the little pile of straw, awful instincts emerge. It would happen that a prisoner, blinded by animal urges, could not resist assaulting the prisoner next to him. Often these types of male prisoners were spies and thought that they could make a new contribution to Enver Hoxha by treading on the bodies and souls of his enemies. Imagine what happened when the victim woke up with a start, faced with the aggressor's impulses while they were all stacked against each other, like a row of bricks.

In prison, insanity took over. Things often ended with multiple kicks in order to put out the animal desire that pushes us humans to lower ourselves to the level of the four-footed. It even happened in these confrontations that prisoners would puncture each other's eyes. I witnessed such scenes, which ended up with a court process that was as awful as it was ridiculous and that always ended with the condemnation of the victim. What that meant in the end was the aggravation of the initial pain and renewed attacks from the beast.

One significant torture consisted in shooting the most respected individuals in the prisons and camps, with everyone else being condemned to watch as spectators. After the executions, the torturers unceasingly repeated the scene played out in Zalli i Kirit. They placed the bloody cadavers in a circle with a bonnet on each head and a cigarette in hand. And then the execution team sang and danced around the cadavers with the songs of Labs (people in the South of Albania, close to the Tosks) and those of the *Korçare*.[2] I do not think anyone has ever seen a more macabre concert! Some of my companions in suffering, when taking in these unbearable atrocities, lost their minds. In the best cases, they pretended to be insane, eating their own excrement, in order to save their lives from an ever-harsher life behind bars. I even remember their names, the first one coming to mind being Muhammet Kosovrasti.

It goes without saying that I also faced the communist mosaic of the torture of living flesh and nerves. Each time I was interrogated, the magistrate would order that my irons be tightened to the point at which they would dig into me. Drop after drop of blood would redden the metals and end up on the floor. Then the magistrate would give the second order, to shake my hands, which were already raw, until the pain became even more intolerable. And when I lost consciousness, "the good Samaritan" bent down a bit and took care of my wounds with tobacco. Then, as soon as I opened my eyes, he would begin to kick me. When his feet got tired, he took his truncheon and tied me up again, threw me on the floor and started kicking again and hitting me where he could. The criminal!

When he returned home, he naturally complained of fatigue because he had been working so hard at the building of socialism. Exhausted after one of these meetings, he sat down in the chair in his office and asked me spitefully, "So, are you going to tell me who your collaborators are?" And I would respond: "Yes, I will tell you right now. I collaborated with Moses, the prophet Elijah, Isaiah, Ezekiel, and then with Christ." "What are you saying?" he would ask me, looking at me speechlessly. Then his face would light up with the hope of discovering the whole spy network: "Who is this Christ, what is his family name, where does he live?" "He lives in the Gospel," I would calmly respond with the humor of a man with half broken bones who relied on a force that the magistrate could not understand

---

2   *Korçare* — Of the city of Korçë, in the Southeast of Albania.

any more than he could understand the names of those who really were my closest collaborators and from whom I anticipated salvation from the evil that weighed on my head.

During a boiling August day, the Police officer of the Burrel prison came into my cell with thirty-five other, mostly ordinary, people and said to Sokol Martini, a well-known gangster: "Sokol, beat up Dom Simon because he speaks against the Government!" In fact, none of the gangsters moved. They had reacted in similar fashion in other circumstances when given an order because some of them did not easily obey police officers. People like Sokol Martini quickly became spies, but they nonetheless retained a certain sense of honor. He regarded beating up a poor old guy with white hair like me for no reason to be a vile act. Moreover, the difficult prison life did not completely wipe out their respect for priests. At the bottom of their tormented hearts, they still heard the voice of God.

A little time after that, for a reason that escapes me, we saw the door of our cell open. The same officer, Mustafa Lika, stood behind the door. I seized the occasion and walked over to talk to him. "I am condemned," I told him, "because I speak about and protest the injustices of this Government. I am condemned, but not to be beaten solely on your orders. You wear the uniform in order to maintain order, not for sowing disorder. You use your uniform to divide people and cause trouble even here in prison, in this place of misery into which we have been thrown by your boss, Enver Hoxha, whose jaw I would break if I could find him right now. But because I cannot do anything against him, I will break your jaw, since you are one of his worthy offspring!" No sooner said than done, I punched him. His kepi flew five meters in the corridor. Then the prison spies Jorgo Laboviti and Rexhep Lazri joined in the fight, disfiguring me with their punches and insults because I had dared hit a Police officer. And to think that those two were political prisoners like me! We found ourselves under the same roof as strangers; we lived without love and died without mourning. The death of one even signified the survival of the other.

I recount this episode of offence against the Police to help you understand why I could not control myself and fell into a trap — me, a man of the Church, who was not permitted to punch others or even to think of doing so. There is a story that one time a Capuchin, in leaving the church, found himself face to face with a sworn enemy of

Jesus. For no reason, the man, like the Police with me, slapped him violently on the cheek. Seeing the inflamed eyes of the Capuchin and that he was quite well-built, he asked immediately after the strike: "Are you thinking of hitting me back? Have you forgotten that the Gospel, which you have vowed to preach, teaches: When someone hits you on the cheek, you have to turn the other?" The Capuchin humbly offered the other cheek and waited for the second slap, which, when it came, left the outline of five fingers on the Capuchin's cheek, despite his beard. After that, the Capuchin said, "Finished? Did you get enough? The Gospel mentions only punches and cheeks, but it says nothing of kicking. That is why, as I apply the letter of the Gospel, it is my time now!" And so the Capuchin's kicking pummeled Jesus' sworn enemy, who did not receive any punches. There you go!

Even the foreign missionaries got the news from those who were with me that day, that I had looked for a fight by provoking the director of the prison and the Police. To be precise, I ended up on the receiving end of police truncheons with multiplying tortures and punishments. In a word, it would have been necessary to follow the morals of the evil ones: become hypocritical, servile, and spineless by saying nothing. If Jesus had followed this type of morality, he would never have been crucified. He would have submitted to Pilate's Judas, and anyone could have replaced him. We would have remained under the weight of sin and death without hope for redress.

The Christian moral path does not accept the middle way, but only black and white choices, the positive and the negative. In Christian morality, "whoever is not with me is against me." It is evident that in prison, the Police were not with me. They were so against me that they had rejected all my rights. What was left for me to do in such a situation? Submit myself? Praise the regime, like some of my companions did in the hope for an early freedom? What value would such a day of freedom have for me? Leave the small prison for the big one, with a bad conscience as well? My cheeks had been disfigured by spit, slaps, and punches. I confess that I also punched others.

But the most important form of my opposition consisted of the letters that I wrote to Enver and to other main Communist Party directors. I do not know where my letters ended up. I would have loved to have included them in this book. But Dom Simon did not have the right to consult the archives. The only people who had that privilege were those who had received the obligatory instructions on where, when, and how to search the archives. Dom Simon never recognized those measures and instructions, and so he also did not have the right to see his own letters, written in prison with his own blood. I must give thanks to God that, upon my release from prison, I still had a clear head. And I therefore had my own archives, in which I passionately guarded all my memories, which are etched in the winding pathways of my brain. Perhaps I am committing a grave error in revealing this secret, for fear that the Government will completely remove my skull with my brain inside in order to put it in the secret State archives and, after having emptied it there, move the skull to the National Museum as a typical Albanian skull!

In fact, the truncheon blows, punching, and kicking incited in me a greater desire to fight with the regime in a way that would lead to my execution. I wanted to be shot. That is why I wrote all those letters. Execution would free me from the danger of the moral despondency that I saw every day in the faces of my companions in suffering. Often without wanting to but without any pangs of conscience either, those companions became spies and sold each other out. But Hoxha knew that there was a big difference between ceaseless suffering and death. That is why I stayed alive.

A Kosovar, Qamil Hajdini, also began to write letters, but he could not continue for long. He was released, with certain conditions, before the end of his term. In fact, it was not worth it to live in prisons or concentration camps, where the suffering and nonstop torture transformed humans into beasts, a word which contains in it all the vices. I do not regret my resistance even a tiny bit. The only medals I merit are the traces and scars of the wounds of past times, still visible on my body. These scars are witnesses to the coherence which I never renounced and will never renounce. Some can judge me to be abnormal, but one day they will say, "Dom Simon was right!" I hope that day does not come too late.

I took a lot of kicking from many investigating magistrates while on my knees, but not all those magistrates deserve to be mentioned for posterity. Without denying the merits of others, the blows of Bib Ndoci, who came from Fan Mirditë, of Shkelzen Bajraktari and his comrade Cirjaci or Cirjazi (whose name I can never remember), left unerasable traces in my memory, and not fewer on my body. The tortures that Cirjazi directed with the mastery of a symphony conductor led to the point of almost making me pass to the other world. Cirjazi had been sent directly by the Interior Ministry to be a macabre conductor who would play the symphony of crime on the nerves of my brain. They had to get me to say, once I had been arrested and at any price, that I had been on the verge of giving the signal for the general insurrection which aimed for the removal of the communists from power.

However, the worst torture was that of a prisoner who, having entered prison as an honest man, buckled and then gave in. Suffering turned him into a spy. In the thinking of the prison director, such a man had been rehabilitated. But then, to the normal suffering of prison can be added another — the worst — that of pangs of conscience, which never left one in peace, day nor night. The snakelike hissing of this conscience came at night in the prison, and tormented and tortured the soul in the cell. Added to this suffering were the tortures of other prisoners and the tortures of parasites. Lice were a real weapon in the hands of the communists. No one ever had the idea of dropping the use of cannons and guns to fight solely by lice, which would be a way to unconditionally annihilate the adversary, who would be able to think of nothing but how to scratch, an endless scratching, everywhere. Lice ate me for twenty-five years, and the gangsters tortured me at the same time! Spies and gangsters, who did the impossible in order to reduce their sentences, did not worry about the fact that they traded in the blood of others.

It goes without saying that these laws and tortures are not included in the code of *Leke Dukagjini*[3], which is still used by the clan in Tirana against the people of the North of Albania, a clan that continues to humiliate the Ghegs. The code does not approve treacherously killing a citizen. It harshly condemns poisoning and aggression from behind. These laws never figured in the code of the secret service of information, which has changed its skin but not its vice! This secret Police is more present than ever in this somber and immense forest that we call Albania. Lekë Dukagjini's code is much more progressive than all the laws applied in Albania since the terribly sad events of November 29, 1944. It is only when Albania considers this day to be the darkest in its history that we will be able to hope for the recommencement of life at the point where we left it before 1944! It is only then that our hair will turn black and our teeth will push through our gums again!

---

3   *Lekë Dukagjini* — Albanian prince of the fifteenth century, to whom is attributed a code that regulated vendettas.

13

Burrel Prison

Burrel prison, a hell worse than that thought up by Dante Alighieri, was very well-organized. An infernal rhyme had been created—"Burrel, the eternal prison!"—because its walls rested on the bones of the dead. The graves of prisoners were scattered all around the grounds. After inhuman tortures, the remains were simply covered with soil, without any ceremony, like for animals, for the simple fault of believing in God and demanding respect for the rights of man. The bones always stayed where the bodies had been buried, without the monuments or statues that these people merited more than anyone else, while our public places are filled with monuments honoring those who, all wolves and sharks of every sort, had fought under the flag of pirates.

At Burrel, we lived in cells that were eight by four meters, with cement floors. There were thirty-six of us piled up one on top of another on stinking straw mattresses. We were like sardines in a can. The same room served alternatively as a dining hall, dormitory, washroom, and reading room. Its constant stink kept us all on the verge of fainting. The never-ending racket made us think that we were at the bottom of hell, condemned forever! We felt worse than beasts in a barn because at least they can get out and go to the sunny pasture. We, however, were destined to disappear in the darkness, suffering from never seeing a ray of the sun, a flower, or a child's face.

Everyone could see the wretched state of each prisoner's nervous system in this life of hell, where caning and blood constituted a day's main events. In order to forget their misery, the prisoners played cards. The loser would pounce on the winner, and a fight took the place of the game. Then knives intervened. Having arrived peacefully covered up, they turned into weapons. In prison, like elsewhere, everyone joined the stronger side, which laid bare people's characters. Everything was like on the outside, with the secret agent playing the role of head of corporate personnel, and the prison director as the corporate CEO. As for the network of spies, they were even more dangerous in prison than on the outside. Then, like now, the

Sigurimi[1] was made up of unrefined, tactless, indelicate, direct, and harsh men.

Those unable to face such a mode of living became insane. At that point, "the Meat machine" would come looking to send them to psychiatry, which was even worse because the doctors and nurses were docile servants of the torturer in chief, Hoxha. They ignored absolutely everything from the Hippocratic Oath. Enver had erected his throne on the life of all of Albania, persuaded that the dictatorship consolidated itself more when it stood on the debris of human lives. Psychiatry was therefore one of the most dangerous circles of our hell. Supplementary wounds were inflicted on the patients in order to keep them pinned to their beds and, above all, to encourage them to more quickly get to their graves because they were the enemies of the people. Horrible cries often came from psychiatry. Some, no longer able to deal with it, hanged themselves at the bars of a window. In a certain way, everyone envied them for their courage, because they felt they were treated worse than animals, especially with the arrival of spring. In spring, the animals go out on the green fields, grazing on tender shoots, bellowing and listening to the sound of the bells around their necks. The concert of the shepherds! "And the butcher?" people asked. Were not we also destined to experience the cutting edge of the *kandjar*?[2] The difference was that we did not have the right to sun or herb or the sounds of the bells! Worse, even on the day of our death, the bell would not have the right to lament, because it had also seen its last day when they had knocked it out of its bell tower.

We were shut up in that stinking cell until our last breath, gazes fixed on the small piece of sky striped by the bars, listening to the lies of Radio Tirana. We always looked at each others' faces, as well as those of the police and the examining magistrates, which shot out sparks of hate against us. The thick, gray walls separated us from those who were dear to us. It was these walls that isolated us from the world and from the liberty for which we had been created and had come into the world. It was the same walls, the same faces, the same barbed wire, the same spies and comrades who terrorized, stole from, and hit us, and who also testified against us. We watched them write up their reports against us in the hope for a better life, they who shared the same pain as us.

---

1   The Drejtoria e Sigurimit të Shtetit, commonly called *Sigurimi*, which was the information service of the People's Socialist Republic of Albania.
2   *Kandjar*—An Asian cold weapon, which is a sort of dagger.

We very rarely had the right to go out into the courtyard of the prison after the opening of the padlocks. In the courtyard, we washed our clothes, did our hair, shaved, and even took a shower if there was more water than normal. That all lightened our bodies. For two or three days the bad stink stayed away and we smelled soap, even if the soap smelled like toilets. Nevertheless, our close ones who came to see us after our shower did not hide their noses in their handkerchiefs as soon as we started walking towards them.

It was a great joy when there was water, electricity, or kerosene-emitting lanterns, when we had a place to hang up the linen if the linen had not been stolen by our comrades. Above all, we felt great joy when we had the right to go out into the courtyard. We otherwise remained closed up day and night in our dungeon, where we sometimes had to wash our linen and hang it to dry in cigarette smoke and in the dust that floated over our heads like clouds in the middle of a storm every time someone moved.

Water was always a problem, and not only for washing. We even lacked drinking water and sometimes we could not rinse our mouths. The odor became unbearable particularly when someone ate garlic. If someone caught the flu, the whole room began to sneeze and cough like a choir because the sickness passed from one to another. Hiccups, smells, coughs, and stench that no human had ever had to smell before mixed together: Smells of garlic, onions, throat or nose secretions, unwashed feet, lice-filled bodies, rotten teeth, mouths that belched out all the odors to the outside because everyone, freezing and sick as we were, breathed with open mouths. Even the arrival of our eagerly awaited close ones became a cause of chagrin for our souls that nonetheless hungered to see others. We knew that what they brought would not be for us. Gatherings with family members were transformed into insults, protests, depression, reproaches, and instructions on how to manage the family that we had left. In this kingdom of ennui and depression, we could never have a party or moments of joy that could clean our faces of bitterness and profound chagrin or of the sadness of prison, where all hope had been buried once and for all.

Like a storm that raises the ashes that cover embers, unveiling and bringing these embers back to life as they begin to burn again, so our meetings with our close ones blew on the drama of our souls. Such meetings replaced the monotonous impressions of prison with those of the past family life or with our friends, from whom we had been uprooted. From the small window through which our close ones saw our disfigured heads, we felt like bramble bushes that tried to catch hold, embrace, and rest in the arms of our mothers. But there were bars between visitor and prisoner, and even in the imagination, this embrace retracted into the cold metal, to return to us, broken into pieces.

Even the mail for which we impatiently waited had the same effect on us. Independently of the talent of the letter writer, we knew that this mail came from a world that we called "the great prison." The only variety consisted in the fact that because of a fight or some sort of incident, we found ourselves in the isolation cell, where in general we were shut up for a month without a blanket, surviving only on bread and water, with humidity which burrowed into the soul as a companion. If someone dared protest, he was tied up, hands and feet. In that way, the person took on the form of a sausage ready to be grilled in the immense frying pan of the Government in order to feed its never-satisfied folly.

In that way we created some verses: "When will our suffering finish? For henceforth we cannot go on. They have sent the wolves to guard the sheep. Until there is no life in the sheepfold." It seems to me that this poetry of the people is still relevant today, perhaps more than ever. When someone died, we grieved like this: "When in the other world you arrive, you will meet older people. They will ask you for news of our lives. You will tell them, 'Everything is all right, thanks to the hope to no longer be here!'"

It goes without saying that after fifty years of the torture, terror, and tyranny that Albanian exercised against Albanian, brother against brother, Albania had changed. Whereas, in 1944, the bad could be counted on one's fingers, today it is the good who can be counted on one's fingers. It seems that there are even too many fingers.

When I was arrested and put in prison for the first time, I was still naive. I thought that all the prisoners were men of ideals. But it was not like that at all. Very quickly, my naivete fell like dust. Spies paraded past my eyes, people without morals, or thieves and every sort of prison sickness. I also must add all those who had many faces.

The arrival of a new prisoner was an event. He was immediately the center of attention. He was put in the middle of all of us, and the first question was why he was there. But the next day, it was he who wanted to know why we were there! Little by little, the newcomer learned all the prison's stories and vices, and when he left a few years later, he had a lot to tell those who were constructing socialism and who had recourse to the hammer and sickle to bring down on the heads of Albanians. He left prison in perfect condition, as the authentic man, the man newly created by communism, the man ready for everything.

There were also some prisoners who read, although only sporadically. Very few prayed. Most of them insulted God and, despairing, shouted, "God himself has become red!"

The climate was also our enemy. In summer we died from the heat and shook the room drapes like they were ghosts. In winter we died from the cold. We would cry for no reason and, again for no reason, would be seized by crazy laughter! We did find a few oases because man is polymorphous and fights against evil, which he opposes because his entire nature is made in the image of God who is joy. We felt the greatest joy when we had water. We considered such a situation abnormal. Water created an unusual calm and peace, and we forgot our need to fight each other or play cards.

Then we would begin to talk about politics, above all when there were polemics between the clique in Tirana and the rest of the world. These polemics taught us the truth, above all about 1966, when the ranks in the army were suppressed, and after the terrible year of 1967, when the communists began their attacks against religion. When we received newspapers in prison, I focused on what the West said. Enver Hoxha's nonsense did not interest me. I had subscriptions to twelve newspapers and magazines and bought many books which had been translated by the bureau of translations in Tirana.

The fact is that all of the world masterpieces in literature were translated, one after the other, and even works dealing with the history of Albania, naturally according to the communist point of view on historical events. But all of the insults and slander against religion, against the West, and against the Albanian writer Fishta had the opposite effect on us. We always read things in their contrary sense: That which was good for them was bad for us, and vice versa.

I read the works of Enver Hoxha with curiosity. After getting hold of them, I soon realized that I could read in one hour what he had written in six hundred pages. If there were ideas of justice, we understood immediately that they were not his. I even heard that he had not written a single line, given that he preferred to spend his time with his harems and other distractions. Certain translated works that were able to pass the censor, such as *A Trip to the USA* or *The Banker* gave a clear idea of life in the USA. Books, not magazines or films, cultivate intelligence. Books contain analyses and minute descriptions that can help the reader see reality like a photo can. The only benefit I got from prison was the fact that I could read the majority of great authors at a mature age, when we can understand and savor them as we should. When I began to read in prison certain books that I had already read in my youth, I realized that I recalled almost nothing. After having finished a book, I made my commentaries to the other prisoners, which led to very animated debates. Each one spoke from his understanding of the book. He would start by praising or criticizing the characters, taking one side or another, as if these poor characters had come out from the book and into our prison to share the sad destiny that weighed on us.

Try to imagine, dear reader, the beauty of these reflections. Don Quixote with Rocinante, Madame Bovary, and Anna Karenina all came to sit with us in our prison cells in Burrel. My companions in misery unhesitatingly justified the immoral conduct of Tolstoy's Anna Karenina. Always ready for this, I explained to them in their manner, so that they could understand without too much philosophy, "If it is as you say, Tolstoy would never have ended Anna's life in throwing her on the train tracks. It was precisely in order to punish her that he had her disappear from the scene."

At first, the communists presented themselves as pure futurists who wanted to construct a present and future without a past. They quickly realized that their sterile brains were not capable of producing anything. They then returned to the world masterpieces, interpreting them, as they never ceased to say, from the Marxist-Leninist point of view. They did so by pushing things to the point at which they did not make sense. In fact, Marx and Lenin were nothing but two adventurers who were totally unaware of the interpretation of the masterpieces of humanity, which all bear the imprints of religious beliefs. It is enough to mention the great Dante, whose "Divine Comedy" is from beginning to end a philosophy and a theology. The giants of world literature eclipse the nonsense of the classics of communism.

At the end of this chapter, let me recall that in Burrel prison at least five hundred Albanians who were massacred by the communists are buried together. That is a number that needs to be added to the general figure of those who lost their lives in the quixotic fire of the communist dictatorship.

14

The Isolation Cell

It goes without saying that from my first arrest, I was forced several times to spend time in isolation. I spent several days there in isolation. But what really was the isolation cell for prisoners? The word speaks for itself! It was the place where a prisoner felt constricted, where he was in danger of falling to the ground in pieces, of losing his characteristics, where he had to shrink to fit into the dimensions of the room. It was the antechamber of submission and subjection, where you could enter just as you are and leave as someone totally different. In this humid, freezing, and narrow cell, you were all alone with yourself, just like you were with your death.

In order to avoid totally changing who I was, each time I was shut up in isolation, I thought that God had opened this very nice door to me to meditate on the great truths and eternal principles that are at the basis of our lives. These are the same truths and principles that I had professed every day to the Mirditors, the poor inhabitants of the mountains who lived in houses that did not differ so much from my isolation cell. It was there that I came to understand that the regime, unable to convince the people and even Party members who in the daytime followed Hoxha and at night followed the priest, had decided to get rid of priests. With a totally clear field, Hoxha could deceive and uproot people without resistance.

In the isolation cell, I recalled principles, but also the events of my life, which passed by like in a film on the screen of the dirty and dark walls. I remembered that before throwing me in prison, the communists had come one night, to my house that was not so different from the houses of Mirditors. They put their pistol to my temple and threatened to pull the trigger if I did not decide at that instant to abandon my parish. At that time, I saw images of my mother, my brother Dom Lazër, and other members of my family who certainly suffered more than I did and mostly because of me. I thought of my personal belongings, few though indispensable for my existence, which had to be sequestered and which would be very difficult for me to replace if I would ever leave this hell alive. My worry became even stronger when I thought that Mirditë in this way would have no priest, that is to say, no soul. It hurt my heart to think of all these innocent people who would suffer because of me.

But I grew stronger when I thought that I was there because of the Gospel and the Cross. I was there because I had never lied to people, which gave me total confidence. This experience told me that human nature cannot easily confess itself. I was there because the money that the people had entrusted to me, that they had saved by taking from their children's daily bread, I used to build churches with all the necessary equipment, with everything that was necessary for a building that contained the heart and soul of a Catholic village. I was there because I had never thought of revealing the secret of the confessional because I accorded greater weight to my faith than to my own life. I was there because I believed in what I preached and was ready to put it into practice, not content with words alone. I was ready to sacrifice my life for the triumph of the Cross, which is to say the triumph of Christian civilization in the mountains that loved me and that I loved.

I also remembered the eleven o'clock Mass that was celebrated in the church of the Franciscans. The preacher's proclamations became engraved in the memories of the listeners. The preachers there lived their words before expressing them. And in a small Balkan village, where everyone knew what you ate and drank, or the hours at which you went to bed and got up, it was not difficult to discern sanctity and unwholesomeness. Inspiring an unconditional respect for themselves for their living example of Jesus, the preachers oriented people towards earthly progress and heavenly beatitude. I remembered the moment at the end of the Mass: the most civilized part of the population of Shkodër flowed like a river from the *Gjuhadoli* valley[1] to the walkway of the "Plain of Çela." This enraged the communists. The latter realized that, in the duel between Enver Hoxha and Jesus, it was always the word of God that triumphed.

But would this tradition be passed down? Would other preachers see the day? Would we ever again see the river full of the nobility of young girls and women, and wise men walking with Jesus in their hearts? I do not know. Maybe everything would change with time and the only thing that would remain of that would be a nice memory.

Then I dreamed of the reopening of the seminary. But where would we find my former professors, Fathers Faust, Dajan, Gardini,

---

1 *Gjuhadoli* is one of the historic districts of the city of Shkodër.

and Valentin? They spread the light everywhere they went. Can any among the younger generation of churchmen replace these giants who left traces of their sanctity and blood along with thousands of pages of their writings without which Albania would be missing a good part of its history? Were there theologians or philosophers as well-prepared and people as saintly as my missionary teachers had been? The people had loved them because they loved the people. People do not love missionaries until their infallible intuition helps them see that they are worthy of their confidence. When the people do not love the missionary, it is better for the missionary to take another path, because as preacher of the Gospel such missionaries risk becoming the most dangerous enemy of the Gospel.

The Gospel does not accept any sort of compromise: Either you are with it or against it. The old clergy had the evangelical virtue of poverty. The more materially poor they were, the richer they became spiritually and the more souls they won, with which they built other churches which were made of living stones. Could the young clergy resemble the older ones in a world in which, as we were told, the dollar reigned on the other side of the iron curtain, opening and closing people's mouths as it saw fit? And among the religious, will we ever have another *Father Gjergj*, a *Father Anthony*, a *Father John*, a *Father Augustine*, or a *Father Alex*?

In this obscure isolation cell that had no iron bars because it did not even have a window, I often felt very small and, as a consequence, happy. I think that the smaller a person is, the happier he is, because Jesus came precisely for the small ones in order to give them the force to confront the powerful on Earth who fight among themselves like dogs over a bone. I was in isolation, but I was not alone. God, in whom I believed with all of the power of my soul, was always near to me. Faith gives sense to life, and softens and educates it. Faith consoles man because it shows him his Creator, who taught him the moral laws and who takes him by the hand to sacrifice, which is the ultimate point for his creation. God does not send more sufferings and temptations to a man than he can handle. And when suffering falls on us and temptations come to shake our souls, we only have to call out to God, and He will respond to our wishes.

And if our most ardent desire was not satisfied, namely the fall of cruel communism for which all the inhabitants of the surrounding cells of bloody and stinking tombs also prayed, that meant that the moment had not yet arrived. That is why I prayed every day to the Lord to grant me the grace that I needed, without mentioning specific prayer intentions. Being convinced that the Lord was in the soul of every one of us, I knew that He well knew what I really needed. I was not the first slave to suffer. See! How many slaves suffered and died, hands and feet bound, throughout the centuries from the most ancient civilizations until the present, from one end of the Earth to the other! Who knows the names of these poor nameless people who died in the most terrible situations, who did crushing work, were tortured in a thousand different ways, and were even buried alive. But their masters also died, masters who believed that their slaves would continue to serve them in the other world. I too was one of them, a modern slave who had to sacrifice himself on the altar of folly. I was happy with this difficult role, because it is always better to be a victim than to be guilty. In that way at least I would not have a bad conscience. Peace of soul is the greatest treasure that a man can desire. Does a dictator have a bad conscience? Do the devil's soldiers have bad consciences? Have not they lost their consciences because they are in the ranks of the armies of evil?

At the same time, armed to the teeth with the Cross and God's blessing, I joined the army of good. I was therefore at the height of my historic task, there in my cell, covered in blood, knowing very well that the history of humanity is nothing other than a nonstop battle between the kingdoms of good and evil, the kingdom of God, founded by Jesus Christ and the kingdom of the devil. And it will be like that until the last judgement. I was invaded with a great joy at the thought that an ideology that had taken over half of the globe, armed with the most modern materials, feared me, trembled before holy water, the Cross, and the Bible that I held in my hand when I was arrested. The communists believed that in taking away the Bible, they could also take away my religion. No, no one can touch my faith and religion. My faith was in me at a depth where no human hand had access. Only the hand of God could access it. That is why I could loudly affirm that I was the freest man because my soul was totally free.

Prison succeeded in closing the eyes of my body, but opened the eyes of my soul. I began to see in depth certain phenomena that I had only superficially known. I began to clearly distinguish good from evil. In prison I began to succeed at finding a solution to certain problems that I had not at all understood when I was on the outside and was preoccupied with a thousand daily worries. I was like an infant who started to learn causes and effects. When I had to face my destiny in prison, I understood the extent to which Albanian harmed Albanian. An Albanian had destroyed his own brother Albanians in order to please Serbs, Russians, Chinese, and Americans.

I began to meticulously and calmly examine the environment where I had lived until then, the people who acted like my friends, who breathed so closely to me but who in one jump would turn to an *operative*[2] to make a report. How many times did I breathe the blessed air that God had created for all, for spies, for good and bad? There, in the isolation cell, when I returned from being tortured, and was exhausted, I remembered all of them, each by name, and exactly how the examining magistrates had tortured me. They did this in order to prove my guilt and intimidate me by citing witnesses apparently ready to offer proof of my guilt. And that guilt would lead to a bullet to my head.

In my seventy-five years of life in Albania, I have seen enter and leave like horses to and from the stable, five political formations very distinct from one another just as much in their attire as in their political spin and speculations with which they deceived, looted, and tortured the people. When we were under Turkish domination, the people said: "The devil may come and govern us, but not the Turks!" When the Turks left and Italians came, once again, the people, despairing of foreign domination, said, "Better to support the devil than these pasta-eating people." Then came the Germans. And the people then said: "The devil is a hundred times better!" And after the Germans, as if to satisfy the wish of the people, who did not understand that one devil had kicked out another, it was Lucifer in person who sat on the throne of Albania, where he found an ideal terrain for constructing a very original hell. Be that as it may, "the forces of hell cannot triumph in the light." Injustice condemns itself, and it is the power of Jesus that triumphs because it is a power founded on love, charity, justice, and fraternity.

Worldly and heavenly powers travel in the same ship, breathe the same air, and direct the same people. The politicians aspire to dominate the people with countless laws, but the citizen respects the law only when he sees a Police officer. The Church, however, reigns by love. Politicians reign by court proceedings, deportation camps, prisons, isolations, and assassinations. The history of humanity has

---

2 *Operative* — Secret service agent.

shown that violence has never conquered respect. That is why those who have a truly human view, in contrast to politicians, prefer to follow the way of Jesus because Jesus does not distort people and the human soul with despicable vices. On the contrary, he makes the soul more human and, even better, divinizes it, and pushes it to resemble Himself, He who is perfect as God and as man. That is why for more than two thousand years the Church by its prayers, penances, and sacraments directs humanity towards the celestial homeland.

Someone can say to me: "And what about the mistakes of the churchmen? We have seen and known awful people among them, totally unworthy in relation to what they represent, in flagrant opposition to the Gospel who came to preach to us." I respond to this question with another question: "How can you explain, then, that the Church, despite strong opposition even to the martyring of its greatest sons, never closed its doors, and that it continues to draw millions of people who, every day, kneel in thousands of holy places in the most backwards places of the world? It is true that in the Church you can meet and come to know people who are unworthy. They existed, exist, and will continue to exist. But the difference is that this category of people is the exception to the rule. And what is even more important is the fact that it is not humans who created the Church, but God. That is why it is better to have the priest as an adversary and God as friend when the priest does not do his duty."

Once someone told a Pope: "Holy Father, our enemies are ruining the Church!" And the Pope responded: "Do not worry, if we could not have destroyed it with our own errors, our enemies will not succeed either!" The Church is not a military power. It has no other weapons than the Cross and blessings. Therefore it was easy for its enemies to drench the Church in blood, which increased the number of its martyrs. But it is surely in the blood of the martyrs that Christian civilization had spread throughout the centuries. The history of the martyrs of the Catholic Church is the history of both ancient and modern civilization. This history was not written by the hand of humanity, but by the hand of God.

That was how I meditated in my isolation cell, and that gave me the force to deal with my suffering. I sometimes had the impression that, unworthy as I was, I was shut up in the dungeons of the ancient amphitheatres, waiting for the lion that was supposed to devour the civilization of the Cross. I regret nothing. I feel noble and proud to have been thrown there in order to defend the religion of Jesus. I remembered the great Popes and Christian kings who brought today's civilization to the world from the great Constantine to Charlemagne. I also recalled the famous monasteries and wise monks who conserved and developed culture and civilization and helped the world escape barbarity. It was this barbarity that had thrown me in prison, into this life where the greatest terror reigned.

My thought, in finishing with the Popes, Cardinals, and Emperors, returned again to our poor Albania during my miserable life. From Richelieu, my thought drifted to my childhood friend *Tonin Harapi*.[3] I remember that when terror reached its height, he, my best friend with whom I was closely tied through common ideals, sent me the photos that we had exchanged in the beautifully ideal years of childhood and youth, when we had one heart, one dream, and one future. I remember that I had not managed to send him my photos, because the Police had seized them at a checkpoint.

Then came other times. Everyone makes his own path in life. He had benefited from a bursary to the Moscow Conservatory and I had benefited from a bursary to prison, where I had studied for the next twenty-six years. I obtained an unequaled diploma from this university. It was the only one able to be called as such in Albania under the dictatorship, because there prison was a school, and school a prison. I do not know which of us was happier and profited more from life. Tonin, having become a great artist, gave to Albanian music a few masterpieces. Perhaps he profited from the fact that, at that epoque, in which the muses of words were forbidden, the muses of sounds were freer. Imagine what he would have composed if he had followed the other path, where he would have made such beautiful steps! Perhaps he would have created another "Ave Maria", famous for world music, because his heart, where Jesus had taken a large place, could not sing, "Ave Enver" except under the classic form: "Ave, tyrant, your condemned are ready to die for their noble ideals!"

Who knows the torments that the notes produced in his heart when he sang the counter-song, the counter-melody of the artist's

---

3 *Tonin Harapi* (1926–1992). An Albanian musician who first studied at the pontifical seminary of the Jesuits at Shkodër, where he became friends with Dom Simon. After the expulsion of the priests, he continued his musical career in an official framework in the artistic Tirana lyceum and then at the Moscow Conservatory.

soul! That is a greater torture than that found in prison, where you fight with forces that are outside of you while your soul is filled with peace and serenity, and with the conviction that you are conducting the fight for a good cause, without any detours. What would I have gained if I had changed paths? What would Dom Simon be today? Could those who know me well imagine me any different from what I am? Dom Simon left in order to be Dom Simon. He became Dom Simon and will die Dom Simon because he could not be otherwise!

In the serenity of my isolation cell, after the memories of my seminary friend, Tonin, I recalled Xhafer Lezhet, a communist from the start who, poor guy, got caught up in fighting with the loquacious Hoxha. Supported by the British Air Force, they caused the Germans trouble. Xhafer was basically a backseat driver in all of that. As for the Germans, they had already lost the war and were retreating back home, humiliated and crushed, dishonored and bombarded, pursued step by step, covered in shame and dust. The Germans came from Greece to pass through Albania and had only a very narrow corridor to return home. When they made their entry in the village of Borovë, as was the norm they met the head of the village, and explained to him that they were just passing through Albania and that they had nothing to do with the Albanian people but that if ever someone threatened them, they would leave nothing behind but smoke, ashes, and burnt cadavers.

The poor village head had no authority over the communist partisans, who hid behind the hedgerows and laid ambushes to shoot any lost German soldiers. The goal of the partisans was to get the Germans to burn down the village, and to kill the women, children, and aged while the youth, in order to escape reprisals, would join Enver Hoxha's partisans with whom they had nothing in common. As was often the case, many others joined the partisans because they considered this path to be the sole way to kill their adversaries. As soon as the partisans had killed a lost German, the Germans totally burnt the entire village of Borovë, which allied itself, despite everything, with the self-proclaimed national liberators. Poor Xhafer.

Xhafer was sent by the communist regime to the Jesuits to lecture and explain to us young Roman collared that, according to the instructions of the new leaders, we had been mistaken for reactionaries and would in fact remain safe and sound by putting ourselves in the service of the new regime. Imagine poor Xhafer, coming from his cabin in Borovë in the middle of the mountains, smelling like horse manure, sensing the communists' savagery, transformed into a lecturer in the Jesuits' lecture hall, where he suddenly sensed the perfume of culture.

After the lecture, Xhafer wanted to know if we had any questions. The first to speak were my superiors, Fathers Gardini and Vata. Father Gardini, who had been trained in the best schools of the world, asked poor eighteen year-old Xhafer, who came from the school of the mountains and the forests: "Given that communism is the only system that can save humanity from misery, and that your Marx and Engels are sufficiently knowledgeable to find the recipes that will heal the wounds of society and resolve all the moral, political, and economic problems, as you have just told us, why were not the Germans the first to apply their genial system, given that Marx invented it in their country? Why was it adopted by the Slavic peoples?"

Poor Xhafer, who knew nothing about German, Russian, or Albanian history, stood there, speechless, gripping onto the papers that he had just read with his trembling hand. He did not know how to respond to the Jesuit. A glacial silence reigned in the hall. In looking at poor Xhafer and the state to which he had been reduced, we laughed under our capes while our superiors kept their eyes fixed on him with implacable seriousness. While waiting for the response, the outer courtyard door opened and the ass in charge appeared coming from Bardhej in Shkodër. This latter, happy at arriving, started his braying.

It was good timing because the sound, crossing the courtyard to the hall where we were attending the imposed course on Marxism, broke the silence which had started to weigh on us. We two hundred Jesuit students burst into laughter, which was a very rare thing in such serious halls. Someone said: "We will not get tired of waiting any longer. The ass has come to give us the response." Another said to Xhafer: "Do not worry, your friend has come to give you a hand." In this way, the lecture was ruined. Red like a tomato, Xhafer left to rejoin his friends in his village of Bardhej. Xhafer had shed the weight of bloody capitalism. The poor guy was likely cross with himself for having accepted to go to such a place. The Jesuit college probably appeared to him to be truly reactionary given that he had come off as an ass there while representing the Party.

In the misery in which I found myself, I was seized by a crazy laugh as I remembered a story: "There was once a rooster, a dog, and an ass that lived well in a Western country. They wanted to take a trip to Albania, which the communists presented as an earthly paradise. The rooster went to Albania at the worst possible moment for roosters, when the inhabitants were chopping off rooster heads so as to avoid sending them to an agricultural cooperative. The poor rooster, not hearing a rooster crow nor seeing a single hen, ran like the wind back home. Next, it was the dog's turn. When he found out it was forbidden to bark, he also beat a hasty retreat. The last was the ass. His two friends awaited his return, but there was no sign of him. Finally, the two comrades received a card on which was written: "Do not wait for me. I am not coming back. This is the only country where I am called 'comrade'!"

My smile vanished when I thought of the day after the Marxist lecture. It was not Xhafer who came that day, but the Police. They were armed to the teeth. It was July, 1945. The great destruction of our seminary began. Our superiors left in handcuffs for execution or life imprisonment. We, their faithful students, would follow them, becoming preachers of prisons and deportation camps. But we were prepared for this novel situation.

My meditations continued to be filled with memories and faces from the past of both friends and enemies. I imagined the head of the first Secretary of the Communist Party for the district of Lezhë, Xhorxhi Robo. By association, I next thought of the head of the Department of the Interior[4] and after that a mayor, Shaqir Dibra. These three, the princes of Lezhë, were all wolves who trampled on the district's population, which was 90% Catholic.

They called on me several times to come before them to be insulted and threatened. Each such trip from my village of Ungrej took at least sixteen hours on foot. In their eyes, I was a sign of contradiction. I had to bite my tongue in front of these thieves who appropriated everything that they could, even the goods of the Church, without the slightest scruple. These individuals were not only useless, but even harmful to the people. They destroyed everything within their reach, starting with souls. They went around all day in their luxurious cars while I did not even have the right to get around with a horse or mule among villages that were situated on steep slopes where I sometimes had to climb on all fours.

When the communists saw that they could not convince the people to stop going to church, they turned their attention towards me. They

---

4 The Police.

said that if they arrested me, they would succeed in getting rid of God from the peasants' souls, as if I was the replacement for the Holy Spirit. The miserable communists did not understand that, with or without me, God would never disappear from the human heart. He would stay there, sometimes hidden, sometimes more visible, until his free manifestation one day when the idols would all fall down as was always the case in the history of humanity from creation onwards.

I reconstructed in my memory the reunion organized at Ungrej, presided over in person by *Xhorxhi Robo.*[5] He had succeeded in assembling by force five hundred people to denounce Dom Simon. The Party's servants and lackeys in the parish had in their hands as eloquent testimony against Dom Simon an old Soviet radio transmitter that no longer worked — just like the administration of the Party, which was also Soviet. As the denounced one, I kept my cool. I firmly believed that the future belonged to me because I was a humble servant of God. Chaos, fratricidal hatred, and death reign wherever people seek to denounce and condemn God to death. That will continue until the return of God, He whom they vainly tried to kill, and then life can recommence.

Xhorxhi Robo looked ridiculous in this public assembly when he accused me of baptizing communist infants by force. The people, so simple as they were, could in no way imagine the priest dragging children from the breasts of their mothers to be plunged into baptismal waters. No, no one believed it! What actually happened was that a communist, working as a store clerk, had baptized his son in the middle of the night, at his place of work, and had then organized a great feast attended by Party members. The same people who lit candles of fat to the Party leader in the day lit candles of wax to the Good Lord at night. It goes without saying that Dom Simon had occupied the place of honor in that night-time ceremony.

The communist authorities even often invited me to play football. I went gladly because I needed to keep in shape in order to climb up to the mountain villages where the people constantly awaited their minister. But in 1959, when *Nexhmije Hoxha*[6] spoke of culture in a public discourse published in the communist newspapers, she

---

5 *Xhorxhi Robo* — Albanian politician: After having fought the Nazi occupiers, he did his graduate studies in Moscow and became a high-ranking member of the Communist Party of Albania.

6 *Nexhmije Hoxha* — Enver Hoxha's wife.

mentioned the fact that a priest, because he had failed to propagate his religion in church, was now trying to do it on the Party's football pitches. It goes without saying that the men who had invited me to play were severely judged and let go from their functions. And so the people, whose intuition never fails, came to the surprising conclusion that I had been denounced solely because I was better at football than all the communists were. Unable to beat me on the football pitch, they denounced me in the full assembly of the people because they held all the cards. Yet their terrible goal was fatal to their side in the end.

Only memories came to visit me in my isolation cell, where rats, fleas, and lice accompanied me. The ennui was terrible. Nothing could help me get rid of the blues. I therefore appealed to my memories. They were of some help and consolation, but then I fell into an even deeper depression. There was not and never will be a pen to describe the anguish of each second in the isolation cell. Physical death occurs every minute and the heart rebels every hour when you see that the future offers you nothing but torture and death, when you are hungry and your wounds of body and soul bleed and burn.

When I was totally exhausted, the hand of God intervened. And I do not know why, but in those difficult moments *Tuk Jakova* came into my imagination and spirit. Though dead, he became my best friend in prison. I wondered how it happened that this Nicodemus of Shkodër, this member of the Central Committee of the Communist Party, close comrade in arms of Enver Hoxha, was able to sacrifice his good salary, rank, privileges, honors, and place in the residential quarter of the communist leaders in Tirana, and had the courage to openly speak to the tyrant in the defense of religion. He dared openly say to the dictator that it was not just to kill the nation's heroes. These heroes were the religious who had established the foundations of European civilization in Albania, formed and preserved the Albanian language, and educated the first members of the Albanian intelligentsia, who were in turn the representatives of all the national values.

In that cell where no one aside from death visited me, my exhausted imagination, wandering through time and space, fused Tuk Jakova and the Nicodemus of the Gospel into one character. I felt like I was among the Pharisees of the Gospel. I heard Nicodemus defend Jesus among his peers who had already taken the irrevocable decision to crucify the Lord. Nicodemus defended Jesus in saying that the Lord had spoken better than anyone and that he had preached and lived with a moral so elevated that if humanity followed it, humanity would be totally different from what it was. People would love each other like they loved themselves. Would they nail a man to a cross before hearing him? Could they condemn him without giving him the right to defend himself? Could they crucify him today when he had only been arrested yesterday?

Tuk Jakova had done the same thing. He had defended Christianity, and with it, clearly, the North of Albania. He who one day had been crowned as king and triumphant in the Jerusalem of Albanian culture was the next day mercilessly and ruthlessly nailed to the cross of communism. And when he was nailed to the cross, the inscription CRN (Crucified for the Religion and the Nation) instead of INRI (Jesus of Nazareth, King of the Jews) was placed above his head.

The crucified North of Albania boasted some of the best sons Mother Albania brought into the world. The communists were pleased to remind us that they had turned her into a mother that eats her own children. This cross remains where the communists drove it down into the ground, and the North of Albania today is still suspended "between heaven and Earth."

In this isolation cell my soul was transformed into a theater. There, the greatest tragedy ever to have fallen on the head of an honest Albanian was played. I was the sole playwright and actor, like in antiquity, while the whole suffering herd was the chorus, whether they were inside or outside the humid isolation cell where no ray of the sun ever penetrated. The role that I had to play required that I face torture without losing or sacrificing my soul. Perhaps some will accuse me of exaggeration when I evoke these terrible scenes. Even the pagan Greeks killed their characters in plays backstage so as not to overly stimulate the spectators. But me, dear reader, I am doing the same thing: I take the people behind the scenes where the torturer's ax never stops the beheading. My tragedy is not a theatrical production, but life because the blood that flowed was not red ink diluted by water, but the heart of my life and people. That is why, as a victim of the most terrible violence, I am constrained to become its interpreter. I really wanted to escape it, because there is no one in the world, no matter how saintly, who would want to be dismembered while alive. In writing out my life's tragedy, I hope that the scene of my soul becomes the flesh of a new humanity.

Now that I have returned to my home, I hope to live in peace. But I have realized that life has become more and more unlivable. The great misfortune, the isolation cell, sharpened my spirit. It taught me to address God with fresh prayers because I lived the scene of a new tragedy, previously unknown, the scene of the isolation cell. How many plays were written until the day of this isolation cell? Few or none at all! People dislike isolation cells because humans are not made for such places. Humans were created to fly freely, like birds in the infinite space of the sky. But the isolation cell was so gloomy that prisoners who were closed up there came to believe that even on the outside the sky no longer existed. And as for wings, indispensable for flying, their bloodied feathers had ended up in the trashcans of the examining magistrates!

The shouting and menacing of the Police that came from the outside helped me see that Hoxha feared the people more than they feared him. I can see religion's invincible force and liberty's real meaning. I grew in power, courage, and also inner peace, spiritual serenity, and confidence in God. I saw up close the hell that the devil put into the hearts of the political class. This class was always preoccupied with holding onto power.

I came to the conclusion that I was better off in prison than the dictator was on his throne! When I was thrown for the first time into this terrible place, the isolation cell, the walls and floor were covered in blood. After getting over the initial shock, I touched and smelled the walls while shaking. No, it was not blood. It was ink thrown on the walls for psychological impact. However, there was plenty of blood. Each time I left the cell for bodily needs, and again on my return, I could not escape the punching and kicking. They hit me where it would hurt me the most, in the most fragile parts. I would be in terrible pain for days. But neither the pain caused by the hitting, nor the irons that bound my hands and fixed me to my chair, nor the humid ground could trouble my spiritual serenity.

When I was alone, in reality I was with the entire world. But when my torturers saw that solitude made me stronger instead of weaker, they made every effort to give me company. To do this, the prison leadership had already trained very effective cellmates. One specialist was Pjepri. I had the luck to have a companion in suffering, an ignorant Orthodox, Spiro Tata, who was selected to draw on all his talents to get me to reveal my secrets. Everyone who was arrested was in effect considered by the Don Quixote, Enver Hoxha, as a political personality who thought only of ravishing Dulcinea of Toboso, that is, of ravishing his power, which was his only love. The rest of us were only windmills against whom the tyrant charged at with his lance and sword according to all the rules of chivalry. He acted like that only because he wanted to close a church or terrorize a group of people that he had seen, in his nightmares, hatching a plot against him. That is why the hymn that his slaves consecrated to this Knight with the Aggravated Face began with these words: "Enver Hoxha brandished a sword."

As soon as I saw comrade Tata enter the prison cell, I said what I should have said at the end of his visit: "Welcome, comrade spy!" Poor Spiro! He was normally insulted in every cell that he entered. Punches sometimes came with the insults. In that way, after having faced the feeble attacks of the prisoners, a race who resembled hedgehogs, Spiro was transferred to another cell, if possible to where he was less known. Nevertheless, he did his best to carry out his mission.

As he realized that, in terms of politics he had nothing to gain with me, he oriented our discussion around moral subjects. Being an ignorant person, he thought that all morality in the world was based on one point. He asked me why priests did not marry, and since they did not marry, what they did to lead a normal life. "What is more powerful", I asked him, "the will or the bolt that keeps us locked inside? While we can tolerate the bolts that the Government has forced on us, how come we cannot tolerate what we ourselves decide to do of our free will?"

Sometimes I mocked Spiro. I told him one day, "You resemble Lenin. Just to let you know: When Lenin was in prison, he was accompanied by a Catholic priest. One day Lenin said to the priest: 'Morally, the world will be dominated by you Catholics because your religion is divine and your hierarchy finds its source in the people. But politically, the world will be dominated by the communists because they also come from the people and do not inherit power like the sons of monarchs.' The priest responded: 'It is true that we will dominate the world because truly our religion is divine and we—the ministers and all of the hierarchy—are of the people and for the people while you, you will never dominate the world because your monastery is beautiful but you have very bad monks. This is because your comrades are conmen. Your system resembles slavery more than anything else, and the more backward your country is, the more powerful you feel.'"

Spiro Tata did not stay for long in my cell. He left just like that, just like how he had come in. I saw him again in the work camps.

He told me that he had been beaten by many cellmates. Naturally, I had not done anything like that to him. I knew that he was already condemned for the rest of his days. I think that even today, if he is alive and in good health, as is often the case for torturers, he has to rack his brains over the Medusa of a thousand forms that the rest of us do not possess and that we gave him as a present.

The greatest benefit that I got from the isolation cell was time for prayer. Prayer chased away all my other ideas, gave me courage, and weakened the terror of prison where God himself descended. I realized concretely that the more difficulty a man is in, the more he addresses God to come to his aid and the more he prays. I, who began life with the wish to follow a religious calling, was given by God the most beautiful solitude of a true monk's dreams. That isolation cell was truly transformed into a monk's cell, and I became a man chanting the Psalms and hymns that, throughout the walls and bars, rose to heaven. Later, when I was free, I could visit the dwellings of anchorites hidden in the middle of the mountains and forests of Europe. I remembered my isolation cell. I realized that it was one of the most suitable places for the life of an anchorite, a solitary, someone who wanted to be alone with Providence.

Ten years after leaving prison, I returned to see the isolation cell, this time as a free man. At least that was what I thought. I was no longer accompanied by rough Police officers and Enver Hoxha's criminals, but by the cameramen from *Italian Radio Television* to give an interview there. I never dreamed that I would be offered such an opportunity. Speaking of this valley of tears, of the five hundred innocent Albanians who were chained there, with their broken bones, living under savage guards, I thought of the tears, complaints, sighs, and pain that surpassed the limits of human thought. I thought of dishonor and the loss of dignity. No one else had ever been judged and condemned in this manner. The guilty did not ever enter these cells, which still reeked of death.

I asked the Italian journalists for a moment of silence in honor of the dead. They did not wait a minute, not a second. Nevertheless, I started my work, guessing that in that way I could give the victims the honor they wanted, which was to show the world what had happened in the depths of these tombs in which the living—a whole crowd of people—had been buried alive. I had to bring to the light what had been committed in the thick darkness of this place. I did not have the slightest intention of appealing to vengeance. Everyone knows that a Catholic priest seeks to resemble his divine Master, and therefore does not know how to avenge himself. He does not even think of it. He knows and wants to repeat with the Lord Jesus: "Forgive them, for they know not what they do!" I wanted the interview to show the sad truth to the entire world, to the world that we thought was the free world. My only goal was that these atrocities would not happen again.

I went therefore from one corridor to another, one cell to another, recounting everything that I had experienced, and afterwards impatiently waited to see on the screen what had been recorded. But when, a few days later, I saw the show, I was shattered. Apparently the free world did not exist. It had no liberty, not even free speech or a free media. I saw scenes that showed nothing important or that did not want to say anything. Some of my words had been cut and treated worse than the words of my prison comrades before their executions. I was able to get out of communist prisons alive, but my interview had been shot down by journalists from the free world. This showed that it was not allowed either in Albania or overseas to speak the truth about the powerful. It was not permitted to demand justice from the criminals. It was not permitted to open the eyes of the people and show them that someone was still playing with their destinies. It was not even permitted to speak of the evil of the United States of America. Imprisoned until yesterday as collaborators of the United States, today we are menaced with prison again for being their enemies.

Unfortunate as we are, we have never found our friends and enemies at the right moment. We did not know how to betray them at the right time, nor how to be with them and embrace them at the opportune moment. In a word, we had needed to hoist the flags at the livestock markets in Greece, Italy, or the United States. And sell to the highest bidder. We would still be the enemies of the powerful, and still carry the same hole-filled flag, tattered by the gunfire of the fighters for ideals that are great, unchanging, just, and therefore eternal. This is because precisely those who had put us in handcuffs and accused us of being the spies for American imperialism have today become the greatest friends of the United States, from where they come and go as if they are visiting their godmothers. The fact is that life does not merit being lived without the consolation of religion. Religion reveals to us our real homeland, that of heaven where, at last, man, who had always based his life on God, escapes once and for all from all these horrors.

15

The Organization of Spying in Burrel Prison

The prison was enclosed with a thick row of barbed wire. Above this, Enver Hoxha's guards watched day and night, armed with automatic guns, under the orders of the prison direction. The prison also had secret service agents, a few bureaucrats, and numerous Police officers. We called them "The Exterior Government" because they were very vigilant for fear that we would escape. But there was also an internal government who was in the cells, corridors, and prison courtyard. My friends from the South of Albania called them intendants or "scoundrels." The intendants were some of our comrades in suffering who had been turned into persecutors. They earned a salary, got better food, and wore different attire. For all of that, they had to file a regular report to the prison direction. First, they spied on each other. Then they reported on whether the Police officer was armed when he opened and closed the doors. Finally, they spied on all the other prisoners.

The assembly room and office of these men were always located in the office of translation, where they worked under the Ministry of the Interior. The intellectuals of the prison, who were the educated spies, were directed by the most refined spy, *Pjetër Arbnori*. We mockingly called him *"the Melon."*[1] As soon as he left prison, he was elected the president of the Albanian Parliament. The Melon was not someone who gave his reports in a vulgar manner like any other spy would. He knew how to weave together all the information, as he had a talent for depicting the characters and conduct of the prisoners in a romantic way. I do not know if the works of this man, who would then attain the peak of power, still exist, because then he would not have to publish any other slander. His prison writings would suffice to help him climb the Mount Parnassus of spy literature. Every country and era have masterpieces on this topic. There exist in the world kilometers of archives containing legal processes and defamations from spies.

---

1   Play on the Albanian words Pjetër and pjeper. The latter means "melon".

Let me cite another example. When the communist regime wanted to publish the work *Ali Pacha of Tepelenë* by the writer Sabri Godo, it asked the Melon and his specialists about Pacha's personality. Someone who knew about the relationships of the secret agent with the office of translation told me that the Turk Pacha was known as Albania's little Napoleon. Albania's Napoleon was small, but the lie big. Individuals such as the Melon had responded in this way because they wanted to get out of prison earlier, or at least before having possible problems with the prison direction.

Burrel can be classified among the most famous schools of espionage for untrained spies. Pjetër Arbnori, like his comrades, was one such untrained spy. He grabbed me by the throat one time as if he wanted to extract all the words I had ever said in my life and present them to the *Sigurimi*.[2] All the prisoners, aware of my hot temper, encouraged me to pay him back. They had even gotten a boiling soup ready for me to pour over his head to disfigure him for the rest of his life. It would have marked his head with his betrayal. But vengeance should not be counseled for anyone, above all a priest who lives with the firm belief that it is the Lord who punishes all the injustices because nothing escapes Him. If I had physically mutilated Pjetër Arbnori, I would have mutilated myself morally. And then, how would he, poor guy, be able to direct our parliament with his bald head that was disfigured by the boiling soup? But with or without the scalded head, everyone wanted to know: How could this guy rise through the political ranks with such a surprising ease in a time when more qualified people than he lived, forgotten, in their dilapidated homes in Shkodër?

After the office of translations, there were other untrained spies which included the cook, the road sweeper, the woodworker, the shoe repairer, the tailor, the accountant, and the store clerk. All of these men were important. They presented themselves as witnesses when it was necessary to re-condemn us. They beat us and stole our tiny seven-gram portions of oil, and the batter that the intendant put in oil to make crepes. Family members of most of these spies were also incarcerated in the same place. At the moment they rest two or three meters from there, in the cemetery which surrounds the prison that reserved the same destiny for their children. Naturally, the parents had

---

2 *Sigurimi* — The information service of the People's Socialist Republic of Albania.

been much better than the children. The former had been condemned for a single crime, that of resisting. They had continued to believe in God, had not lost their dignity, and had not renounced their desire for liberty for themselves and for their people.

At the beginning, Burrel was in effect filled with true fighters for liberty. Later, the unbearable terror began to weigh so heavily on the prisoners that the most honest would have had a difficult time finding someone suitable to talk with. The most honest counseled us not to speak loudly against the regime because, besides the spies that I have just mentioned, many others did not hesitate to inform on us. Those who spoke received the same destiny as a frontier guard who was executed if a slave escaped from him for the free world. Prison was the same. There was a line that could not be crossed. The prison's padlocks were not enough. The most important padlock was reserved for the mouth.

But I could never shut myself up. If I could not express myself, I would already be long dead. Therefore, when I was filled with thoughts and could not stand it any longer, I told the spies to get their paper and pens. And from time to time I even gave them my own notes. And I would begin my discourse, which was generally not in the style of Cicero: "The Bible says: 'When God wants to punish a people, He gives power to children.'[3] Me here, in prison, I am convinced that 'every people has the Government that they deserve!' Our Government is nothing but a pit of thieves and immoral, ignorant individuals who spend their days thinking up assassinations, arrests, and deportations." Every time one of those who had signed onto spying entered our cell, you could see it in his eyes. I waited for him with the terse words, "And you too, Brutus, my son?"[4]

An old leader of the Communist Party with whom I spent time in prison told me that a dreadful secret dossier was released by the Central Committee every day. It contained the names of six or seven Albanians who had to mysteriously disappear that day, followed the next day by another six or seven names. Evidently, these were the boldest and most just individuals. Some even belonged to the ranks

---

3 Cf. Ecclesiastes 10:16: "Woe to you, country with a lad for king," (Jerusalem Bible).

4 *"You too, my son?"* Words attributed by Suetonius to Caesar at the moment of his death by assassination when he saw that Brutus, who owed him everything and whom he considered as a son, struck him.

of the communists and held ideals. These communists would very quickly see the great distance between theory and communist criminal practice. The Party would make the malcontent intellectuals disappear, one by one. Those intellectuals preferred dying to submitting to a yoke which was worse than an ox's yoke, a yoke that Albanian had put around the neck of Albanian. This process forced out Albania's brains and left only those who did not know why they existed or why they were living in the shadows. This information formed a discourse type that I occasionally held in front of the thankless spies, who trembled at the idea of listening to me.

Those who did not surrender and who refused to become government spies had a peaceful conscience. They were physically tortured, but not spiritually. Spiritual torture is the worst kind of torture. The real tragedy of the prisoners began at the moment they decided to "be rehabilitated," as the ignorant secret service agents would call it. The "rehabilitation" would lead the conscience to feel so much pain that "the new spy" would end up hanging himself with the bars of his window.

I remember a thankless fellow who left the prison in order to testify in front of the examining magistrates against his son who worked in the Department of Interior Affairs. There he found himself face to face with his son whom he had betrayed because of his fear of torture. He came back to prison totally changed. He did not want to stand up. To compensate him for his betrayal, he was put in the prison infirmary where he could lay down in comfort in a separate bed. But even the bed did not help. In betraying his son, he had betrayed himself. He could no longer sleep. He no longer had a peaceful soul, and he could not find inner serenity. His remorse was so powerful and intolerable that, after two days, we heard that he had cut open his veins with a piece of glass in order to free himself once and for all from the tortures of his damaged soul. The poor guy believed that death would be the end of everything.

Evidently, none of the prisoners could accept that they were spies. They all said that they were forced into this task. Even Osman Kazazi, when he had become a nurse, told me: "I had no choice. I had to accept it or spend the rest of my days in prison." The most unfortunate spy was the doctor; when he could no longer successfully treat the prisoners, they would lash out at him and beat him to let off steam from their overloaded souls. To face this situation, the prison doctor had to be a St. Anthony. As soon as he appeared at the counter, the condemned gathered around like hens around a pile of grain. They jostled with each other to get medicine, thinking that the tablets could cure them of the terrible ennui of prison, the evil touching their families, and above all the evil of those living in freedom on the outside which, in reality, was less free than we were in our irons.

But the doctor's medicine did not heal anyone of these incurable illnesses. That is why when leaving him, prisoners would insult him in every sort of way and treat him like a spy, like the intendant, who belonged to the same category of people. The doctor was often punched. When he was absent, at the concentration camp, often someone claiming to be a doctor would be imprisoned, and the doctor's role would be filled again. What the new doctor had or had not done before was of no consequence. The prison needed a doctor, and at the time of need the doctor was there. It was not at all difficult because Albanians were constantly candidates for arrest. Everyone was malcontent, everyone spoke against the Government, and, deprived of all spiritual value, everyone looted what they could and committed all sorts of offences. We were all under the same yoke, like oxen, but no one aimed their opposition in the right direction. We all deviated from the Party line day after day and night after night in such ways.

We often talked about things in prison. The conversation would start off on serious subjects, but it would quickly degenerate into trite remarks. Familiarity encourages contempt, and we were, from that point of view, worse than a family. We were a family united by violence. We lived close to each other but without love to such an extent that when someone died, we rejoiced at having more space. Instead of crying, we battled over the freed-up forty centimeters.

Life was made harder by the tensions that two or three gangster spies created. Just like ancient emperors, they dominated the devil's kingdom. They would start their activities by shouting insults aimed at no specific targets but affecting everyone. Nonetheless, everyone backed them and even gave them food out of fear for them. Me, I never spoke to them. They would ask me: "Tell us, do you think you are better than the others?" I would always reply with a stubborn silence. I knew that these vile individuals wanted us to believe that they were honest, that they were on good terms with everyone, and that everyone appreciated them. Maybe everyone else believed that, but not Dom Simon who, even with his broken teeth, could not play that game.

I am not only writing to jar my own memory. These lines can help us to easily understand the events that took place after the opening of the prisons, events that appeared surprising and inexplicable to some. In seeking an explanation, we need to start first with the prison cells, then with those who were thrown inside and who, on their release, were not the same people as when they entered. Then, we should continue with those who, once out of prison, found themselves at the summit of Government while many others, who had suffered a lot, remained unknown fighters for an illusory freedom. That is why I decided to call certain people by their real names. Otherwise, we would not be able to learn the lessons of history, and history would continue to mock us even more cruelly. That would last until the Last Judgement, when the politicians of all time would finally be forced to publicly reveal their sins and crimes. Although these spies took every precaution to prevent the letters that they sent to the prison leadership from falling into our hands, we often succeeded in getting hold of some of Pjetër Arbnori's reports. He spent the nights writing while we were all deep asleep. He said that he was writing novels and other works that would make him immortal.

When the spies got together, they would do so in the presence of a secret agent, whereas when other prisoners were together, a simple Police officer was enough. Even when the spies were permitted to sleep with their wives for a night, somewhere nearby, there would be another, more sophisticated spy, a micro spy, who recorded all that took place in bed. That was the gift that the prison offered its spies. In all the special meetings of the prison spies, the micro spy would be there, ready to record every utterance. The secret agent would also be present, but the real agent was the micro, whose identity as the micro was officially hidden, though everyone knew. After the family meeting, the prison spy would meet the secret agent and verbally report the information about what had happened in bed that he could not put down in writing.

Countless times, I saw these spies meeting while I was being taken to the Department of Interior to listen to a fresh condemnation against me, as if I were so incorrigible. They spoke in total confidence of "the enemies," as they called those of us who had never accepted the dirty job of spy. One time, when Pjetër Arbnori and his comrades had beaten a spy, the Department of the Interior, concerned about keeping unity among spies, condemned Pjetër to one month in the isolation cell, naked except for boxer shorts in the middle of winter on the cement floor. Beating up a spy was like beating up an officer of the Department of the Interior.

In contrast, on another occasion, when Pjetër stabbed his fingers into my neck, no one said anything despite my protests that he be sent to the same cell as the other ordinary prisoners. I even wrote to the authorities about this subject. The main point of this letter was the following: "You want to dominate the prison according to the divide and conquer method! You have divided us to the point where we fight against each other!" The consequences of this letter were not unexpected. I got to understand it several times. I was condemned once again, without recourse to a trial. But I had already been condemned several times. This time they preferred to violently torture me. Covered in blood, I was then thrown into isolation, where I languished for a month without personal food or clothes.

The secret agent Esat Lata had the honor of being able to meet other pseudo intellectuals because he himself was a giant ignoramus. He spent many hours talking with them, gleaning information on what he thought to be the principal source of culture. It was logical because this information came from the mouths of cultured people, no? One day, leaving the room without any consideration for anyone else, he shouted at me, insulting me at his pleasure, and then savagely beat me and put me in isolation for a month in the middle of winter without clothes or covering, without a jacket or sweater, and naturally without food.

While meeting with family, prisoners warned the others to be prepared. When the prisoner was a spy, and the secret agent was absent, the spy had to wait for many long hours for the arrival of the secret agent. In our misery, laughter was a delight. We would say to each other: "He has two interviews. That is why he is late. But the second is more important than the first. What is the wife of a spy, in relation to a secret agent?" Me, I also could not escape the "noble" invitation to serve the Government. After having finished with the examining magistrate, another torture would begin. The captain Xhevdet Miloti, one of the men most loyal to the Department of the Interior, became one of the most honored employees of Caritas, in Rome, in the period happily qualified as democratic. He was supported by a woman, an officer of many years in the secret service, Alma Galani, who currently works in Latina in Italy.

Miloti submitted me to yet another interrogation. He offered me a proposition that he thought was very advantageous for me: become a spy of the isolation cells! Did I do wrong in refusing? If I had accepted, I would have taken the place of Pjetër Arbnori! Can you imagine Dom Simon, with all his teeth lost in prison, leading the Albanian Parliament side by side with those who had yanked out his teeth? Xhevdet said to me: "You can really help us in the prisons and camps because you are a priest and everyone trusts you. As you know (he would swallow sounds as he spoke, like he swallowed the days of our lives), confession opens all the doors and allows you access to where we can never go: to people's deepest secrets."

Vile Xhevdet! He believed that confession was like communist self-criticism, which could be sold on the market! The evil fellow was not satisfied with my ten years of prison, nor the tortures of the examining magistrates, nor the destruction of five churches that I had built with so much effort. But he wanted to take my honor once and for all in making me lose my soul that I had guarded so selflessly. He never said the most awful word in the whole world, "spy"! No, he called this dirty word, "work for the common good."

He called this "good," but he would be the one profiting, he who drove around in a car on foreign trips when Alma's family welcomed him any time he wished, he who dressed like he was the *count of Milot*.[5] I would also profit in the prison cells, where I would be betraying others in order to give the marquis of Milot pleasure. What a disgusting creature! I unhesitatingly refused. Then he started to threaten me: "Shut your mouth and be careful not to mention the names of the camp spies who gave testimony against you. They are convinced that the fairest route would be for you to accept this proposition that we have made. I will stick those testimonies on your back. They will be stuck on you like a stamp on an envelope."

I paid a heavy price for my attitude when the spies came for me after their meetings. Upon their entrance, I would play the role of Vatican correspondent. I balled up my fingers as a microphone and asked the recently-arrived a series of questions which were good enough to be transmitted live. But a real Vatican news microphone was far away; it was inappropriate to make a microphone with my balled-up fingers, and my punishment was ready. Holding my improvised microphone

---

5 Dom Simon plays on the name of this unfortunate king, *Xhevdet Miloti*, whom he mentions above.

up to someone's mouth, I asked: "Tell us first of all, how is the health of the President of the Department of the Interior? What would happen to us if something bad happened to him? That would not be pleasing to God!" The interview was brutally cut short, and Dom Simon received two or three more broken teeth as compensation. It got to the point where I lost all of them. Then it was my jaw's turn.

Today I need to have recourse to this same microphone, even if people say that liberty has arrived and democracy is progressing. The microphones have been shut off for the "nut with a hard shell." This is so because, above all, the truth is very bitter for everyone in this world. I am not a politician, but I cannot stand either communism or the mafia that dominates today in our country. And it seems to me that many others also cannot stand these two because men and women prefer drowning in the waters that separate Albania from the West to living under terror, lies, and permanent persecution from the tribal Government of Tirana. The end of Albania, which is between life and death, is not a new phenomenon. The barbed wire is still there, invisible, but very real! The new democracy preaches peaceful living between the wolf (the Government) and the sheep (the Church). Curious! Who can say who will eat the other?

16

Comedy Hour

Do not think that everything in prison is a tragedy. In life, everywhere where there is a human, there is always a comic aspect beside the tragedy. It was the same in prison, where many people suffered from inferiority complexes. Having never read a line in their lives, there were moments when, to annoy cultured people with whom they were stuck all day long in the same sardine can, they began to cite the names of authors and book titles of which they had never even dreamed. They deformed the names and words to the point where it was impossible not to burst out laughing.

There were also those who set out to write books. Then they gave them to me to read, hoping that I would class them among the most celebrated authors and the masterpieces of world literature, somewhere between Shakespeare and Molière. The writings perfectly resembled their authors. Here and there in the writings, there would be a pearl stolen from the world treasures, woven in among the lines with the prison wire. When I took out this finery, these writings resembled bad high school compositions. I told them directly, which enraged them. They thought I did that out of envy. They thought that once they left prison, their works would shine their rays in libraries around the whole world. Unfortunately, those works that could have been printed would have sold at half price because the contented people of the West do not like stories about martyrs, neither before nor after their meals! To one of them, after I had read his masterpiece, I said that he was below the intellectual level of Skanderbeg's horse! To someone else, I said that he lived only for eating!

The Melon told me one day that he did not read the letters of peasants because, though a peasant himself, he did not understand their nonsense. But the peasants, with their big boots, had keen spirits. I will give one example: One day, a friend of mine from *Bushat*[1] received a letter from his wife. She said, among other things: "In prison you are a hundred times better than I am, because there, with six hundred grams of bread covered in mud, stones, and whatever else that is given freely to your mouth. Me, I have to earn it, working in

---

1   *Bushat* — Village and ancient municipality of the country of Shkodër.

rain and sun, and covered in sweat. You rest all day in prison while I dream of having a day of rest because even Sundays impose useless work and unending conferences." Such a declaration made us happy. She showed us that those who were considered free envied us, we who were in handcuffs. Marvelous! We enjoyed such comedy, which even cancelled out the prison director's threats, when he said, "Behave yourself, or I will have your family transferred from the cooperative to the concentration camp. If you continue to act badly, I will have them imprisoned." The letter from the peasant of Bushat showed us that this path led to paradise, to the paradise where we had already been for a long time.

Newspapers and the Radio were other sources of comedic inspiration. We started with the newspaper, *Zeri i Rinise*[2], which had given itself the task of resolving the problems of youth. We read aloud the ready-made formulas and recipes for the reconciliation of couples whose relationships were racked with jealousy and who did not get along anymore because of the way they treated each other. Youth was presented as morally sound, but we did not believe what we read but what was between the lines. We thought of Rinia Park in Tirana where, if you did not pay attention where you stepped, you risked stepping on couples having sex. If you had to spend a night there, you would get the impression from the groans and cries that rose like a choir over the green lawn that the dead had come out of their graves. This was where people took their first steps towards abortion because they were forced to put their infants in the weeds after having dived into the sea of Eros and Aphrodite without knowing how to swim. And what to say of youth movements, military service, and other follies that were organized to educate, but which assured only the poor education of youth.

We would continue then to read in our way the other organs of the press:

> Prisoner 1: They accuse us of not having cars!
>
> Prisoner 2: What would we do with cars, we who so love each other that we are happy to travel communally, collectively, with public transport, on buses. We even prefer to travel in open-roofed trucks because in doing so we profit not only from each other, but also from the air.

---

2 *Zeri I Rinise — The Voice of the Young.*

Prisoner 3: Those who live in the West do not love each other. That is why they all travel alone in their individual cars. Additionally, the poorest spend the largest part of their day lining up in front of stores in order to buy pears imported from Albania.

Prisoner 4: Westerners do nothing else but pick through the garbage.

Sometimes, unable to control myself, I would stop reading. One day I said to the prison director: "Why do not you send us to suffer our punishment in the capitalist world? If we are to believe your newspapers, we would suffer much more than we do here in Burrel!"

On such occasions, the tragedy's curtains would lift. Do not ever forget the common proverb, dear reader, that says that exaggerated joy sometimes turns to grief. And people would also say: "When the mouth speaks, you need to think of the backbone!" After this joy, I would face torture and end up like the Phoenix, in ash and dust. But when the terrible door of the isolation cell opened in order to clear the dust, like the mythical bird I would get up again from the ashes, ready for another comedy! What was the secret? Prayer. That is what gave me life, even when my physical strength had abandoned me. Believe with your heart and pray, and you will see how the human is transformed into a phoenix! He is transformed into something even more divine: into a dead person who rises on the third day and then rises to the higher circles which have neither prisons nor handcuffs.

The Radio provided another source of comedy. It was supposed to educate us because prison was also called "education." From that, the word prison disappeared from the dictionary and the world could no longer complain that Albania had any. But even worse, there was not one corner of land on this territory where graves were not opened in order to throw in the bodies, skin and bones, of the prisoners, who are the real martyrs in the fight for freedom.

In order to re-educate us, they turned Radio Tirana to maximum to give us the chance to hear the most amusing news of our lives. The first scene of the much-anticipated comedy was the news that *Mehmet Shehu*[3], after a fit of hysterics, committed suicide. This

---

3 *Mehmet Shehu* — General and Albanian politician, Hoxha's right hand man. In the end, he opposed Hoxha's isolationist politics. He was found dead in his room on December 17, 1981. Dom Simon mentions suicide, but he may have been executed by the *Sigurimi*, the information service of the Hoxha regime.

comedy attained its height with the news of Enver Hoxha's death. The joy that this announcement produced must be registered in the world archives of crazy laughter, because there is no comedy that could provoke more laughter and joy, wilder, more powerful or deafening, than that news set off in Burrel prison. My ears still buzz with the suffering voice of my comrade, the late Ded Begeja, who distinguished himself among others in this ecstasy of folly and unheard-of joy. Even the face of the Police officer who opened the small window to see what was happening displayed the inclination to break out in laughter. He too, the poor guy, was a sort of slave like us. He guarded us because it was easier than guarding the fields of the collective. Often, in our presence, he ate bread with the nuts that his wife had stolen from the fields of the cooperative.

I amused myself by chatting amicably with the Police officers to whom, when I was in a good mood, I said: "I understand why I am here, because I speak against communism and communists, but you, what crimes have you committed that you are obliged to be on guard for twelve hours straight!? And when you are hungry, you are fed worse than me — a piece of bread as hard as wood or a stone with nuts or tomatoes that your wife stole from the cooperative. What pain you give me, poor guys. Me, I am condemned temporarily, but you, you are condemned forever!"

Under dictatorships, those who revolt without fear for their lives live better than anyone else. Everyone else, from the most important to the lowest server of the dictator, lives in anxiety, unable to differentiate friend from enemy. They wait for the small post to be set up and the ladder readied for the execution. Evidently, it never occurred to them to participate in the comedies that we had played with so much constancy and passion in the prison cells. The unfortunate come into the world and die in the tragic scene.

Another comedy scene in jail was the arrival of the prison inspectors, some from Tirana. All cell comrades fixed their eyes on me, as if to regain courage, because we did not know what these undesirable friends would inspect. Thus, I prepared myself by letting off steam so that I would not explode. For the occasion, those who came from Tirana had put on their Sunday clothes. They walked out in front with a haughty air, followed by the Burrel prison authorities with their military uniforms. Locks and keys creaked, doors opened and closed with a din, and the guests appeared in the doorframe, overflowing with the emotions of the moment. They grimaced because of the stench of rags and, above all, the smell of pots in the corner of the room. In this scene of such aromas, the important figure from Tirana started speaking in front of thirty or so ragged listeners, covered with their Stalin covers, some mats filled with bad cotton that, euphemistically, we called furs: "We have come to examine the legality. Therefore, if someone has any remarks or complaints to make, if there are any injustices, we are ready to listen!"

The thirty ragged people stared, wide-eyed and open-mouthed that someone had come from Tirana to defend them. Our rags had the not-yet-dried bloody traces from the examining magistrates, traces that at the same time served as warnings. No, we do not have any complaints to express, we have experienced no injustice, none of our rights were violated! We can speak in complete freedom. How could they violate our rights in a time when we did not have any rights? And so the ragged fixed their eyes on Dom Simon as if they wanted to say, "So speak in our place!" And naturally, Dom Simon could not disobey these eyes that sought justice precisely in the words of the priest, who for them was the representative of Jesus. So I stood up and commenced my litany: "You have come here to speak to us of laws? Of what laws? Of the written or of the non-written laws? Because we here, we are treated according to non-written laws. This is not a prison, but an institution of extermination, and it is not difficult to comprehend that we live lower than the level of animals." Obviously, I did not get to the end of my litany, because the comrade who had come to defend justice that is connected to handcuffs ordered me to dance. So the prison comedy, for me as for many others, always ended in tragedy!

17
Dreaming with Wide-open Eyes

Discussions between prisoners were generally vulgar and mediocre. The principal focus always returned to eroticism. Most of the people had their stomachs, and Eros or Cupid, as gods. Each also sought to present himself as a great adventurer who would carry on for as long as he would live, which meant outside of the prison walls because inside no one could see what sort of people we were. The gods of sex particularly dominated the souls of those who were in prison because of their chance to study overseas, or because they were former functionaries of power who had obliged poor young men and women to sell their honor when seeking work or even for an additional portion of rations. So, even in work camps and prisons, places of misery which should have made people a bit more serious, the names of poor young men and women were cited. They had been the victims of this sort of "male," because I cannot call them "man." Obviously, they had entered prison with a vice, but lived with other prisoners also adorned with all sorts of vices. They enriched each other and became real masters in this domain. Prison can be classified as being among the best schools of vice that the world has ever seen. This school throws people into the worst depression, deprives them of every human dignity, and always directs them closer to the most savage animals.

I knew very few true men in prison, which can be explained in part by the fact that the heroes of the Ancient regime were already sleeping the sleep of the just, their chests riddled with bullets or their necks broken by a rope. When I was arrested, there still existed a few from the Ancient regime. They were still authentic persons. Prison had not succeeded in dishonoring them. They still felt the pulse of the global situation in a time when others, plunged into pessimism, dreamed of a great day. In whom could we hope? In the superpowers that had left us in the hands of communism? It was because of them that we were in prison in the first place, reduced to being subhuman.

Our only hopes were in a possible war between the two camps, the Russians and the Americans. We would gaze at the sky with the crazy hope of seeing it go up in the flames of war. We were convinced that just as the Second World War had given us the gift of communism, so a Third World War would free us from communism's eternal slavery and a new world order would give us back our lost dignity. Dreams with wide open eyes! Nevertheless, even our dreams could be the pretexts to a worsening of our pain because here spies sought even to penetrate our dreams. They warned us that if our dreams came true, if Enver Hoxha's power were ever threatened in the slightest way, we would be executed first. To mock them, I told them that they would then be forced to also kill the spies that they had taken so long to train.

Everyone, certainly Catholics, but also the Orthodox and even Muslims, when it comes to the future of humanity, considers this type of situation according to religious principles. Now, the principal citadel of these principles is the Catholic Church, the only force that opposes evil. It paid for this opposition with the blood of its greatest sons, blood that flowed freely throughout the centuries in the name of liberty and human dignity. Enver Hoxha, even if he had a brain tinier than that of a small chicken, had borrowed ideas from American law. He nonetheless inundated newspapers with insults worthy of the Chinese against American imperialism in calling America "the world's policeman" and "the giant with feet of clay." That is why, every time that an official conference held in the prison courtyard came to a close, I would tell the instructors not to insult American imperialism because it was precisely President Roosevelt who had brought them to power at Yalta when he gave little Albania to Stalin's side.

We often discussed Albania's political history. Everyone gave their opinion. When we talked of Governments, most of us came to the conclusion that the consciences of Albanians had been so tormented that we preferred foreign occupants to home-grown dominators. We had better things under the Turks, Venetians, Austro-Hungarians, Italians, and Germans—and the list goes on. But the fact is that none of the occupants came down on God like the communists did. An honest Albanian, encountering every occupant including the Turks, was able to conserve his religion more easily than under the communist regime.

When it came to discussing which was better, a monarchy or a republic, the discussions in the "parliament" of prison grew quite spirited, more so than in the biggest Parliaments of the world. This was because the condemned fulfilled the conditions of making up a parliament: It was composed of all the parts of the political spectrum.

It is this parliament of prison that would be the first Parliament of a truly democratic Albania. Some did their best to defend the monarchy, for whose cause they were in prison, even while the king lived a filthy life in the free world. A thousand sweet thoughts for the king came out of their mouths. This for a king who managed politics from a harem and who had put the crown on the head of a man unworthy to reign. They told us that the king loved this man more than his own head and reign. He had succeeded in transforming Albania from the feudal era in instituting the law of the first night for women at the beginning of their wedding. When the young women refused, it did not bother him to kidnap them. From that, he merits the title "Father of the Nation" because, wherever you looked, you saw the eyes of children that made you think of the eyes of the king!

Others who had the sad fate of believing that Albania's salvation could come from the Italian occupation and who were linked to fascism tried to convince us that everything that is good about Albania was the work of the Italians. Well, they were not totally wrong. What pushed them to sympathize with fascism was that it had promoted Albania's ethnic sense and, above all, because it had dethroned the king Zog. We counted up the names and events. These prisoners brought up the fact that the Italians had directed all the Albanian ministries while seeking to teach this art to Albanians so that we could then become masters of our future. They say exactly the same thing to us today to the point of swearing that the Italians have nothing better to do than to save the Albanians, making sacrifices to the point of living with us in our lack of water and electricity. This is all supposedly because of the small spark of love for us that has been suddenly kindled.

Only a few prisoners studied seriously and sought to fill the culture of misery in which we found ourselves — as much as prison conditions allowed them. Most of them had no hope because they saw clearly that they would rot in prison, that they had caused the ruin of their whole family, and that no one thought of them. The world never stopped talking about rights and liberties, but it never acted because every day one of us ended up with broken ribs or in the prison cemetery. You are going to tell me that death is the same everywhere and that the grave is cold for the president as well as for the prisoner. But he is also born to a mother, and has a sister and brother, wife and children. This man also had eyes, and perhaps a hand would have wanted to touch the eyelids to close them at his death. Prisoners were not able to have the consolation of seeing their close ones at their last hour. The poor family members could not even cry. They quietly sobbed with tears of blood which flowed from the bottom of the soul — silently, for fear that others would see them and realize that they cried for the death of an enemy of the authorities. In any case, we were designed by destiny to replace our handcuffs with other handcuffs, sometimes Russian, sometimes Chinese, sometimes American.

Those who read novels relaxed when they brought to us the novel "The Banker." They understood the cat and mouse game in the world. They learned a few new words, unknown until then, such as Protestantism, CIA, and masonry, without which it was impossible to understand the White House, on which they had fixed their hope-filled eyes because the White House was the symbol of their dreams and illusions. Dreams of the sun, dear reader. While we dreamed of knowing how the President of the United States of America was going to free us from our handcuffs, who knew what the American President dreamed of? Certainly not of us, nor of our handcuffs, nor of our starving families, nor of our futures in the savage prison, where even the cuckoos preferred not to come and sing a song of bereavement on our heads. And to say that we were agents of the United States, a place we had never seen and that apparently had no need for the help of a half-living rag-tag folk like us.

Nevertheless, it needs to be said that certain prisoners merit an eternal commemoration. I will not say much about the Churchmen, as their examples are already known around the world. I will mention first a layman, Bep Mala. As one of the founders of Shkodër communist group, during the fascist occupation he was deported to Italy. After the capitulation of the Italian fascists, he returned to Albania, where Enver Hoxha and Mehmet Shehu tried to assassinate him. These latter two were part of the base of resistance at Pezë. Bep only just escaped, solely because it was nighttime.

Here is what he himself told me in person about the assassination attempt: "Enver and Mehmet gave me a letter to take to the *Dajti Hotel.*[1] I waited until night to leave the base and walked through Pezë

---

1 Under Albanian communism, the *Dajti Hotel*, situated in the center of Tirana, at the foot of the mountain of the same name, was reserved for international visitors and diplomats. The rooms were equipped with microphones, and staff for eavesdropping were located in the basement.

streets to get to Tirana. While I made my way along the shrubs and hedges, I heard shots fired at me. Miraculously, the night prevented the assassins from accomplishing their criminal act. I barely had the time to jump into the shrubbery of a hedge, where I laid still for quite some time, hidden like a hedgehog while controlling my body in order not to be shot somewhere. An hour later, when I no longer heard any steps, I came out of the bush and continued on my way. It was dawn.

"Something made me think about the shots and, even more, about this letter which was addressed to an orthodox communist who worked at the Dajti Hotel. It was a letter that was signed by Enver, in which he wrote: 'If we fail to put him down while on the way, you need to do it as soon as you read this letter.' It was one of those ambushes that one often encountered in ancient and modern tragedies. I realized very quickly that the two communist leaders hated me because they saw in me, like a mirror, their own profound ignorance. They knew nothing about communism. They had no theoretical training, and even less philosophical. Among all the Albanian communists, a genuine theoretician was Sejfulla Maleshova. He told me one day: 'They were very afraid of my learning. It is why they sought to liquidate me. And they succeeded.'"

The assassination attempt against Bep Mala was identical to that organized by Mehdi Frashëri, who was linked to Hoxha, against Father Anton Harapi. Father Anton was on the Shkodër-Tirana road. Another car of the same color and type was traveling just in front of him, a fact that would lead to a happy ending for him. When the thugs were about to throw a big tree trunk onto the road to stop Father Anton, they spotted a family inside the vehicle (of course, this was the car just in front of Father) and assumed that their target had changed his mind about going on the trip. The conspirators let the car with the family continue on their journey before leaving in theirs. Father Anton arrived safe and sound in Tirana. When he had learned what had happened with the other vehicle, in which his friends from Shkodër were traveling, Father Anton could not but think of Mehdi Frashëri, who was the only person who knew when he was going to leave for Shkodër.

Totally disgusted by the politics of Albanian politicians, Father Anton wanted to completely withdraw from political life. He left for Austria, where he had studied, with the idea of devoting himself totally to the problems of the soul while enclosed in the calm of a monastery. But Mehdi did not leave him at peace even in the monastery. He went all the way to Austria and persuaded him to return to Albania because of the needs of the people. He could not withdraw to a monastery and leave his patriotic duty unfulfilled. Touched by this proposition, Father Anton returned to where death, falsification, ingratitude, and forgetfulness awaited him.

It was like this for the best sons of the land. Father Anton and Bep Mala were very different people, but they shared a vast culture and the capacity to fascinate all those who had the chance to be close to them. Bep surprised many in the prisons with his erudition and, above all, his vast philosophical knowledge, just like Pjetër Gjini delighted the prisoners with his inexhaustible humor and Dom Njaci Gjoka shone with the example of his sanctity. In my own modest way, I also gave the example of resistance by my rebellion to the point where even today people ask me how I provoked the Police and secret service agents when they inspected our cells in Burrel. Actually, I was the only one to rebel when they appeared in the primitive stables where we lived, holding their hands over their noses in order to escape the "aromas" emitted by our miserable, fatigued, and filthy bodies that were adorned with all sorts of deathly odors.

That was how we spent our days and nights when we were not getting tortured: ceaselessly dreaming of what would never come to pass.

18

The French Revolution and
the Albanian Clergy

D
ear reader, do not be distressed when you discover in reading these modest lines that the majority of Albanians became communist spies. If you believe me, you can even be proud of your Albanian clergy, who showed a much more heroic attitude than the French clergy during the French Revolution. I reminisce in these lines only to add testimony to the history of the martyrdom of both the clergy and the faithful Catholic laity in Albania without engaging in analyses of context. I only recall decisive exterior factors which brought Albania to the precipice. But I cannot avoid looking at the origin of this evil, which was the bourgeois revolution in France, in which there are deeply rooted crimes against God and against men who believe in Him.

The reader will realize that the attitude of every kind of communist towards religion was nothing other than a bad copy of the attitude of the enemies of God in revolutionary France. But Albanian communists did not make a direct copy of France. Rather, they borrowed their blueprint from their Yugoslav friends, who, for their part, photocopied their blueprint from their big brothers, the Russians. The Russians took it directly from the source and used it after the necessary corrections according to the Asian-communist-Byzantine taste. The waters of communism, issuing from the troubled French source, came to the Balkan hordes, on territories already sown with the seeds of the most ferocious Islamic fanaticism. The Balkans was rapidly muddied with Christian blood. That is totally true. Whatever else they say is just demagoguery.

We can say that the French Revolution began with a Mass. And did not Shkodër faithful, hidden and petrified by terror in their houses, also invite the Albanian communists to a solemn Mass in the cathedral on a night of ill omens, Christmas 1944, at the exact moment when the communists had taken power? On May 5, 1789, in like fashion, before the beginning of the Assembly of the Nobles, the Clergy, and the Bourgeois, the latter of whom were known as the Third Estate, a solemn Mass was held. Shortly thereafter, on June

17, this assembly transformed itself into the National Constituent Assembly at the initiative of the bourgeois and with the participation of certain noble and clerical groups. This birthed the movement that would substantially alter the State's structure, thereby creating the preliminary conditions of modern democracy.

Catholicism was the official State religion in France under the absolute monarchy, the *Ancient regime*. Nevertheless, something had begun to change from the middle of the eighteenth century. The dispersion of the ideas of the illuminated, known under the banner of "enlightenment," demonstrated that Christianity no longer constituted the sole point of reference for explaining historical processes and natural phenomena. The same thing happened in Albania. While communist ideas spread, the monarch continued to reign throughout this latter country. But the monarchy differed greatly from that of Louis XVI. Our Salep Sultan was intelligent enough to flee before the communists brought in the guillotine. Further, the country's social and religious situation underwent great change, with one foot in Istanbul and one in Moscow, always looking east and trying to get away from the "first Rome, the true one."

The seed of atheist ideas, arriving from our Slavic neighbors, found fertile ground in Albania, as this land had been carefully worked over by Islamic extremists who did not hesitate to put on the mask of the *sans-culottes* only in order to extinguish Christianity from the region once and for all. Therefore Hoxha, the little sultan, was a great homosexual and, by that, a great partisan of unlimited liberty. It was not the liberty of the nation, but the liberty of the most repugnant vices.

Hoxha was a former student in the daughter of the Revolution, France, and a friend and permanent guest of the Northern and Southern Slaves. After his adventurous travels, he brought back to Albania a large sack filled with the seeds of vice and atheism. He immediately took the plow in his hands and mercilessly went over the field that had been sown with seeds of virtue. He carried out purges everywhere before sowing his own seeds and lifting up those who would serve him day and night until the harvest. We are still dealing with this harvest, and we will be for some time to come. He sowed wind and harvested a storm!

At the time of the French Revolution, the most eminent French Catholic theologians, who understood the transformation that was taking place, sought to elucidate the social role of the Christian religion. They testified that the Church was not opposed to, but was even totally in agreement with, the oppressed masses to whom its mission was indissolubly linked. Did not Albanian Catholic priests do exactly the same thing at the outbreak of the epidemic of communist cholera? We only need to mention the inspired sermons in all the churches, such as the preaching of *Father Anton Harapi*[1] when he accepted a part on the regency consul, and the conferences held by Father Anton and *Father Gjon Shllaku*.[2] This does not count the precious contributions of Catholic magazines. If you read them, you will see that they are similar to what is written and read today. They are still valid today.

Nevertheless, the efforts of French theologians were still in the project and discussion phase, without any visible influence on political reality at the outbreak of the French Revolution. Even if they had not yet started to take an extreme antireligious attitude, the members of the National Constituent Assembly were inclined to think that it was necessary to rethink in depth Christianity's role in the Ancient regime. It was a question of guaranteeing the same political and civil rights to all the French, independently of their ideological and religious convictions. On this occasion, it was necessary to adapt institutions to the new reality in which Catholicism would be only one constituent part. This meant that the principle of religious liberty had a place in the Universal Declaration of the Rights of Man and of the Citizen. This right was also initially included in the constitution of the Albanian communists.

Members of the National Constituent Assembly did not want to push this principle to its extreme consequences. They knew very well

---

1 *Father Anton Harapi* — A Franciscan, he was a prominent figure in Albanian Catholicism. He was first professor at the Franciscan College at Shkodër from 1923 to 1931, and then became the director. When the Italians left the country on September 8, 1943, he was designated by the occupying Germans among the four members of the Regency Council charged with governing Albania. He only accepted after receiving authorization of the Holy See and on the condition of never signing a warrant to condemn someone to death. When the Germans left, he refused to leave the country because he wanted to stay with his flock. The communists accused him of collaborating with the enemy and he was the object of a long manhunt. The Police finally found him hiding in a house. He was immediately arrested. He was condemned to death and executed on February 14, 1946.

2 *Father Gjon Shllaku* — Franciscan priest executed by the communists at the end of 1945 or the beginning of 1946. He should not be confused with Monsignor Bernardin Shllaku, cited below.

that without the help of simple believers and of certain "enlightened" bishops, their plan would not be successful. They knew very well the Church's influence among the people. These latter were the sole forces to whom the Constituent Assembly could appeal to in order to legitimize its existence. The nobles and high clergy considered this assembly to be illegitimate. So also, the Albanian clergy considered the installation of communism to be totally illegitimate. It could not be otherwise because Christ and the Antichrist were face to face.

In France, the introduction of the "Civil Constitution of the Clergy" (July 12, 1790) determined the necessity of the separation of Church and State. The constitution excluded all concrete interventions of the Pope, including the nomination of bishops. These were issues that had until then been regulated by the Concordat of 1516 which accorded the Pope "canonical investiture." This required papal approval of an episcopal candidate who had been designated by the King. In revolutionary France, one part of the clergy took an oath of loyalty to the Government, as was demanded of them, but the other group refused and was called refractory.

In that way, half of France's priests and bishops, headed by the archbishop of Paris, backed the revolutionary side. They became nothing more or less than spies who worked behind the scenes. They went even further: They married and took up arms against the other half of the clergy which had remained faithful to Christ and his Church. It was 21,000 against 21,000, with one group armed with guns and knives and the other with the Cross and God's blessing. But the spies, even with Government support, did not prevail. They all disappeared when the French revolutionary Government did because evil always has the tendency to disappear. And it is the irony of destiny that their heads were guillotined, which was an instrument invented by them to execute their foes. This was a great shock. Every day heads rolled and ended up in a big boiler. The Albanian dictatorship also devoured its own children one after the other.

In France, discordance arose between the Church of the "oath-takers," who were legally recognized and subsidized by the State, and the Church of the refractories who, opposing the new institutions, were not recognized by civil authorities. The situation in the Albanian Church was even worse. Priests who worked for the Government included those who were already affiliated with the Government and those who would get their first affiliation later on in the offices of the

Department of the Interior. Neither group took a public oath. Both groups sought to hide this allegiance as effectively as possible. In this way, the Communist Party creatively developed the teachings of fanatical Islam alongside those of the French, Yugoslav, and Russian Revolutions. The Party knew full well that hidden evil is the biggest evil.

When the bourgeois forces began the Revolution in France, they also started the politics of laicization, towards which they advanced in very measured steps. But, in 1793, there arose on the political scene a new social force, the *sans-culottes*, the working classes who did not wear the upper classes' *culottes*. These were, in other words, the proletariat of the towns and countryside. At first, they sought political and social rights, which were formulated as equal rights for all of the citizens with equitable distribution of material goods. In the autumn of 1793, the revolutionaries adopted the policy of dechristianization in the country. This was directed by the leftist Jacobins, who sought to keep alive popular pressure on the Convention and thereby consolidate influence. But the Jacobins feared losing their privileges if the proletariat continued to demand only political and social reforms. They therefore encouraged the *sans-culottes* to go after Christianity, thereby killing two birds with one stone just like their pupils in Albania would three hundred years later.

It needs to be emphasized that the antichristian current was never general nor total. During the French Revolution, Charlemagne's France did not slip to the bottom of the atheist precipice nor declare itself, with a crazy pride, to be the first country without God. Yes, dear reader, the revolutionaries used gloves because they were French revolutionaries, dealing with the French and not the Albanians. The latter were habituated to changing religion and the law as often as desirable. St. Jerome was a fourth-century A. D. Illyrian from Stridon and the pride of Albanian Christianity from that time on. He observed: "In my country, a sole and unique God is recognized: the stomach. Life has the value of one day. Whoever is the richest is the greatest saint!" An honest Albanian, if there is any, will ask himself, "Who is the most famous person nowadays in Albania? And what did he do so that we have his name on our lips? What good did he bring to this beautiful yet unfortunately crazy country that continues to applaud its torturers, hucksters, and flag sellers?"

Many documents from revolutionary France testify to a certain respect for Jesus Christ, who was portrayed, obviously, as a good *sans-culotte,* which is to say, as Judea's greatest revolutionary. As has happened so often in history, the image of Christ was used to justify antireligious measures. So it seemed that the Church, after having lost its political and cultural influence, would completely lose its influence over the masses. But in fact, the situation was more complex and troubled. The confrontational nature of the first phase of the Revolution made it the tensest part. After that, the Catholic liturgy was demanded by the people in several regions. Religious functions, based on memory, also sprang up spontaneously. In other words, dechristianization was incomplete. Did not those priests who displayed courage during communist criminal processes demand the same things? Was not religion in all its forms practiced in the catacombs? Did not this save Albania from dechristianization? Otherwise, how could fifty thousand people reunite, one at a time, out of the catacombs and without any sort of announcement, at the time of the first great public Mass on November 11, 1990?

In France, the bourgeois revolutionaries perfectly understood the importance of a religion "directed" by them to control society. In fact, they believed in that to such a degree that Robespierre came up with a State religion, which was the cult of the supreme being. Likewise, the Albanian communists profited from this French experience by seeking to place religion under their direction. Is not the Statute of the Catholic Church in Albania significant in this regard? It was approved in virtue of article 7 of the project of the law number 743 of the 26th of November, 1949 on the religious communities. (See *Dom Ndoc Nogaj*[3], "*The Albanian Catholic 1944 - November 1990, Defeat and Victory,*" Shkodër, November 1999, pp.101-109). You have to read between the lines in article 1. Fundamentally contradictory, it is the most significant of the whole statute because it camouflages the backroom accord between *Monsignor Bernardin Shllaku*[4] and *Mehmet Shehu.* The following words are written there: "She (the Catholic Church of Albania) is inspired by the principles of the

---

3 *Dom Ndoc Nogaj*—Encouraged by Pope Saint John Paul II, this Albanian priest helped to bring back the Catholic media in Albania after the communist years.

4 *Monsignor Bernardin Shllaku*—No doubt in the hope of assuring the survival of the Catholic Church in Albania, he understated the situation in Albania regarding religious liberty in front of Italian parliamentarians while visiting the country. Dom Simon was aware of negotiations carried out with the same hope. Monsignor Shllaku died in his eighties on November 9, 1956. He was the last representative of the Catholic hierarchy in Albania.

worldwide Catholic Church, founded by Jesus Christ, under the presidency of the Pope, successor of the apostle Peter."

"She is inspired by the Pope" while she is completely separated from him!? I am not going to linger on this argument, which is objectively treated in detail by *Father Zef Pllumi*[5] in his book *Live to Witness* and Dom Ndoc Nogaj in the book mentioned above. Article 8 stipulates, "Hand in hand with the development of religious sentiments, the functionaries of the Catholic Church of Albania will cultivate in the faithful their sentiments of loyalty regarding the people's power, the People's Socialist Republic of Albania, and love for the nation, for peace, and for the general well-being." Let us remember that after the clarifications by Monsignor Shllaku, the Statute was unanimously approved by Albania's Catholic clergy.

Viewed in its time and place, the Albanian statute was really a photocopy of the civil constitution of the clergy that was devised by the French Revolution. This constitution divided the country's clergy into two groups of almost identical numbers. The constitutionals had given the oath of loyalty while the refractories had not and so remained unrecognized. The episcopacy, generally originating from the noble class, almost totally supported the refractory side. Only seven of the one-hundred and thirty-five archbishops and bishops of France gave an oath of loyalty to the Revolution and its constitution.

This reality did not replicate itself in Albania because the bloodthirsty communist State had taken every measure to prevent such regroupings, in particular by physically eliminating the Catholic hierarchy. The list of priests who approved the famous statute begins with Monsignor Bernardin Shllaku, archbishop of Pult. The statute is the object of discussions because it is analyzed by the thugs of

---

5 *Father Zef Pllumi* (1924–2007) — Franciscan. In his book, he testified on Albanian life under the communist regime. The site *"Livres en famille"* notes: "Father Zef Pllumi's book is the witness of a man who considered his task to denounce the years of blood and terror that he himself and thousands of Albanians faced during the communist period. Between 1945 and 1990, Albania could only be known through fiction that captivated the French public. Since the fall of Albanian Stalinism, other books have been published, of which certain have started to reveal the painful reality. However, Father Zef Pllumi's contribution is unique because it is not limited to describing the realities of the Albanian gulag. This book recreates national history. It helps the path of rehabilitation in considering the lies perpetuated by the Stalinist dictatorship. One constant idea that appears is that of a European Albania."

our sad history, even in our day, and in Church symposiums. It seems that Albania has become deaf; it has no ears to listen to the lived testimonies of survivors. Albania hopes that with the deaths of these survivors, which will not be long in coming, she can shake off all traces of the truth. She should instead aim to rid herself of the thousands of pages of lies that were written more than a half-century ago concerning every domain. Those are books that the Albanian people need to publicly burn in order to have its own history, like all the other cultivated nations of the continent to which, come rain or shine, Albania belongs.

During the French Revolution, it was difficult to refuse to collaborate. Failure to swear the oath meant exclusion from every religious function. Religious organizations were threatened with changes that were unacceptable to the Catholic Church. In the spring of 1791, for instance, the French were called to vote to elect new bishops who came in their entirety from the constitutional clergy. (What choice would Albanians have made according to this formula at a time when the country's religious hierarchy was just recovering?) In these conditions, the persecuted bishops emigrated en masse after delegating their jurisdiction to the refractory vicar generals who had the courage to continue their missions in France. The bishops were able to freely leave for anywhere in the world. No one arrested them at the border to shoot them as was the case in Albania. The French revolutionary Government was even content that priests and bishops left of their own accord, which our Government came to appreciate only later.

At that later point, the Albanian communists figured that instead of creating problems for themselves in poisoning or shooting the clergy, it would be better to open the doors and let them out. This would make it easier for the Government to choose the new leaders from among those who remained. So, one nice day the massive emigration started. The most capable of the regime's adversaries were made to leave. Afterwards, they followed events from afar with their hearts torn by the farce of Albanian democracy. They had neither the power nor the desire to oppose what was happening in Albania. Some of these Churchmen no longer consider Albania as their country. One of these clergymen is very close to the celestial country due to the numerous years he has already passed far from his earthly country. Because the Church is universal, he prefers to remain far from hell, where he was already burned once before.

But let us return once again to France. Ecclesiastical events shook things up so badly that the Constituent Assembly was forced to backtrack and transform the Civil constitution of the clergy, a constitutional norm, into a law of the civil code. This made it easier for the clergy to swear the oath because this act only covered politics, not religion. Nevertheless, everyone retained their original position. This prompted violent confrontations between the two clergy groups that continued until the Napoleonic era. Such confrontations did not take place among Albanian Catholics because most of them remained faithful to the Gospel and refused to divide the Body of Christ.

In France, religious upheaval became more and more politicized. Opponents to the constitution, encouraged by Pius VI's formal condemnation, united all the forces of opposition to the Revolution. November 29, 1791 turned out to be a day of ill omen. Following the request of the Jacobin left and the deputies of the constitutional clergy, the New Legislative Assembly approved very tough measures against the refractory clergy. Their churches were to be closed and they themselves, if suspected of insurrection against the law, were to be arrested and held under strict surveillance.

In Albania, things proceeded differently. The clergy were shot or poisoned and the churches were closed. There was no one to oppose this with a veto as happened in France with poor King Louis XVI. He did his best to stop punitive measures that were based uniquely on suspicion. Yet local authorities did not take into consideration the King's opposition regarding anything. He was decapitated on January 21, 1793.

The situation worsened when France went to war against the House of Austria on April 20, 1792. On July 6, Austria was joined by its ally, Prussia. This prompted the pursuit of all those who had been accused of links to the enemy. You can see here the clear parallel with the persecutions of the Albanian clergy. In most cases, the latter were accused of spying both for the Vatican and for traditionally Catholic countries. In France, such an attitude of suspicion was adopted regarding most citizens, but it was particularly severe against the refractory clergy that obeyed the pope. The latter supported Austria and Prussia. Some members of the refractory clergy began leaving France as quickly as possible. If they were caught, they were deported to Guyana. But the majority did not leave their flocks. This was also the case with the majority of Albanian priests. It is enough to mention the martyr *Father Anton Harapi*. He had refused to withdraw with the German soldiers because of his firm conviction that his place was in Albania. It did not take long for him to be cut to pieces.

Here a recurring problem arose once again: Was it better to leave Albania and pursue your mission overseas, or to stay and be shot? Perhaps both! Albania needed both free voices in foreign lands and the prayers of those who sacrificed their lives or became spiritual fathers in prisons. In France, the persecution peaked with the September Massacres, which also saw the monarchy's impeachment and the failure of the constitutional regime. The Legislative Assembly then decided that all men of the Church, without any exception, had to once again take the oath of loyalty to defend liberty and equality. This time it was purely political. The clergy who had refused the oath in 1791 once again split from the other priests. Each group adopted different behaviors which of course depended on each view of this act's legitimacy. This came after the pope had condemned not only the civil constitution of the clergy but also the Declaration of the Rights of Man.

The situation became more and more strained. On April 23, 1793, the Convention gave the order to deport all the members of the clergy who had not yet taken the oath for the defense of liberty and equality. In autumn of this same year, the terror was launched. Its principal objective was the country's radical dechristianization. It goes without saying that the terror attacked the refractory clergy more severely than it did the constitutional clergy, who were largely unbothered. That was a clear indication of the bankruptcy of the principles of liberty and equality that the Revolution had proclaimed with much pomp. The same thing took place again afterwards with all the regimes that wanted to imitate this. Holding onto the truth, the refractory clergy opposed the convention with all its forces.

The convention, however, was already dominated by extreme Jacobinism. An unprecedented wave of attacks thus began. Later, these were repeated in many countries around the world. In France, churches were closed or set on fire, steeples demolished, bells made silent, and liturgical ornaments and sacred vessels looted and later used in antireligious demonstrations or destroyed in fire. Those ornaments and vessels, first-class artistic masterpieces, testified to human genius and to the inspiration of the supreme Creator of beauty. The revolutionary calendar was also modified to suppress

Sundays. The week would be ten days, with civil solemnities on the tenth. The names of the months were also changed. Priests, monks, and nuns who were not massacred were constrained to make a public denunciation, that is, to declare that they renounced religion.

The Albanian clergy acted like neither the French nor the English clergy before that. Some Albanian priests submitted to the regime out of fear. Yet when they were forced to state their renunciation publicly, like the Muslim and Orthodox clergy, they chose to die for their faith rather than renounce it. This highlights the powerful education that Catholicism gives to people, which Catholic priests had received body and soul. This Catholic education in Albania was better than it had been for the French clergy. It teaches first of all not to change colors according to the circumstances. Priests were no less helped by their vow of celibacy, which they rigorously and faithfully practiced. Celibacy freed them from family obligations. They had nothing to lose. Their children would not be tortured in deportation camps and their women would not be dishonored because they had neither. They knew that if they were shot while vigorously demanding the Lord's pardon for the grave sin of the spy who had turned them in, they would be free forever from the hell of their conscience and other burdens.

Whether alive or dead, whoever has God in his heart is free in every situation. Many times, I thought with chagrin of my many peers who had ceded. St. Paul and his conversion came to my spirit many times. I believed that God would have mercy on them and lead them to the right path by showing them how to unite themselves to His Cross. That meant facing suffering and torture in the name of the greatest ideal of the world, which is the ideal of the Gospel.

The French Revolution's fiercest period saw many monks and nuns assassinated. The persecution was led by increasingly fanatical and corrupt individuals. They even started to attack the priests who were revolutionary deputies. This happened to Abbot Lamourette, a republican and proponent of reconciliation. He was sent to the guillotine in 1794. It also happened to *Abbot Fenelon*, who faced the guillotine at the age of ninety.[6] In Nantes, the sixteen thousand "counter revolutionaries" who had been drowned in the Loire included

---

6 *Jean-Baptiste de Salignac-Fénelon* — Born in 1714, he was the great-nephew of François de Salignac de la Mothe-Fénelon (1651–1715), archbishop of Cambrai, the best known Fénelon.

one-hundred and forty-five religious. At *Rochefort*, a concentration camp for the religious was established, and five-hundred and forty-two died. In Albania, we do not yet have precise statistics on the extermination of the secular and regular clergy and the number of Albanian Catholic laity who were martyred, but we can say with certainty that the tragedy of revolutionary France was enacted on our territories with still more virulence than there. The tragedy happened at full force in our country because communist and Islamic hate were interwoven against Christianity. The horror that resulted from this atrocious twin is our new man!

The extermination of the French clergy was perpetuated in France in the name of the defense of the nation. It was in this context that the disappearance of religion was mentioned more and more as a necessity. In their public speeches, the revolutionaries lashed out like drunkards against the Church's faithful. They repeated accusations of treason and appeals for the death penalty without any supporting arguments but with an ease that makes one shudder.

The situation got to the point that the people, acting like a drunken herd, became unstoppable. Then even the orators of the Terror were sent to the guillotine. The guillotine's inventors began to experience it with their own heads. Accounts from the era speak of a political class that first incited the people into a frenzy with the idea of the guillotine and then could not retrace their steps out of fear of these same people. In lowering itself, the political class doomed itself to the guillotine. Reports indicate that the Terror got to the point where every act of pity was considered a "betrayal against the people." Clearly, the guillotine waited for the traitor.

But among those who faced the guillotine, many men and women religious gave brilliant examples of heroism. At Paris they stretched out their necks with a smile on their lips, pardoned their executioners, and prayed with the firm conviction that they were going to see the Lord very soon. Let me mention one example: While the fifth anniversary of the storming of the Bastille was being celebrated on July 17, 1794, sixteen *Carmelite religious*, singing the *Salve Regina* and the *Veni Creator*, walked up the steps of the sinister platform at the Place de la Revolution in Paris to their execution. They had been accused of espionage in the service of the enemies of France and of conspiracy against republican institutions. They all came from the convent of *Compiègne*, sixty-five kilometers from the capital. Ten days after them, on July 28, Robespierre himself, failing to kill himself with a bullet to the temple, was also led to the guillotine where the blood of the Carmelites was still fresh.

This tragedy inspired the creation of the well-known play *The Dialogue of the Carmelites* (1949) by Georges Bernanos, who wrote many other famous works including *A Diary of my Times*. This play, inspired by chronicles which were written by a Carmelite nun who was present at the events, inspired the production of a full-length film, *The Last of the Scaffold*. This was written by Father Raymond Leopold Bruckberger and Philippe Agostini. The film shows that heroism is not simple at all. We are seized by fear and anxiety when we sense that we will be touched by the sharp blade of the murderous sickle. But when it comes to being a martyr for God, He never refuses to give the force for the person to face death. The author calls this process "the holy agony."

The dialogues were recreated in a dramatic manner and with much finesse regarding the state of the souls of the sixteen delicate creatures. They were ready to die for HIM, to whom they had consecrated their lives. Some of them were even happy to think that God had designated them to take His place in the testimony of blood. But that is a useless heroism and a temptation to empty glory. A sister who hopes to be an early martyr is a bad Carmelite, just like a soldier who wants to die before the battle commences and does not have the time to carry out the commandment's orders is a bad soldier. If we look at the lives of the great saints, we realize that many rejoice in various ways at the idea of death, while some disdainfully push it away. Still others actively seek to evade death. Desiring to die when one is in very good health amounts to filling the soul with wind and is just like the fool who believes that he can nourish himself with the aroma of the meat that he is cooking.

In *The Dialogue of the Carmelites*, the youngest religious, the novice Blanche de la Force, suffered enormously at the idea of the guillotine. She feared death, but also felt shame in separating from the destinies of the other sisters. She was too young and cute to give her neck to the sharp blade of the ax. An inner battle developed in her conscience that led her to leave the convent. Once home, depression replaced fear. This depression inspired a new life for her. She could no longer distance herself from the site of the guillotine. On the day when her sisters climbed the stairs to the scaffold while singing, suddenly, one heard from a corner the sound of her voice, which united with the chant of the Carmelites climbing the scaffold. Raising her childish voice higher and higher, she continued to approach the place of execution as the crowd parted to let her pass. Her peaceful face showed no more signs of fear. She had been freed from her anxiety. She continued to sing until her head fell like those of her sisters. She had achieved her own revolution (extract from "Storia della Chiesa," from the *Duemilla anni di cristianesimo* edition, third volume, Famiglia Cristiana).

We can juxtapose this history of the French Carmelites with a single event at the beginning of the martyrdom of the Albanian clergy. This was the end of the life of the first martyr, the poet of tenderness and love for country, *Dom Ndre Zadeja*.[7] It is up to you to judge which history has the worse ending. On February 4, 1945, when he was arrested, he was the curé at Sheldi. He had become very well known due to his very animated sermons in which he warned the people of the danger of communism because it did not recognize God. The believers always kept in their hearts the memory of three sermons given at *Shirokë*[8] and at Shkodër in 1944 on St. Roch.

On February 3, 1945, the peasant Tom Marku, accused of carrying arms without permission, was executed. Dom Ndre Zadeja, with unparalleled courage, dared to approach the body to pay his last respects. That was enough for them to put him in handcuffs. A week earlier, another priest, Dom Lazër Shantoja, had been arrested along with the peasant Kole Sheldija, who had housed him. Now, the authorities made Dom Ndre Zadeja march on foot to Shkodër. He was thrown into prison, where he found many of his peers, in particular Dom Mikel Koliqi and Father Dionis Maka. On May 25, 1945, Dom Ndre Zadeja and thirteen other religious left prison to go to their death. The authorities did not even organize a simulacre of a process as they had done for many others. Also present was *Prek Cali*[9], built like a cypress and a hero who had given Vermosh to Albania while also being an ardent *anti-Zogist*.[10] He was more than

---

7 *Dom Ndre Zadeja* — Catholic priest, writer, and playwright, he was arrested by the communists on February 4 and executed on March 25, 1945.

8 *Shirokë* — Town close to Shkodër. Father Anton Harapi was born there.

9 *Prek Cali* — Hero of the anti-communist resistance, he was born in Vermosh, Albania's southernmost village.

10 *Ahmet Zogu* — Albanian politician and twice Prime Minister and then President of the Republic from January 31, 1925, and finally king of the Albanians under the name Zog I from September 1, 1928. He replaced the first Albanian Republic with the Kingdom of Albania.

a foot taller than the others. They would all lose their lives from the bullets of a traitorous brother.

While this small group of condemned left the prison court, the religious remained in their cells, leaning against the bars. They stood up to give the final blessing to the condemned while their warm tears fell on the bars. As soon as they saw the guns pointed at their heads, in the half-light of the window, the thirteen, acting as one, went down on their knees on the prison's court pavement. In that way, the condemned symbolically received the viaticum, the food for the last voyage on which they had departed. Their lives would not end at Zalli i Kirit, like their communist torturers believed. The heads of certain of these last did not wait to fall. Pitiable, my God, worse than the head of Robespierre.

It was the dawn of a wet and gloomy winter day. As usual, the execution was to take place in the night's darkness so as to leave enough time for everyone to go to close the roadblock in Zalli i Kirit, where piles of garbage grew higher — yet another blessing. Dom Tome Laca approached the group. With Jesus in the men's hearts, fear and anxiety disappeared and their faces shone with an otherworldly light. The priest, who soon thereafter would be the protagonist in a similar scene, had been unable to get away from the group when, in the streets and lanes of the ancient city, gunshots were heard. Since the communist arrival to power, the city of Shkodër no longer needed roosters, clocks, or church bells to wake locals up. The new regime had given the gift of this fresh way to wake people up: machine guns. Machine guns cut down and harvested the city's best sons. Those sons had elevated Shkodër to the peak of culture and progress. Those who are no more will never come back. I do not know if we will see their kind again. These bullets overcame the city of the North itself.

The thirteen fell one after the other. It was not anything extraordinary. Others had fallen before them, and others would after. Extraordinary things happened later. At daybreak, the terrified Shkodrans went down to the roadblock of Zalli i Kirit to see whose turn it had been the night before. They repeated the same ritual every time they heard gunshots. The Communist Party gave them the right to contemplate the children riddled with bullets all day long. A similar scene played out in the amphitheaters of the Caesars. But now they saw what no pen could describe. Not even all the water of Zalli i Kirit could wash this away.

Bursts of gunfire from the same height of the firing squad ended up in different places of the body depending on the height of each of the executed. Apparently, more metal was put into Prek Cali. The guns had targeted him at chest height, like a cypress just in front of the real cypress trees. The burst hit him square in the heart. While the burst had struck the brave, it also hit Dom Ndre in the front, totally detaching the skullcap from his skull. This left his brain exposed and a rain of blood covering his face like a purple handkerchief. The bullets had struck the others somewhere in the front of the body or the heart, depending on their height. This dreadful sight cannot and should not be forgotten, just like those who died while forgiving their executors should not be forgotten. But the guilty culprits did not stop there. They dragged their lifeless, bullet-riddled, and bloody victims up to a pile of manure and put them into a sitting position in a semicircle. It was as if, in this assembly, they wanted to sort out the problems that had remained unsolved in these poor areas. It was as if they wanted to weave the thread of what they had only just started to live in order to leave a heritage for future generations. They also put a cigarette into the mouth of the already dead Prek Cali, out of which flowed a tiny river of blood.

They were happy to see people like that while the faces of the members of the crowd, looking on with terror, still carried the shadow of death. After having executed Prek Cali and other men, the murderers grabbed the murder weapons, took each other by the hands, and began to dance around the cadavers in *Labërisht*.[11] They sang, "Dance, dance, mother of the *Gheg*.[12] We have blasted you." It is something that is still present in the destroyed city of Shkodër, which is a city devoid of construction, streets, or glory and filled with mothers who lost their sons.

In truth, it is totally understandable that among those who performed this macabre dance some converted to Christianity. They even fill the first rows of the churches. Bravo, they are skilled. Nothing more to say! Because if we were not the sons of God, if we had not met the One who gave his soul in praying to his Father, the One who in all his being could shake the world, "Father, forgive them, for they do not know what they do," it goes without saying that today, a

---

11   *Laberisht* — A dance from the North of Albania.
12   Northern Albanians are called *Ghegs*. The mother of the Gheg is the mother of Prek Cali.

half-century later, we could have sought this very natural pleasure of dancing the *Ghegerisht*[13] in the same way! But for us, such behavior is unimaginable. Even if such an image appeared in our dreams, we would go running the next day to confess, having been persuaded that dreaming such obscenities was a sin. But the sad reality is there, as I have described it. It was not a dream, but the unadorned truth. That is why we cannot forget.

But the young can say: "Why do we have to remember these atrocities?" Yes, my children, you can and must forget them only if you are sure that one day you will not see your father, mother, and perhaps yourself at the execution post at Zalli i Kirit? History repeats itself. If you do not believe me, believe at least in these two moving scenes, one from France and one two hundred years later at Shkodër, in the century in which you came into the world. Perhaps it is more real when the torturers are your neighbors and come knocking on your door to request a pinch of salt. They are all alive, safe and sound, and have the great desire to start the dance all over again on the garbage mound of Zalli i Kirit. If the world had really changed, the *most beautiful national monument* would have been erected there a long time ago. And at least one of those who had been drenched in blood at Zalli i Kirit *should have been brought to the altars* as they had fulfilled and even surpassed the necessary conditions for being considered *Christian martyrs.*

Why has that not come to pass? This simple believer wants to know. It is because we have not shown that the Church's concerns need attention. Nevertheless, we must console ourselves with the idea that the living's attention or the lack of it does not bring prejudice against these heroes. They undoubtedly benefit from the vision of God. They wear immaculately white clothes that are washed in the blood of the Lamb and hold the martyr's palm. Even if humans forget, God never forgets to compensate his sons! The true city of Shkodër is henceforth one of the principal quarters of the heavenly Jerusalem.

But let us return one more time to France in order not to forget that those who took in or *defended the persecuted priests and religious* were also condemned to death. Even at the peak of persecutions, many did not hesitate to extend their necks under the guillotine in order to save the religious, or to protect Bibles, rosaries, statues, and other sacred symbols. It was the same in Albania. And it is necessary that

---

13 *Ghegerisht*—Dance from the North of Albania.

someone, naturally from the Church, take care to make the names of these individuals known. Those who were tortured yesterday are forgotten today. They are the real heroes of twentieth-century Albanian history. Naturally, we also must support their children, who were born and brought up in deportation camps for the sole fault of having parents who defended the clergy. It is a crime that the Church sends the sons of lawbreakers whose hands are bloodstained to the best schools. *Dom Prenke Ndrevashaj* testified that the Albanian students who directly benefited from communism's fake fall with religious bursaries to America's best schools all came from the nomenklatura.

When it comes to educating those who were unable to glimpse a ray of the sun, stupid questions arise: "Can you speak English? Do you know how to use a computer?" Obviously, such students do not know. Where could they have learned, dear reader? Perhaps in the muck of the swamps? Prisoners' infants only knew how to use pickaxes and shovels due to those who supposedly took our defense. The Church must instruct her own children — those who have proven their faithfulness. The Church must familiarize them with modern culture if she wants to have her own people in every domain, and not only Judases. The Christian people must know these truths. Some never stop saying that we always speak poorly of others, and that we need more discretion and reserve because we harm the Church when we reveal all of this to the world. That is a useless and valueless consideration. Members of the Church must ensure that they resemble Jesus as much as possible by moving as far away as possible from the devil's temptations. Then, they will not fear anyone or anything. But if we sin, it is the duty of every Christian to criticize us without any fear of harming the Church. It is precisely in that way that we teach the Gospel whenever someone keeps on falling away and persisting in evil: First, face to face. Then, with two or three witnesses. And finally, in the midst of the community. We cannot forget that the Church has nothing in common with the Department of the Interior.

It is the same with priests. The Church belongs to all the faithful, and if one priest does not behave according to the Gospel, if he does not live according to what he preaches to others from the altar, he obviously does not represent the Church. We are told that even other religions specialize in hiding the shortcomings of their clergy. Naturally. They have other principles than we do. The Gospel of Jesus Christ teaches us that the Church is not headed by humans but by Jesus Christ Himself. This is why if someone is off the track, no one should worry or be afraid. The believer needs to look to God, not to Monsignor!

Let us return once again to Danton and Robespierre. They then tried to slow down the exaggerations committed in attempting to dechristianize the country. Although the Convention had proclaimed "religious liberty," Christians were not permitted to reorganize their churches. It was only in February, 1795, which was seven months after the fall of Robespierre, that the constitutional and refractory Church succeeded at returning to its pastoral activities in the shadow of the Thermidorian regime. Meanwhile, an atmosphere of disgust for the former exaggerations combined with the reappearance to an unprecedented degree of popular religious sentiments and the desire to follow the liturgy. Only two years had passed. But in Russia, whose example we had followed, and in Albania, more than half a century was needed — in fact, more than a human lifespan.

Nevertheless, this was not the first time that the Church was forced to confront savage and powerful enemies. And it will not be the last time. Since the ancient amphitheaters, the Church has climbed up to the scaffolds. The world can see it hundreds of times in various countries and eras as the Church declines, only to rise even more powerfully, and precisely so because she is not a work of man. Not every Albanian priest had been a saint because it was not easy to become saints in the hell where they lived. Some surrendered. Some priests and bishops could not resist this hell. But this did not come to half the number of priests as it did in revolutionary France. In Albania, only a few succumbed to the tortures and accepted the dirty task of spying against their own Church. From this we can affirm that the Albanian clergy, which is made up of flesh and blood men who are therefore sensitive to cuts or burns, when faced with discouragement and the discouraged, maintained a more heroic attitude than the English Catholic clergy of the sixteenth-century. That was when Henry VIII, grandfather of our dictator, found it necessary to chop off heads. He separated the English Catholic Church from the Vatican in establishing the Anglican Church. In addition to the crown, he claimed for himself the headship of the Church, which is to say, Pope, and, above all, torturer.

19

The Dissidence

Who can be considered a true dissident in a time when not everyone was put in handcuffs and only those who had fought for liberty wore them. Not everyone who passed through the silky sieve of the communist interrogation ended up without some brand. Happy are those who succeeded at resisting by not selling their ideals, friends, or family. They did not bend, despite wounds or temptation. Happy are those who did not fold when confronted with the hope that was proposed by the devil. That could have opened to them great paths to power. Some of the weak accessed that. Truly very few managed to miraculously escape because great heroes lie down for their last sleep in pits that no one can find anymore, dug in a heap of garbage around cities and prisons. Can you imagine that the bloody dictator who would order heads to roll merely due to a hastily-spoken word left the great dissidents alive?

That is why poor Albania had lost its joy — because the true dissidents are no longer with us and those who denied the Albanian people even the most basic rights have once again taken the seat of Government. These rights include the right to exist peacefully in your home, village or city, and country. Tell me what sort of men of Government are those who first were servants of the dictator and then servants of his enemies, while giving beautiful speeches and composing philosophy, poetry, novels, and music? A prisoner at Burrel, exhausted but rebellious, had more dignity than whoever declared themselves dissidents. Those dissidents shook at the idea of someone making their exploits public at some point. They therefore lived a repugnant and servile hypocrisy even as they smiled from ear to ear at the Police dog and the truncheon. What tasteless servility from all those who call themselves dissidents yet today receive compensation for their past spying! — for espionage, for the books that they wrote, for the chants that they chanted, and for the faces that they portrayed. It was not these individuals who overturned the dictatorship. Nope. They supported it and continue to arrogantly and brutally support it.

When I went to the UN, I asked some American statesmen who they considered to be Albanian dissidents. They lowered their heads, and after a moment of silence, gave a laconic response: "You carried on your own back Enver Hoxha's dictatorship. What is better, him or the multi-Party system?" As if there were no other alternative for Albania, Hoxha or the multi-Party system! It is either this or that, and that is it. Either be suffering Socrates or a malcontent pig! Either a sole dictator or a crowd of mini dictators who are all faithful sons to the guy we had assumed was already dead and long gone. And all of that is a gift of America, where we had set our eyes. We had been ground down by torture and hoped to benefit from a ray of liberty. Thank you, America! The merit for Albania of yesterday and today returns totally to you!

But what can we expect from America? It can in no way tell us who is and is not a true dissident. In the U. S., which considers itself the symbol of liberty, the individuals who had put the true fighters of liberty under their yoke found refuge and continue to find refuge there. Do you know who I met during one of my visits to the United States? Ndoc Vasili. What do I call him? When he was born, he was known as Ndoc du Vasil de Berdice, then as a Franciscan by the name Fra Tarçis Vasili, just like his close comrade, Luke Kaçaj, who went by the name Fra Severini. It was this man who, in 1946, at the assembly of Gjuhadoli, was unmasked as a spy of Fadil Kapisyzi. It was he who stole the keys of the church from Fra Ndou and who helped Pjeter Kçira hide weapons in the Franciscan church. It was he who, the day after the dismissal, as eyewitnesses confirmed to me, went among the priests, introduced himself to the provincial, *Father Mati Prendushi*[1], and said hello with a punch to the head while saying, "Death to priests." That is to say, death to all those who until then had been his brothers. Therefore, "Death to religion, to the nation, to culture, to peace!" He was accompanied in this approach by his new master, Fadil Kapisyzi. The next day, Father Mati told the other priests all of that while morally prepared for the first act of the tragedy.

This priest-clown criminal was not content with his betrayal. He went further. He brutally tortured the other priests in the prisons. Professor Sami Repishti witnessed this. Father Çiprijan Nika informed

---

1   *Father Mati Prendushi* — Franciscan priest and great patriot, he helped to defend national interests, notably at Deçiq, in Montenegro. The communists demanded his return to Albania. Condemned to death, he was executed by the communists. His last words were: "I pardon the Court and all those who will kill our innocent bodies." He was beatified in 2018 with 37 other martyrs.

him of his last wishes while they suffered in the same prison. The spy Ndoc Vasili, after having realized that he had not gotten what he had expected, or perhaps to pursue around the world what he had learned to do at the Department of Internal Affairs in Shkodër, took the path of exile and presented himself as a dissident in the freest countries. In this way, the monster found refuge in the United States. He changed his name, naturally, to Anthony Kapaj and was put under FBI protection.

It shocks us to see these individuals leave for the United States and immediately settle in comfortably. We long ago identified them as traitors and spies. Then they became famous dissidents who received compensation and, of course, started to write books in order to camouflage their betrayals by continuing to falsify history. That is what Anthony did. He never stopped speaking poorly of the same priests who had brought him up and nourished him. I read his lies and Nikë Stajka's just responses. Therefore, when this man salutes me, with his great height and dark face, I get the impression of having come from the pit of hell. He wanted to gain my confidence, as he had done with Dom Zef Oroshi. This latter had also demanded exile in the free world and was accorded a place in this group of dissident Albanians. But I have to stop myself with these words: "I am astonished that you are not still stuffed with all the bread that the monks had given you!"

Instead of fabricating endless lies, it would be better to castigate yourself and beg for pardon. I hope that you recall the time when you were a deacon, because God pardons even the greatest criminals — obviously when they repent! Similarly, you must remember Judas, who did not repent and hanged himself. I thought that, as the Judas that you were, you would find a fig tree in America and hang yourself. It would be just to do it with the St. Francis cord that you had betrayed so treacherously. Or you could have hanged yourself at Berdice, where I find it necessary to remind you that fig tree branches are not lacking.

If America had been the country of liberty for everyone, as it symbolizes, and not only for itself, it would have no place for the Judases of our tragedy. And those who had not forgotten the dictatorship's misdeeds, even recently, would not have been burned. How can we call American presidents like Carter, Bush, and Clinton Statesmen when they permit Enver Hoxha to belong to the Organization of the United Nations? It was this Enver Hoxha who shot people solely because they looked beyond the barbed wire which surrounded the slaves of Albania. It was this Enver Hoxha who shot a priest for the simple fact of baptizing a child or who arrested a father of a family who, living in the misery of the agricultural cooperatives, admitted to stealing bread to feed his family. These so-called Statesmen continue to applaud the politicians in power who commit more refined crimes today. The wages they offer for the pain and sweat of the honest make life impossible in Albania. Albanians are caught between miserable wages and European prices in a market where they sell the castoffs of the East and the West. This entire type of Statesman, near or far, will have to respond one day. The curse of these people weighs on them, above all on the men in Washington because violations of the Rights of Man start there and end up in Tirana.

The small seek to model their lives as closely as possible on the examples of this world's powerful. But when the powerful are completely rotten by vice, what can we expect from the small people? All political prisoners, even the most ignorant, who have nothing to do with politicians aside from accusations against them, knew that the communism installed in Europe by the Yalta Conference in 1945 had been the work of the USA. The Americans gave the ancient and recent "democracy" of Tirana as a gift. Albania was a land seeded by bones where only death grew. This so-called democracy, even today, is supervised by American counselors who live "in the shadow of the khakis" on the romantic hills of Tirana. With the same indifference that European embassies observed, the suffering of the Albanian people under Hoxha's terror, European Union observers today contemplate the Albanian mafia gallivanting in luxury cars on our pothole-filled roads, preoccupied only by the abundant craters that disturb their journey in this virgin country.

20

Released

April 13, 1989: I was about to come out of my eighteen-month isolation when the small blinkers of the cell opened. What resembled the eye of a Cyclops appeared in the tiny hole. This eye that became scarier in the backlight was looking for someone. It was the eye of a policeman who had always caressed me with his kicks and endless violence. He was looking for me. After spotting me, he made a sign at me with his finger and yelled, "Tell me, then, you, get your things and come out into the corridor!" I pretended not to see or hear him. My eyes scrutinized the ceiling as if searching for the enigma of life. The policeman's voice exploded with anger as he repeated the same order. The even more indifferent "nut with a hard shell" remained in the moldy corner of the cell. While I played the role of a person who is preoccupied with nothing, I felt my body and soul vibrating, as I knew full well that obstinacy came with a high cost here. Every gland in my body was animated. My brain sped and heart pumped rapidly in the expectation of being punched and kicked. All of my being, at the peak of tension, expected the eye to pass through the hole in the door and transform itself into a real cyclops, into a being who with a single strike could also break the hardest nut that exists.

The policeman opened the door and came into the shabby room. This time he fixed his two eyes on me — he had two, not one, as the small opening had given me the impression. He was as red as a tomato. He pointed to me with his finger, repeating for the hundredth time, "You say something." I responded, "What does that mean, 'you'? Me, I have a name, and as long as I am not called by my name, I will not budge from my spot." He then called me by my name, Simën Juba! And even if this was not exactly my name, I got up and got ready to leave. The first thought that came to my head was that I was going to be transferred. The second was that I was going to be attended to by another examining magistrate. What would that change? I had the tendency to pass from rain to hail and vice versa. A bit of variety!

That was the sole variation in our lives: from the prison cell to the examining magistrate. At least for a few instants we changed

147

the environment. We would no longer have in front of us only the ragged walls of the prison, the same faces which were even sadder than the dull walls, like the sky on the gloomiest autumn days. The door opened and, to my great astonishment, I felt a regret in leaving, perhaps to never return. I was a priest. I was connected to these people with a thousand threads which were rooted in my soul. They loved their priest, even if he was mediocre. With the priest, they found the moral force to face the coming suffering. I left, touched by my comrades in misery, for an unknown destination.

The policeman had me walk in front of him and leave through the prison court. It was the first time that I was in the court without handcuffs. I started to feel free. Astonishing! The policeman pushed me forward, which interrupted my dreams, and had me go into an office where I found, in front of me, all of Burrel's authorities — in a word, "the triangle," as we tended to call them at the time. It was my first time in the presence of people who thought they were free solely from the fact that they did not have their hands and feet tied. The head, the President of the Department of the Interior, pounced on me, saying, "You do not behave at all like you should!" I replied, "Does that have something to do with what I said against you? Obviously, I talked, and will continue to do so. That is why God gave me a tongue: to demand the rights and freedoms that belong to me, and also, obviously, to eat, though not the pig slop that you have nourished us with all these years." We had several rude exchanges which are not worth remembering because other former prisoners have recounted all that in their memoires. It would be good to find, read, and mention them here: see page so-and-so in such-and-such book, etc. But where could I find such patience, now that I already find it difficult to end my reflections that, thank God, are nearing their end. I think that nothing should get lost, neither the events nor, above all, the names of the criminals who destroyed religion, the nation, and life.

These testimonies are an integral part of the history that we hope to see written in the future and that merit to be called *The True history of Albania and the Albanians*. Will the truth of the history of Albania and the Albanians be written when until now only lies have been published? A lot is said regarding patriotism, fraternity, and, above all, unity in a time when no one speaks of the harsh suffering that the Albanians of the South caused to all Albanians, especially in the North. If we, with our still-festering wounds, dare to call the facts by their names, there suddenly arises booing against us. We are treated as fools, secessionists, and anti-patriots. All of that is from the past, certain voices will nervously say. Those are the ones who think that the events can be struck out with a blow. Therefore, from one forgotten thing to another, we will succeed, they tell us, in living together — wolves and sheep in the same inn and same stables. We have already made general moves, to the great satisfaction of the wolves, which replaced the shepherds at the head of the flocks.

Burrel was Albania in miniature for as long as Albania was a great Burrel, which signifies a perfectly organized disorganization. In order to attain the peak of this type of civilization, the communists had created a university and an academy of sciences which had for principal mission to sow the greatest confusion possible in order to make life impossible for Albanians and to make Albania unlivable. These glorious institutions offered the people splendid masterpieces, all of the genre of the *Albanian Encyclopedic Dictionary* in which we learn that we have to erase our memory once and for all. The authors of these works are still around, adorning their toilets with academic insignia and continuing to boast. In fact, they need to thank God for not having their wrists adorned with the same handcuffs that they put on us for more than a half-century. At the end of the day, the communists richly deserve these handcuffs! Someone needs to bear the responsibility for the destruction of so many works, so many regions, so many human lives, and so many souls, for the ruin of Albania and the Albanians.

While I expected the resumption of tortures and had prepared myself to take them, the President of the Department of the Interior announced the most unexpected and hoped-for news: "You are free," he said, almost enraged, "and from this moment it would be better if you used your mouth only to eat. Do you understand? Get your stuff together. In five minutes, you must be out!"

I was amazed. I was truly free. The Chief Officer of the Department of the Interior stared at me with his criminal eyes, expecting me to thank him. But my toothless mouth remained nailed shut. No words of thanks, no servility. Why would I thank him? For my still-fresh physical and spiritual injuries? For my handcuffs? Or for the teeth that I had lost? What would he have learned the most if I had addressed him with a smile? The terrible cave of my mouth, reduced to this state by men like this one standing right in front of me. After mercilessly torturing me, instead of demanding forgiveness from me, he continued to threaten me. I could hardly believe it. I told him, "Finally, you have come to understand that your system has crashed down on your heads. Is it true that you are really freeing me? Or have you just changed tactics, replacing torture by mockery? I am sure that first you will release your spies. At the moment, they are more indispensable outside than inside the prison. Then it is my turn and that of my dissident friends, whom you would wish all to die, stupidly believing that the dead can no longer speak. They speak, mister, they speak! We will make them speak if they are ever forgotten!"

The Chief Officer of the Department of the Interior was filled with rage. Using vulgar language, he ordered the Police officers to kick me in the ass all the way to the prison gate. This came after his meticulous control of me to the extent that I could not even take a piece of paper from outside. The policemen rushed to carry out the order. "Check me out, check me out," I said to them, ironically, "because I have in my pocket the letter to give the signal for the general insurrection!" The policemen, now infuriated, kicked me one last time and threw me outside with my rags that reeked of the prison. I was free! But I began to doubt it. I was brought into prison with punches and I left with kicks. Funny freedom!

I had not yet set foot in the space that I assumed was free when I realized that I was going from prison to chaos. I could not find a trolley to carry my necessities. I would later find out that there was not even a spoon in my twice-sequestered house. A few hours later I managed to find a truck with an open though loaded back. Much later, it dropped me off at Milot. There, the first spy that had been released from prison awaited me. After greeting each other, he started talking to me in a familiar tone, as if we were old friends. I told him that I did not normally have such conversations with people I did not know. He then started praising my prison behavior, providing me with details that I myself had forgotten. He did not give me any space and stuck to me like a spider. He was an integral part of what people in Albania call "liberty." Nevertheless, still filled with the emotions of freedom, I did not worry about his presence, just like I had not felt the cold or wind that had whipped me in the back of the truck.

Near midnight, another truck finally brought me, rags still on my back, and my guardian angel to Shkodër. The thankless guy told me that he lived in a village and had nowhere to sleep that night except for my place. Finally, I neared my house, which was located close to the Rrëmaji cemetery, where two century-old green cypresses stood. That was where the white crosses of marble mortuary monuments would be set up and taken down. Those were the only crosses that could escape the communist storm, even if they were cracked and broken, just like the souls of people who could no longer hope to rest in peace with their loved ones under the cypresses. The Government had created another cemetery at Shtoj, and some said that a new city quarter would be built at Rrëmaji. It was also said that the dead were more content at Shtoj because they were between vines where they could imbibe grape juice and wine in their dead mouths. They thereby passed the time more drunk than when they were alive. In a word, life flourished in death. Shkodrans mocked this because they well knew what type of flourishing could be born from the glacial communist winter. But it never came to their mind that the Lord had designated this plot of bone-filled earth with giving the signal of a true springtime. It never even came to my mind.

At that moment, I looked for but could not find my house, as it was covered in silence and obscurity like a tomb. I knew that one of my nephews, born like all honest Albanians with the malady of persecution, had left for the United States and that my brother had been sent to the gulag. I did not know anything more. When I found the door to what I thought was my house, in the crisscrossing of walls and doors of new structures built in my absence, I figured it out: I had come to the door of my house where no one was waiting for me. I had the impression that it was the thick cover of an ancient book that was written in an unknown language. It was midnight. Even if someone lived there, he was already long fast asleep.

My family had told me that another nephew lived there. He had not been sent to the gulag, rumor had it, because of softer laws. My trembling hand grabbed the new door knocker. The old one was gone, the one that had announced so much happy news in this small house built near a cemetery. The sound of the knocker spread in the night's silence, out into the jumble of half-cabins and to the cemetery to bother the sleep of deceased ancestors. After I had knocked several times, a candlelight finally appeared and the door opened. Behind this light I saw an unknown face, with tousled hair and sleep-swollen eyes. He stared at me as if I had fallen down from the moon, and when I told him who I was, he woke up completely and got into a very bad mood because, as I soon learned, he was sleeping with his mistress in the house where two Catholic priestly vocations had been formed: Don Lazër and myself.

I had knocked at the wrong door. I asked for pardon from the tousled, grouchy person and continued my mission in the night. Later, I learned that in this house other young people, his comrades, also came to satisfy their animal cravings. While this house, which was located in the middle of a Catholic street, had been reduced to such a state, imagine other houses, where for more than a century the voice of the Lord had not been heard! The archbishopric was in an even worse state. The persecution had carried out a life and death struggle with religion and civilization, and it had succeeded in interrupting all development for some time. My nephews lived among these people.

If the country's development had not been interrupted by the Tosk statelessness, they would have been completely different by being educated in religious institutions like other young Albanians. Albania would not have been transformed into a place of thieves, fornicators, ignorant, and impresarios who had only one idea, which was to leave for another country in order to make money in places with the highest prices, where everything was for sale including antiquities, ripped draperies, promises, virility, and religion. This stank out the entire world.

I crossed the threshold of the door, deeply shaken to my soul. While I examined with great nostalgia this place where I had so strongly desired to live, my nephew fed me whatever food he had. I quickly ate with my unwelcome guest before walking into my room on the ground floor. It was a simple priest's room: poor, disorderly, and with a cement floor and walls. I dropped my prison rags to the floor and went to bed, having the feeling of being back once again in prison. Who would be waiting for me tomorrow? And the next day? What would I eat? What would I become? "That the Lord's will be accomplished," I said to myself out loud. I made the sign of the cross and put my dark thoughts behind the door about which I had so often dreamed.

The next day I had to go to the Department of the Interior to present my prison release document. It certified that I had left the herd of handcuffed slaves to join the herd of free slaves. The Officer opened the paper, read it, and, raising his eyes to stare at me better, exclaimed, "Seven years is not enough! It is an insufficient length of time for a man like you to repent, you who had started his life as a priest and finished as an enemy!" I responded: "Even if I said I repented, you would not believe me. You would even only hate me more, and insult me, and say: 'What kind of a priest are you that you would tread upon your religious convictions solely because you are afraid?' So I say to you now and I will repeat it every time that you ask me: 'I entered prison as a priest and I feel one hundred times more convinced that I am a priest. It is not at all true that I did seven years in prison. I did twenty-six and I need twenty more. In a word, I need several lives, all in prison, for your great satisfaction!" He was beside himself with rage, but he could not do anything. He was constrained to leaving me to my new destiny.

I do not know what took hold of me, but in leaving the Officer I began to mutter in Italian, "*Il communismo è un regime di fame e di sangue basato sulla bugia e sul terrore, è una disorganizzazione organizzata nel modo più perfetto e non è altro che la personificazione della degenerazione umana.*"[1] The Officer opened his eyes in astonishment and acted as if he had understood everything by nodding his head menacingly. As I left, I heard his colleague ask him, "What did he say?" The first guy, to avoid appearing ignorant in the eyes of his colleague, responded, "He spoke in Russian. These religious guys are real devils. That guy learned Russian in prison. But what can he do with that? Does he preach in Russian?" "What?" replied the other guy. "It is the Orthodox who preach in Russia. He is a Catholic priest!"

I then went to the Post office, where I sent a little money to my prison comrades who had no family. This money was given to me by the prison's accountant on my release day because we did not have the right to money in prison. A few days later, the administration of Burrel prison sent back the money to Shkodër. The administration, knowing full well that poverty is the most powerful reality that has ever existed on earth, did not want to pass along the money to the guys living in misery. It is also one of the tortures that the prison administrators had and still have recourse to as a way to stomp on a person's dignity. A person with no ideals or wealth finds it very

---

1 "*Communism* is a regime of hunger and blood, based on lies and terrors. It is the most perfectly organized disorganization and is nothing other than the personification of human degeneration."

difficult to safeguard his human dignity. Misery leads to fighting, dissension, divorce, and even crime. The communist clan knew this very well! That is why poverty in Albania actually took on a more dismal aspect than in an earlier time when everyone had been equal in their poverty. When one sees how criminals, smugglers, and slave sellers enrich themselves, it is difficult to resist the temptation to say to oneself, "How is it possible that I am not capable of doing anything?" How can such a person not envy the neighbor's wealth? This is wealth accumulated without perspiration, now as always, with the permission and blessing of the Department of the Interior The Department's subjects, whether before or today, swim in troubled waters while the Albanian boat sank a long time ago.

In the meantime, I received a greater consolation: I began my religious activities in my house. I even began making visits, especially to families in both the city and the countryside. My first activities were public funerals. While I stood in front of the deceased, prayer book in hand and vested in white, most passers-by stopped, as much to honor the deceased as to see who the capricious priest was who dared to provide public religious honors without permission of the secret police. Hundreds of people began to visit my house for religious services and to attend the Mass that I celebrated in every rite and that included a sermon. Other religious who had been released from prison had transformed their houses well before me into living churches where Christians felt more or less like those from the primitive Church.

One of the first actions that I undertook after my prison release was to visit the tomb of my brother Dom Lazër, the martyr who was poisoned by the political Secret Police. I immediately paid the required sum to the State enterprise to build him a tomb. More than ten years have passed, and I have yet to see the tomb or my money returned. Thinking of this money reminds me of the kerosene-powered radio station that I had at Mirditë when I was the curé and the calf that I sold to the State collective enterprise. But this fraudulent State stole my radio and did not give me the money for the calf.

It is a State of thieves that, aside from the death of my brother, his tomb, the radio, and the calf, also owes me much more important things. This State mocks me in thinking that it will never pay me this, not even in the other world. But when we all present ourselves for the Last Judgment, priest that I am, I must once again say, "Forgive them,

Lord, for they know not what they do!" When He hears that I have pardoned them, I who was tortured when alive, will not the Lord also pardon them, He who is eternal Mercy? Can I, who in this world was tortured and burned in their fire, say to them: "Come here!" and then kick them and throw them into the fire in the next life? Whatever. I pray that God keeps them far from me in eternity!

21

The Fantasy of Suspicion

The fantasy of communism, which is still present to this day in our poor land, seeks to profit from the best of Christian experience. Obviously, communism suppressed God and replaced him with the dictator. In its imitation, communism seeks, just like God, to create a new man. All around him it builds up a quagmire and soaks man in it, trying to follow the example of God. But instead of man, who is a creature of God, communism announces the fantasy of suspicion. This fantasy, in turn, does worse than its creative mother, the communist dictatorship, in seeking to penetrate the tiniest flaws, such as in the marital bed, making husband and wife fearful of being heard, in the cracks of rocks and up in the floating clouds. The fantasy of suspicion is the most dangerous creation of dictatorship. It is even worse than misery and is one of the worst evils. It makes our lives ever more uncertain and full of suspicion. Everyone suspects everyone else. Everyone suspects you, and obviously, I also am guilty of suspecting others.

The fantasy of suspicion was everywhere, even when the wind called democracy started blowing. This fantasy was present when I was preparing to celebrate my first Mass. The fantasy was also at the Mass itself, blowing into the ears of the people, even in those of the convinced faithful. It said to them: "This Dom Simon seems very courageous! Tell me, where does he go? Who is behind him? Who is following him? Who supports him? He has nothing. Behind the altar, where he intends to celebrate the first Mass, you will find Sigurimi [the Directorate of State Security]. Or maybe it is under the altar!" "Who then," added another, "under which altar? He who celebrates the Mass is himself an officer of Sigurimi. And even, from this time, all those who will go to the altar are Sigurimi officers. They are present not only here, but also in much higher places, up to the Vatican. You can ask, if you do not believe me! Ask those who know these problems better, who know people's names." But where can they go, the Sigurimi, if they have closed up? People always talk about the same things: "Where will they find refuge now? They cannot stop feeding their children! Is not the Church a source of mercy and charity? They cannot find a better place than to infiltrate Caritas, the sacristies, the Catholic associations and radios, the Catholic media."

The fantasy of suspicion spreads out everywhere in Albania, from city to city, house to house, person to person. Whoever wants to work hard faces this fantasy, whether he wants to or not. This fantasy stinks like a cadaver and is humiliating. The fantasy starts up immediately: "Who is that? Is not that one of those who ate the bread of Enver Hoxha for fifty years? Tell me, how did he live? Imagine someone who had been in prison. Why was not he eliminated? How did he manage to be released from prison, to still be alive? How can he live now without any work? Who are his friends? They must be those who are at the top of politics. There is no other way. He is also a spy. His background seems to be a mystery, but actually we know!"

The fantasy of suspicion buzzes in my ears while I write: "You believe that you have accomplished a holy work in having an accusatory book published. But, my dear, what a work of ingratitude! Who will read your book? These types of books are outdated nowadays. People have shed enough tears—even too many. They do not want to cry anymore. They no longer want to hear these stories of torture, blood, and cadavers. It would have been better for you to write more in the chapter where you talk of eroticism. You could give it a racy title like, *A prisoner's eroticism,* or *In the police officer's bed,* or even *Eroticism in the confessional.* This is particularly appropriate for you, since you have heard so much from confessions. Obviously, your book would quickly sell out! People love these types of stories."

"As for the other types—historical memoirs, fact-based accounts, condemnations of criminals, dangers from the past—people no longer want to hear about these things. They want to forget about the dictatorship's existence, about the caning, bullets, and graves. They do not even think about the fact that it could all start up again from its beginning if we forget." The fantasy says, "I am here to make them all forget it. It is I who inflame their sickly fantasy so that they act foolishly. If the mass of people become wise, we will have an armed insurrection and a bloodbath up to our knees. This is the only solution to truly wash away the crimes and sins which weigh on the Earth. Where have we ever seen liberty win without bloodshed? It is a waste of time to write books. We will throw your books onto the pile of garbage that floods our cities and villages. Alleycats will go there to lick themselves. They will be your sole readers!"

"It is no longer the time for ideals. It is the time of money. Are you capable of paying for the minds of men? Of buying them? Of running to the four corners of the world to throw around wads of cash? You will immediately win the Nobel Prize. You will be famous all around the world. I am certain, as I am an expert on this. They could even erect a monument to your memory after you die. Who has been condemned until now? Everyone who has had our claws around his throat has become a bigshot. They have even bought themselves islands! And all of that came about in ten years."

"Meanwhile, your good friends, if they are not resting in forgotten pits or have not gone overseas, hang around like shadows in city streets, reduced to the worst labor, with their ideals crushed by iron boots. You are so happy to have finished your book on prison because you will not die without leaving your testimony as heritage. You even believe that all of those who felt persecuted will be happy to see your book appear. Do not believe it! Many of your guys will say every bad thing possible about your book. If they have not forgotten you, they will scrutinize the smallest details of your life because they are implicated in your book. They will not be able to resist because they will find their true face in it. Then they will start spewing a thousand spiteful words against you and lay into you worse than in prison because, dear reader, fault is always an orphan. Even now, all those who led the true martyrs to their graves see themselves as victims and martyrs. While the veterans of the battle for national liberation will remain veterans, your saints will be considered as criminals. They will even be assassinated a second time: first with a bullet and second with forgetfulness."

"Whatever," I responded to the fantasy of suspicion that did not leave me in peace. I will write my book and get it published. At least from that I will shut the mouths of the enemies who will go so far as to write books on their crime families, seriously mixing the torturers and the victims. If we do not open our mouths, they will portray us as butchers, we who were tortured. They will present the facts according to their interests. This will bequeath to us a bad history. If no one reads my book, too bad. But I assure you that, by the end of the book, they will be crazy with rage and will pounce on everyone, clawing and biting, believing that everyone had been disfigured. They will become the personages in the book. Thus, there is something to take from even this type of reader.

The fantasy of suspicion continues to roam about because, in the muck where it was created, the rest of the Sigurimi dossier, whether burned or hidden, remains. One black night of suspicion, this fantasy whispered in my ear. It told me what people had said of me from the start of the Mass, when they called me a saint, until that particular day, when some, including certain fellow priests, labeled me with every epithet. Unable to hold in my anger, I said: "You have in your stomach the leaven of the Sigurimi dossiers along with the names of those whom you left drenched in their own blood because they did not want to sell themselves. So vomit your leaven, this rotten nourishment that your stomach will never digest. Then everyone will clearly see who had sold themselves and who had washed every temptation with the blood of the Lamb. That will bring down your curtain!"

The fantasy sneered with a tragic grimace. Its echo still fills my whole room, just like the sound of a hammer on the nails of a coffin. I shook when it said, "We have gone where you cannot even imagine. We have registered the declarations of wife against husband and husband against wife, of father against son and son against father, of bishop against priest and of believers against God. We have organized a vast network of witnesses and always keep it active. Whether we have burned the dossiers or not, do you believe that we are not capable of rewriting them as we want to? The proof is that we have them. You do not. What will you say when you see your name at the head of the list, with totally normal testimonies and witnesses? Shout as much as you want. You will never have the power to defeat these documents and testimonies. People will look at you in a funny way and say: 'Look. Even the priests who we trusted blindly, the ones we confessed to about the most intimate secrets that we would not dare say to anyone, even they have betrayed us! Who can we trust? We had thought of those fellows as representatives of Jesus on earth? How come the Lord did not strike them down for this sacrilege?' So then doubt would appear, the suspicion that even Jesus collaborated with the Sigurimi. And after all the infatuation of the post-dictatorship era, we will return to the beginning, to attacks against the churches that you had built in the Mirditë district, we will return to handcuffs and imprisonments. The world goes around, but only when I blow on it," said the self-assured fantasy of suspicion to me.

This was a worse nightmare than prison. The fantasy was spot on. This son of the devil is the master of the situation, and we are powerless to make it disappear from the face of the earth. It will be like that until we separate once and for all the sheep from the wolves and the wheat from the chaff with a just human judgment. It was only one moment of blasphemy and suspicion, a moment of temptation and sin. I recalled the exorcists, and the temptation dissipated. The fantasy of suspicion will never succeed against the Cross. I therefore gripped my cross (not the metal one that I wear on my vest collar) and felt stronger than the prophet David armed with his sling. The fantasy of suspicion disappeared like the whistle of the devil, leaving behind him his nauseating odor. I lit a wax candle on the small altar in my miserable room, and the dissipating stench ceded to the candle's pleasant smell. I consoled myself with the hope that at least at the Last Judgment the Sigurimi dossiers, whether burned or not, would be opened. Everything would be laid out on the same eternal balance while the Truth would appear — provided that God is not too annoyed by the injustices of people of every epoch and country! And God will bring out an immense pile of espionage dossiers that one man had written on another with the sole objective of destroying the other.

22

The Arrest

In January, 1990 at Shkodër, someone began to blow with all his might on the embers of liberty. Those embers were half covered with the ashes of forgetfulness. The problem was that some people focused on their lives and others on unlimited pleasures after fifty years of persecutions. In my own foolishness, I felt a new hope reborn in my heart — to celebrate a public Mass. It was only in this way that I could blow on the embers of liberty so as to transform them into a pure flame that would burn and illuminate the dark like an altar candle. That was my true task! That was a task that I had begun to exercise publicly at my home, even though it was surrounded by spies. Besides those who were specialists in pursuing our family and had poisoned my brother Dom Lazër, many others also stood night and day at my door. My neighbors knew them very well because the spies stood like idiots in front of the door. That was even the principal activity of the communist State, from which comes a popular expression. "When you have nothing to do, you move your door" was transformed into, "When you have nothing to do, you swing your door."

Nevertheless, true Catholics never feared coming to my house, above all when they heard the announcement of my liberation from the Voice of America on the radio. They had always attended the Masses of other priests, and they came to my house to change their priest, to hear a new voice, and to see a fresh face which had come out of the grave after twenty-six years of imprisonment. During a time of terror, the presence of a priest is an extraordinary force, even if he does not speak. In fact, the less he speaks and the more he acts, the more convincing he becomes through his example. Albanians did not really need formulas and recipes but rather examples to console them and give them the force and courage to pursue their navigation through the swamp that Albania had become from the rot of communism.

I normally celebrated two or three Masses a day. I exposed the Blessed Sacrament each time that someone asked me to, always under the strict surveillance of the "black angels of the Sigurimi," which flew over my head like bats everywhere I went. They stuck by me whether there was a Mass or not. They were easily identified because they muddled up or tripped over their words. They wanted to be taken as fervent Catholics but did not know how to make the sign of the Cross or say the smallest prayer. Meanwhile, the Kremlin's satellites regularly received orders to start political decentralization. There were more and more evasions, but families were no longer deported. People spoke freely without being arrested. Western radio stations were listened to everywhere, and no one knocked at the door, handcuffs at the ready. Workers at cooperatives no longer went to work, and began to loot and steal more and more, and no one arrested them. That was the face of liberty as it began to come at us. It was the face of State-organized anarchy. The State had changed tactics in preparing to present itself in a novel way, but its teeth and claws were still sharp!

The population, raised on the secular psychology of the slave, could not bring themselves to believe it. Nevertheless, at the beginning of this unprecedented anarchy, in the middle of the recently unbridled herds, I began, filled with profound conviction, to exercise the activity to which I had consecrated my whole life. I took the dead to the cemetery by walking through the streets. As in the past, a cross-bearing child would go before me. As I walked along the streets, wearing liturgical vestments and carrying holy water and the book of Roman rites, I felt the presence of Catholics lining the streets. They said to one another, "Look at the brave eccentric!" And they made the sign of the Cross. The Muslims said, "The Catholics have a religion. They have a religious leader. Look at the priest, wearing the vestments for the Mass in the middle of the place, accompanying the deceased." It was this atmosphere that preceded the overturning of the statue of Stalin in the center of the city along with the burning of four-hundred thousand Communist Party membership cards. But we had not yet arrived at the end, and we still have not today.[1]

Tirana, which changed its policies by the hour, gave the order to arrest those who had dared rise up. Some unfortunates whose behavior had gotten a bit out of hand faced severe consequences. I had the honor of being among the first to be arrested, even though I had not participated in any demonstration or protest. It was not fear that prevented my participation, but prudence. Being guided by courage, and not by fear, is prudent. It is not prudent to push things too far.

---

1 This book was written in 2001.

One beautiful day in November, 1990, while I was giving a catechism course to a dozen children, a large bus stopped twenty meters in front of my house. A guy who the neighbors called "Dom Simon's spy" was always standing near the front door. The poor guy was fed up with trying to discover the undiscoverable, that is, my hostile activities. My work had started again with the most peaceful and most human message that the world has ever seen — that of the Eucharistic sacrifice, which expresses the most perfect love, that of God for human beings. Could the regime's special forces, who had been educated and trained like animals with human faces, understand what I was doing?

Three of them violently entered the room where I was working with children who had heard God's call to engage in the path of preaching. The three repeated to me the expression that I had heard so often before: "In the name of the People, you are arrested!" In the name of the poor people, those who had withdrawn into themselves because of the terror of these guys. In the name of the people who had no name! The poor infants who surrounded me, along with their parents, remained stupefied. They had believed that the terror had come to an end. I did not move a muscle. I was used to these jackals. I calmly gave them the exact response that the situation called for: "Oh, no, since long ago I have purged my pain from prison. Now, it is the turn of your *Ramiz Alia*[2], who sold the country to the Serbs, the Soviets, and the Chinese, and is at the moment selling it to the Americans. He has changed tactics, and ..."

They did not let me finish my thoughts. They pounced on me like in the past but even more savagely because by now they had become modern forces of violence, which is to say, trained criminals. They tied my hands behind my back, tight to the bone. I once again tasted the bitter poison of prison, the same taste that God experienced on the Cross when he was thirsty, and bile flowed through him. They led me to the bus, closing my mouth with their dirty hands because each time that I could open my toothless mouth, I yelled at the top of my voice, "Filthy offspring of Enver Hoxha. It is your time to be handcuffed!" I do not deny that I have perhaps erred, because I do not in any way

---

2 *Ramiz Alia* (1925–2011) — He was an eminent member of the Communist Party and president of the Republic from 1984 to 1990. He was recognized as responsible for the crimes of the Communist Party and of the army in the national liberation.

resemble Jesus on the Cross even though I was beaten like a faithful son of the Cross. I could not gently say to them, as my position as a priest obliged me to, "Forgive them, Lord, for they know not what they do!" Perhaps because it seemed to me that they very well knew what they were doing. That reminds me of another sin for which God justly punished me — in not satisfying my desire to die as a martyr.

And so, with my mouth alternating between being forced shut and then yelling, and at the great satisfaction of my neighbors, because these fools always preferred people who yelled over those who kept silent, the police threw me into the bus which now replaced the Department of the Interior's jeep for more discretion. They slammed the door behind them. Then they once again took on their former occupation of butcher. They threw me to the floor and kicked me so hard that I almost lost consciousness. In other words, they finally succeeded in getting me to close my mouth.

They dropped me off at the Department of the Interior. Having anticipated this sort of place, I kept my vestments on, with only staff and sac at hand like Jesus had told the apostles to do in the gospels. In fact, I always remained dressed, day and night, always ready because they could take me back to prison at any moment. Still today I am on constant alert. They left me at the end of the corridor, waiting for the others to arrive. On that day, police vehicles went here and there nonstop, dropping off at the Police station many people likely on their way to Tirana. Meanwhile, all Police officers had been summoned to the Police station. Each passing officer spit in my face or punched and kicked me. These were the last gifts that the popular power took out from its treasure of tortures. Fortunately, all my teeth had already been broken. I was in such shock that I no longer felt the strikes. When I had become totally numb to the hitting, one of the most satanic Police officers, a short guy, put under my nose a medal of the Blessed Virgin, on the edges of which were written, "Ave Maria." The officer did not spit on me. On the contrary, he asked me to spit on the medal. "Spit on this," he said. "Spit on this and I will release you immediately!"

It was a macabre scene that has been endlessly repeated throughout the history of humanity in many different countries. How many times were the martyrs asked to walk over the Cross or spit on it, or on the Virgin Mary or other saintly images! I responded: "Why should I spit on it? It is not the Virgin Mary who is torturing me, but

166

you and other Albanians like you who have been torturing me for a half-century only because I do not love what you love, which is Tito, Stalin, and Mao Zedong. Therefore, if by chance you have one of those guys on you, I will spit with pleasure, and I hope to have enough saliva in my dry mouth." Crazed with rage, he offered me his portion of punching, kicking, and spitting.

A little after that, they again led me somewhere else. I sensed that we had gotten into a taxi, with me between two Police officers, with my irons clamped tightly around old wounds, and with the drool and saliva scattered on my lips that I could not dry off because I could not move my hands. Nevertheless, what bothered me the most was the narrow space: I could not stand my body touching those of the Police officers. The missing thing was the crown of thorns on my head so they could say, "Ecce Homo!"

The officers began to discuss sports, as they knew about my athletic past. They assumed that I would be unable to control myself and would join the conversation. This desire to discuss sports echoed in a way the tendency of the chief of the Department of the Interior of Burrel prison. When he wanted to criticize the government, yet unable to do so himself, he would come into my cell, incite me to talk, and give himself the pleasure of hearing my ridicule of the Government tribe in Tirana and of himself. Sometimes I said to him, "Listen, today you resemble a Chinese guy." Another time: "You have a Soviet demeanor." And another time: "You seem like a real Serb to me, because they have all marked their stamp on your physiognomy, on your mug, in a word!" The fact is that I had a lot of fun when they visited me in order to hear the insults and abuse that I directed to power because I knew that they also hid a lot of poison underneath their slave uniforms.

Abdullah Sollaku told me of Shkelzen Bajraktari when they were university mates. Bajraktari did not stop speaking badly of Hoxha's regime. But to earn a salary, he later tortured people who had been arrested and brought before a magistrate. There was nothing simpler for this criminal than to kill someone in order to get on the good side of his superiors whom he hated and whom he would have killed in a similar fashion if he ever had the occasion. With such ideas swirling in my head, I no longer felt the pain of the handcuffs, which continued to dig into my skin right where the old scars were left from earlier prison experiences.

When they took off my handcuffs at around 2:00 a.m. in a cell in Tirana, I felt the full force of pain, even more so because my arrival in the cell was as triumphant as all my other such arrivals. As was already well-known to me, I did not have to do anything to get into the cell. The Police officer came to my aid by giving me a last terrible kick to hasten my entry into the free hotel that lacked a mattress or light, into this hotel that I had so missed and that the Government in its death throes had given me as a gift.

The principal examining magistrate was called "Colonel" by the other Lilliputian judges who all followed him with unparalleled servility. The examining magistrate and the examination itself did not differ in any way from previous such meetings. It was the same ritual of questions and responses, like those already treated in this book, apart from torture, naturally. The hyenas no longer dared hollow out our cadavers. It was the most natural thing in the world for me not to be vexed when leaving a piece of nail or finger as fodder. Nevertheless, this was the shortest of my arrests. On January 17, 1990, I had my eleventh meeting with the examining magistrate, which did not last more than twenty-four hours. After that, they sent me back to Shkodër so that this eleventh arrest did not make too much noise so soon after my release.

Meanwhile, I saw all around me organized decadence attaining dimensions never before reached in history. The people, depersonalized in the depths of their souls, looted everything. They chopped down trees in the forests, pulled out telephone wires, stole the rails of the railroad, and destroyed everything that they had built with so much sweat under the dictatorship's whip when they pretended to work and the Government pretended to pay them.[3] For this reason, the people detested the fruits of their labor which were never theirs because everything that they had created fell into a bottomless hole. In other words, it ended up in the villas of the slave drivers in Albania and throughout the world, and as parts of other previously unknown follies, which were the fruits of their stupidity. These included not only ridiculous bunkers, which were supposed to protect the

---

3   Albanians stole the wood from trees that were situated along highways in order to heat their houses. They also stole roof tiles from old state farms to make their own personal houses. They were convinced that stealing from the state was not stealing and that everything that belonged to the state now belonged to them personally.

fantasies, but also money that ended up in the pockets of friends of the Communist Party all around the world. These friends were nothing but adventurers. They wore patched up shirts, pants, and sunglasses; they ate and drank what the dog of a dictator gave them, and they enjoyed music at the expense of the miserable people.

The ideas of the Albanian Communist Party were meant to be the future of the world. The entire world was supposed to live under the same happiness as we were. While I would love for the world to live with such happiness even for one year, I know this stupid world and from up close. It never learned the lessons of history that were explained to it in concrete terms, that is to say, what took place in the immense auditorium of Eastern Europe. It is a shame what we call the world free that holds onto that idea of happiness when in fact the West was and remains today the prostitute of our epoch!

The people forgot that in stealing the telephone wires it would no longer be possible to call someone when there was a problem. When you take the railings to sell so you can get drunk, you will not have a train. If you cut down the trees, you will die of heat in the summer. The people had everything stolen from them while the communists tried to educate them about the sense of the common good, which is to say goods that belonged to no one. The people so hated the expression "collective ownership" that they no longer wanted to hear it. At present, people are like a squirrel trying to bring into its little home what had been unjustly taken from it. After doing his best to fill up his little dwelling, he will once again have enough. He asks himself, "Why should I spend my whole life in this little cell?" So comes the black hour of national hara-kiri: Albanians flood into the West like guts splattering out of a cut-open stomach. In continuing to exploit that opportunity, they leave their own country with a giant gaping hole in the stomach, emptied of everything that was inside.

Henceforth free, I continued my religious services without participating in the demonstrations, unlike some unfortunates who ended up suffering. Leaders of anti-communist movements who had said many bad things about *Pjetër Arbnori*[4] and other faithful

---

4 *Pjetër Arbnori* (1935–2006) — Albanian politician. He was condemned to twenty-five years in prison for wanting to form the Social-Democrat Party. After eighteen years of detention, he was condemned to a further ten years in prison (twenty-eight years in Burrel prison). Freed in August, 1989, he then became a

troops of the secret police quickly climbed the hierarchy of the new politics. This hierarchy had received its instructions from the Central Committee. The hierarchy's task was to persuade the people that communism had come to an end and that the new democratic era had commenced. It was a new democracy wearing the old costume of communism, mended here and there by a few prison spies.

But let us go back a bit in order to better appreciate the events to which I have been referring and those that I will mention next. On November 1, 1990, Adil Çarçani, the then Prime Minister, came to Shkodër, to this unsubmitted and continually punished city. He wanted to convince the people that the glowing dawn of democracy was on the horizon. He reunited all the communists. Their mission would be to prepare the people for the changes that would be gradually taking place, always under the direction of the Party Central Committee. The changes would take place in specific sectors that would not shake the Party's power. The Central Committee had decided to allow for religious freedom, to stop the frenetic fight against religion, and to take moderate measures against religious demonstrations. It was about time! Only a handful of priests and male and female religious remained in Albania. They were completely destroyed physically but morally steadfast. They would have a terrible time remaking the knot cut by the sword of Damocles. This was their work of giving the Church back its splendor. The Church that was being reborn quickly took on the aspect of those who claimed to be democrats. In the first row at ceremonies, the Judases and Pilates appeared the most often to present themselves before the people as the highest civil authorities of the country.

In a certain manner, then, it was decided to accord religious liberty. But the communists did not like that one bit because they had fallen out with the people, and even with members of their own families, by preventing religious activities. They had even gone so far in their zeal as to tear down the crosses of their believing ancestors. These faithful believers had left for the other world, taking first in their saintly suffering the nourishment for the voyage that leads to eternity. Moreover, the communists, on countless occasions, had spied on and denounced those who had not accepted complicity in such

---

deputy of the Democratic Party that he had founded. He was President of the Assembly from 1992 to 1997. He died in Naples on July 8, 2006. It seems that Dom Simon considered him to be a "spy."

lowly things. The communists thereby brought on themselves eternal divine vengeance solely for the good pleasure of a few passing idols. What could they do now? Nothing could be worse than dishonoring themselves by coming out and propagating religious freedom.

However, they quickly surpassed this preoccupation. Why bother worrying? Had not they changed their flag so many times before? Who could ever say that it was the first time for them to change their vests!? Had they not disapproved of those they had previously banished a hundred times before? What would one more or less time really change? They even began to boast of the idea of discarding the already-outmoded costume of the East for Western attire that, compared with the shabby things of Moscow and Beijing, would permit them to leave for Paris, London, or Washington. At the end of the day, this really meant that they were returning to their origins because, until 1944, Albania sought to wear Western clothing to break clean of the Turkish yoke.

But without even having the time to get used to Western styles, Albania was constrained to change the hat for the *kapice* and to wear Yugoslav styles until 1948, when the latter were declared outmoded. Albania then adopted Soviet dress, another slave attire, including the Russian bonnet, which helped keep out the cold until it was too moth-eaten by 1960. No longer able to handle the "Winter of Great Solitude," which attracted Moscow's glacial wind, Albania hastened to re-adopt the Chinese style. Albania thereby presented itself before the world with the Harlequin look. She put Mao Zedong's Asian kepi on her head and buttoned herself up to the neck. Albania survived with this attire until 1978, by which time these clothes had become nothing more than rags. However, no one proposed another costume that would fit her. And so, the Chinese material fell off little by little, which eventually reduced Party comrades to the state of nudity.

That continued until the arrival of international emergency aid, which brought attire that was left from Europe's long-dead grandfather. The Europeans, fearing the moths, got rid of this antiquated attire by donating it as humanitarian aid to the nude comrades. Nevertheless, it needs to be said that these comrades remained alone for a certain time. In that terrifying nudity, everyone could see that, in this country, ideals, political conscience, nationals, Europeans, and citizens were always full of hot air and baloney. It was all a lie. Further, the people of the martyr city Shkodër were right to bet everything on God. God does not change. His mercy and love are eternal. God and country go together!

Imagine, therefore, dear readers, what took place when the people realized that the Government itself wanted to offer religious liberty. The people believed that liberty was found where God was. This was indeed genuine freedom. But the poor people! The people love to lie and to believe in the lies which they are told. They tell a lie about the market that is repeated from town to town until everyone believes it. Big gossip therefore spread throughout Shkodër, gossip that is no longer heard. Words became so complicated that they turned into a real knot that could only be figured out from the first string. This leads to the name of Adil Çarçani. It seems that, at a communist gathering, he said, "The Muslims should make a mosque of lead[5] (even though there was no more lead since it had been stolen), the Orthodox should build their church at Vrake where there is an old warehouse, and the Catholics should organize their Masses in the chapel of the ancient cemetery of Rrëmaji!"

---

5 Mosque constructed in the eighteenth-century in Shkodër under the Ottoman Empire. It was thus named due to its lead-covered domes.

23

The First Mass on November 4, 1990

November is traditionally the month of the dead. The ancient Catholic graves of the Rrëmaji cemetery were still being violently preyed on in 1990. Bones of the deceased could be seen through the broken graves. In the middle of the day, people descended into and later came out of a place where before only the dead had gone. The people believed that this cemetery was a goldmine. And after digging around, without fear of God or people, in the best of cases, they would come out with a medallion, two old watches, and two gold rings. In the worst cases, they would take a gold tooth or a crown. And they began to fight each other with the teeth of the dead!

While this happened, the biography of the deceased was examined with the same attention that the Party paid to the biographies of the living. Naturally, they did not attach much importance to political opinions, which had evaporated. But they paid attention to certain indications of primary importance, such as family origins and age of the person, because at Shkodër the rich had been interred with the most precious jewelry of their lives. Once the human hyenas had come out, it was the dogs' turn. Whoever looked in the pit of a smashed-open grave heard the cracking of bones: Dogs delighted all day long in this paradise of bones. What is more, half of the crosses and photos had long ago been torn to pieces with their names half worn off.

These scenes took place under the secular cypress trees and the immense cynara, whose gigantic foliage shook at this never-before-seen spectacle. As soon as you stepped past the cemetery entrance and into the narrow passage through the cypress trees, what struck you was the chapel with its collapsed roof and burned, barely standing arches. The chapel resembled an unburied dead person. The generous spring sought to soften this ugliness a little. It ornamented the ancient cemetery with violets and roses, and it covered the walls of the chapel with climbing plants. Winter also tried to camouflage the ugliness under a thick layer of snow. While the dead continued to sleep without resisting the violence against their resting places, the communists broke the rocky graves. They killed these people once again. The communists reduced the dead to ash and dust, both their bones and their names. Through the broken slabs, the dead, who did not strike fear in the hyenas, showed an eye or an arm, rotten by time's passing. The dead were astonished to see how the living did not move, those who had often visited the ancient cemetery.

Cry for the dead and cry for the living. The dead could no longer scare the living because the living could not find peace in themselves. Throughout the sunny days of the soft month of November, many came to clear out the lush vegetation that grew over the cadavers and to place and light candles for the repose of souls. This gave the old cemetery a spooky allure. The cypresses' sharp peaks, resembling green flames, reached towards the sky. Under the cypress trees, hundreds of small flames played with the breeze, creating thousands of petals and flowers. The characteristics of the dead, long frozen in their last photos, gave the impression of movement, as if they wanted to come back to life and give Shkodër the splendor of yesteryear. In lockstep with the generation of the pre-communist-occupation era, Shkodër began to reassert its original traits. The living stood firm in the hope that though God would sometimes be late, He would never forget.

On November 4, 1990, at nine in the morning, a certain Mark Murana, an ambulance driver, visited me. The family name is curious, as if it had been created just for that day.[1] The man with this family name, which made me think of ghosts, came to tell me that certain people were arriving at the cemetery to clean the graves of their loved ones. They wanted a Mass and had sent him to look for me because my house was the closest. And I, who lived only for the occasion to involve myself in saintly adventures while simultaneously hoping that people would stop gossiping to me, immediately left the catechumens who surrounded me and packed my suitcase with everything necessary to say the Mass. I did not have priestly vestments and had to be content with a stole. I was ready in two minutes.

I left with Mark and the others who were standing behind the door, where they were waiting for me. This time, again, God chose the simplest man for such a great work, he who had the least merits! Obviously, fear precedes courage. That was why the few Albanians who had gathered in the cemetery greeted me wordlessly while busily cleaning up the graves of their loved ones. To escape any danger, they

---

1 *"Murana"* in Albanian signifies "embalming".

stated not only that they had not called for me, but that they had not even let me in. I went straight to the altar's former location, which was precisely situated for a coffin. In past years, that was where the coffin would be forever closed after the service. Then the terrible sound of the nails that covered the deceased would spread throughout the cemetery. It would make for a powerful moment of meditation. I stopped on a pile of garbage and waited while Mark returned to his nearby house to bring back a table.

That was where the first altar was erected in Albania after the great collapse: constructed on the people's prayers, the souls in Purgatory, the tears of the suffering, the sweat of laborers cheated of compensation, the blood of the martyrs, the indescribable suffering of the disappeared, and the survivors now in a sorry state. Close to this extraordinary altar, I prepared for the Eucharistic Sacrifice without thinking of anyone else but He, the One whom I represented at the altar. This altar had been installed in the burned and plundered chapel of the city of martyred Shkodër, in this bloodied city in Albania that was surrounded by barbed wire. Nevertheless, this Albania was in Europe, and Europe in the free world. Europe would no longer permit the clique in Tirana from rising up.

Nevertheless, I have to say that I found myself face to face with the antichrist!

I began with a brief introduction, inviting the people to pray to the holy souls in Purgatory to aid us to definitively conquer this antichrist. I started the Mass in Latin with a worn missal that had somehow escaped the many communist inspections of the houses of two religious. Little by little, the number of people began to grow around the altar. They continued arriving at the cemetery, as it was *November*, to look after the graves of their deceased loved ones.[2] Obviously, the women and children greatly outnumbered the men. These latter feared losing their jobs and, consequently, their daily bread. On this day, however, I nevertheless also saw men around this altar where I celebrated the Holy Mass after twenty-four years of silence in this place. The news spread everywhere very quickly![3]

---

2   The month of *November* is particularly dedicated to prayer for the deceased.
3   This first Mass was heroically celebrated *on November 4, 1990* by Dom Simon spontaneously and discreetly. Due to insecurity, many of the faithful feared attending. Dom Simon and every participant risked being assassinated by the regime at any moment. Therefore, only 200–300 attended.

This first Mass, in all its splendor, remained a unique event in the spirits and hearts of all those who were the first to have the chance to meet Jesus on his return. First of all, this is because they knew very well that Jesus neither undergoes change nor betrays anyone. Second, there was no greater event to bring back so much hope. Third, because there was not a bigger dream than to wait for the happy day on which Albania would no longer work like the slave of the West. The West betrayed our country more than the communists did. On some happy future day, Albania will have true liberty, stamped with the trial of its head and so tortured that it is very difficult to find a cure.

This first Mass was the prelude to the *great public Mass* which I celebrated *on November 11, 1990* before an immense crowd. I will not cite the homily that I delivered on that day and re-delivered later for the fifth and tenth anniversaries of this great event. I have devoted another book to this Mass. That book came out of the Albanian printing more mutilated than its author did in leaving prison. In order to avoid making the same mistake, I decided to have this present book printed overseas.

"Do you want to see a miracle in order to believe? Behold, the miracle is in front of you!"

This and the previous photo show the celebration by Dom Simon Jubani of the first Holy Mass on 4 November 1990 at the old chapel of Rrëmaji cemetery in Shkodër which was the only Catholic place not destroyed after these long years of State atheism in Albania. The inscription on the façade means: "May God give them eternal rest." The chapel was restored after the liberation of 1991.

"Is not this blessed night a miracle, with the cemetery's cypress trees transformed into Christmas trees, with Jesus who, in the time of the first Christians, was born on a bed of bones to bring us life?" This photo shows the reinstallation of the crosses on the roofs of the very rare churches not destroyed by the Albanian communists.

24
Three Homilies among Hundreds of Others

I thought I would insert into this memoir three homilies among the hundreds of others that I delivered around the world. While the homilies changed, one sole thing never did: the Gospel of Jesus Christ. The first is a homily of hope. The second concerns the loss of hope. The third conveys the faith that justice will triumph only at the Last Judgement because in the lapse of ten years no justice was seen. Where there is no justice there can be no peace. Finally, without justice there will not be any confidence in the political class or in any other force. But humans cannot live without peace, hope, or confidence. In that situation, there is nothing left for people to do but lift their eyes towards Heaven and ask for the blessing of He who had created us — to ask for a little justice even before the Last Judgment. Let us pray that He does this for the little land called Albania!

THE HOMILY OF THE FIRST GREAT PUBLIC MASS ON NOVEMBER II, 1990

Homily for the second Mass and first great public Mass on November 11, 1990: The sermon of great hope.[1]

Shkodër

Brothers and sisters,

Let us have a moment of silence in memory for all those who are dead and laying here in this cemetery and also for all of our brothers and sisters who gave their lives in order to have a European Albania during these forty-six years.

In 1443, when our national hero, Gjergj Kastrioti[2] *escaped Istanbul in order to return to his country, he greeted the Albanian people in*

---

1 This second public Mass, also celebrated by Dom Simon Jubani, drew 50,000 people on November 11, 1990, again in front of the chapel of the cemetery of Rrëmaji, in Shkodër.

2 *Gjergj (George) Kastrioti* (May 6, 1405–January 17, 1468), called *Skanderbeg* (a family name of Turkish origin, by which he is normally called in most European languages), was an Albanian lord who is considered to be Albania's national hero

addressing them with the following words: "It is not I who bring you liberty; I found it among you."

I, who am unworthy of this mission, say to you that it is not I who bring you religion, but I found it, living in your hearts.

That this religion was always on fire in your hearts is testified by your presence here today — you who have come from the four corners of Albania to this holy site to adore, thank, and glorify our great Lord for this great MIRACLE that we see today with our own eyes.

That this confidence was always alive in our souls is testified with the restoration of this small cemetery church, achieved with the contribution, in work and money, of our brother Orthodox and Muslims.

That this religion was always burning in our spirits and hearts is testified best of all at the holy place of St. Anthony at Laç[3] when, in the middle of the terror, thousands of Albanians went to those ruins. Each person, in his own religion and language, prayed constantly to St. Anthony for every spiritual and physical need. These prayers are crowned today with this public gathering.

In the name of God and of the faith in him, all of you can speak better than I can of the innumerable consolations that you draw from this religion. It fortifies, comforts, awakes, cultivates, and civilizes the spirits and hearts of all of humanity.

In the name of the great Lord and of his saints, the deaf who hear, the mute who speak, the lame who walk, and the psychopaths and epileptics who are healed can express this better than I can.

Just like the air that we breathe is indispensable to our physical existence, so also the reality of a supernatural Being is indispensable

---

for his resistance to the Ottoman Empire. Born in Krujë, son of the Albanian lord John (Gjon) Castriote and the Vojsava, princess and daughter of the Lord of Pollog, in current-day North Macedonia. His father, lord of mid-Albania, was obligated by the Ottomans to pay tribute. Educated with his brothers at the Ottoman court according to the will of the sultan, he was then a student at the empire's military college. The sultan, Murad II, who ascended the throne in 1421, gave Skanderbeg high military duties. The latter brought victories in Asia to the empire. But at the death of Gjon Castriote, the father of Skanderbeg, the sultan, instead of letting him succeed his father, occupied Albania and installed a governor at Krujë. Skanderbeg shook off the Turkish yoke and declared Albanian independence on November 28, 1443, raising his red flag with the black eagle. Having rejected Islam and the Ottoman Empire, Skanderbeg became defender of his country and of Christianity in the Balkans and in Europe.

3   St. Anthony church, in the small city of *Laç*, Albania, was a church of the seventeenth century.

for our spiritual existence. This Being helps us confront life's difficulties, and is indispensable in giving us optimism, enthusiasm, and courage. This supernatural Being helps us to see with the eyes of the soul the happiness of Paradise, which we wait for after this short life just like we see with the eyes of our bodies the marvels of the Earth.

Everywhere in the world, just as in modern cities as in the most forgotten villages, domes, mosque minarets, and steeples rise towards Heaven. These are the symbols of the contacts, the links that humanity has always had with Heaven, with God.

Their pointed peaks resemble the lances of a silent army that the human race created throughout the centuries in order to safeguard moral and cultural values.

What global interests does religion represent?

Who tamed the medieval barbarians, the Goths, Visigoths, Huns, and Vandals if it was not Jesus Christ and the religious? It is they who tamed the hordes of Evil: The Cross in their hands and prayers on their lips.

All of Europe's moral and intellectual development finds its source in Christian philosophy and theology.

Who gave Europe its spiritual, cultural, and political unity, if not Christianity?

In the seventh century, who liberated the Arab countries from paganism and polytheism and gave them the gift of monotheism and led the primitive tribes to an organized State and thence to the Arab and Ottoman Empires, if not Islam and its prophet Muhammad?

What is the civilizing role of religion at the national level? Regarding the moral level, religion is like a barricade that protects. A barricade prevents water from rushing in to destroy fertile land and people's dwellings. Similarly, religion is a moral barricade that does not allow for vices, perversions, degeneration, and corruption to penetrate into the spirit and heart of humanity. In this sense, religion provides the greatest contribution to public order.

On the cultural level, all the primary schools and lyceums, and all the cultural and social institutions in our country were created and directed by the Basilians, Benedictines, Franciscans, Jesuits, etc. The first printing press and the first modern agricultural enterprise of Bardhej were even founded by the religious of St. Ignatius of Loyola.

Religion is also determinative for the defense of the country. As the ideas of the century were not capable of providing the Albanians with

*political unity, only religion could reunite the Albanian princes of the
fifteenth century against the common enemy, the Ottoman Empire.
All the gatherings took place in the church of St. Nicholas in the city
of Laç. It was in this church that all the decisions for all the military
operations executed at Beselidhja[4] were taken.*

*But the civilized world also knows us for the glorious League of
Prizren (1878). The President of this League, Haxhi Ymer Prizreni,
together with other Muslim, Orthodox, and Catholic leaders such as
Eljaz Pacha Dibra, Vaso Pacha Shkodrani, and Abdyl Frashëri, held
all their reunions in the mosque in Prizren, from where were sent out
all the directives.*

*The Lord, in order to give all the Albanians prosperity, provided
Albania with two lungs, the land and the sea. In order to retain a
healthy spirit, equally on land and at sea, the fifteenth century
Albanian princes all lived, fought, and died, as later the brave and
valiant men of the Albanian League of Prizren did.*

*1989 was the year of peace and liberty for the whole world because
this year saw the walls and iron curtains separating peoples and
countries come crashing down. The gravest thing was that they had
separated the hearts of people. In this same year, blood stopped flowing;
forever-flowing tears became dry. In this year, the sweat that had been
shed in vain and the fight of everyone against everyone came to an end.
All of humanity entered a new era of peace, liberty, kindness, harmony,
and prosperity. The prosperity and harmony of a people depend on the
liberties that are given to the citizens.*

*Liberty in the philosophical sense of the term in a gradual process
that concerns a people's conscience and culture. We will gradually and
peacefully recuperate this liberty and these rights. The peaceful path
is typical of a civilized people. We must resist the temptation to have
recourse to violence or brutality. The latter two have never resolved
national problems nor family problems.*

*It is only in this manner that we will succeed at closing the mouths
of those who consider us "a geographical expression," an unexplored
territory, the nation of no one. It is only in this way that we will close the
mouths of our enemies who consider us to be a bastard people situated
by mother History at the crossroads of four paths.*

Shkodër, city of more than two thousand years of history, in the

---

4   Word of honor, from which the name of *Beselidhja* gave to the League of
Lezhë in the fifteenth century.

past the capital of Illyria, Shkodër, city of Teuta, of Gent, and of Agron, Shkodër which, fifty years ago, gave the moral, cultural, political, religious, and economic tone to Albania, is ready even today to collaborate with Tirana and with all the other cities of Albania because she is the heir of Balsha the Great and Marin Barleti.[5] She is the successor of Fishta and Bushatli, of Oso Kuka, of Dom Ndoc Nika[6], of Dom Ndre Mjeda[7], of Luigj Gurakuqi.[8] She is the heir of the Frashëri brothers[9], of Faik Konica.[10]

Shkodrans are here in these Albanian lands, ready to renew the tradition and authority which Albania had in its best times, both here in the country and abroad. Amen!

---

5   *Marin Barleti* (1450–1513) — He was a historian and Catholic priest in Shkodër and considered to be the first Albanian historian due to his eyewitness account of the siege of Shkodër in 1478. Barleti is also known for his second work, a biography of Gjergj (George) Kastrioti Skanderbeg

6   *Dom Ndoc Nika* (1865–1951) — Born in Shkodër, priest and writer, he fought the Turkish occupation. He was arrested by the communists in 1946 at eighty years old for trying to overturn the Government by force and died in prison on January 16, 1951.

7   *Dom Ndre Mjeda* (November 20, 1866–August 1, 1937) — A priest, linguist, lyric poet, and Albanian deputy. He is described by Jakov Milaj as "one of the great Albanian writers."
Jakov Milaj (March 25, 1911–January 2, 1997) was a journalist, veterinarian, Minister of agriculture, and first Albanian anthropologist. He was arrested and condemned by the communists when they came to power but released in 1951.

8   *Luigj Gurakuqi* (1879–1925) — A Statesman, politician, and diplomat. He was born into a Catholic family in Shkodër. He shone in the fight for Albanian independence with his pen and with weapons. He was Minister of Education and of Finance under the Government of Fan Noli (Orthodox bishop and Albanian politician who was Prime Minister and regent of the Principality of Albania in 1924). He was assassinated in Bari on March 2, 1925 by an agent of King Zog I.

9   *Sami Frashëri* (1850–1904) — He was an Albanian philosopher, writer, and playwright who, along with his brothers Naim and Abdyl, favored the birth of Albanian nationalism while under Turkish domination. Sami worked on an Albanian alphabet and helped in the publication of mostly scholarly works in this language. This was prohibited by the Turks. The goal was evidently to lead a cultural combat which would result in the emancipation of Albania from the Ottoman yoke.

10   *Faik Konica* (1875–1942) — Writer, journalist, and brilliant essayist. He is one of the founders of the modern Albanian language and its literature. Due to that, he is also considered to be one of the founders of the Albanian national identity.

FIVE YEARS LATER: THE HOMILY FOR THE MASS ON
NOVEMBER 11, 1995

The homily was destined to refresh the memory and doubts
regarding the present and the future. This homily rises like a cry of
depression before unrealized dreams, but it does not lose hope. It was
delivered on November 11, 1995 at Shkodër cathedral on the occasion
of the fifth anniversary of the first great Mass:

*Communism wanted to choke, in misery, the Albanian people's thirst
for progress. It [communism] came from the barbarian East to seize
by violence and brutality the fruits of the world of culture that came
thanks to prayer, sweat, pain, and talent.*

*For all of Albania, Shkodër was and is what ancient Greek was for
the world: a city that had once flourished and had now disappeared; a
mother of brave, long civilized men who did not fear giving everything
for ideals, for eternal truths, for fundamental principles that give life
sense; today, a mother without children! Because the best sons fell from
the bullets of their brothers with the firm conviction that their ideals
would triumph one day, in Shkodër and in the whole world. A classic
example from our epoch is that of Imre Nagy*[11] *in the Hungarian
Revolution of 1956. When he was arrested by the Russians and was
put before the firing squad, he declared, "You kill me, but know that
it will be you who will erect a monument in my honor!"*

---

11   *Imre Nagy* (1896–1958)—Hungarian politician who belonged to the
Communist Party and then to the Hungarian Workers' Party. He was twice
head of the popular Government of Hungary. He was seen as a dissident of
sorts. His reforms, which went in the direction of greater democracy, were not
accepted by Moscow. After the popular uprising of 1956, which was provoked
by his recall to the Government and led to the arrival of Russian tanks to
crush the insurrection, he found refuge in the Yugoslav embassy. Trusting the
Government's safe-conduct guarantee, he left the embassy. He was immediately
arrested by the KGB and deported to Romania. The simulacra of a court process
only began two years later. Nagy was executed by hanging in a Budapest prison
on June 16, 1958. The declaration reported by Dom Simon appears to have
taken place near the end of the phony process. Nagy was buried under a false
name in a secluded spot of the municipal cemetery. After the political change
in 1989, Nagy received a national funeral on June 16 of the same year and was
rehabilitated by the Party not long afterwards. A more dignified sepulture had
been reclaimed for him for a long time, such as in 1988 by the student leader
in Budapest, Viktor Orban, future Prime Minister.

184

November 11 is the crowning of the heroic resistance, of the active resistance that the civilized city of Shkodër demonstrated against the murderous clique of Tirana, in starting with the first tract of Mark Çuni.[12] *He was shot just like thousands and thousands of honest people, among whom we will mention Father Faust, Father Dajan, Father Shllaku, Dulo Kali, Monsignor Prennushi, Dom Dede Malaj, Xhemal Naipi, Monsignor Vaalaj, Qemal Draçini, and Dom Shtjefen Kurti, to limit ourselves with this unending list, because it is not complete, not even in our day. Mentioned or not, they are all soldiers, known or unknown, of liberty and democracy.*

The 11th of November is the cry, the appeal, the agony of this infinite number of bones, of skulls that, from common pits of the prisons of Burrel, of Beden, of Maliq, of Vloçisht, of Zall Herr, of Zalli i Kirit, protest more eloquently that words. They demand a process and justice before God and History. But no one until this day took the responsibility or the bother to make it better. On the graves of these true martyrs of democracy, no monument was erected, while people continue to place fresh flowers on the graves of their criminals, those who sparked civil war in Albania, who imposed on our mothers, wives, and sisters, and transformed the country into a zoo. They pierced the hearts of all those who, in love with liberty, tried to break through the barbed wire. Thus, flowers continue to be placed on the graves of those who created the realm of moral degeneration, of ignorance, of misery and rebellion, on the graves of those who suffocate religion and the law, who commit racial genocide, whose politics are anti-national and accumulate a debt that weighs on our shoulders and that, apparently, we cannot get rid of as quickly as we had thought at the beginning.

I have the impression of hearing the rumbling of truck engines that passed in front of my house during the night, breaking the night's restful silence. They took the best men of the intelligentsia of the Nord of Albania to shoot them in Zalli i Kirit. I still shake when I hear the echo of my cousin's voice, Luigj Katrati. From this truck of death, I heard him yell: "Adieu, and good night mother!" I saw file past my eyes the macabre scenes that followed the executions, the violation of graves, the lab dance[13] *around the martyrs of religion and of democracy who had*

---

12 *Mark Çuni* — Born in 1919, a seminarian. He was shot in 1946.
13 In Albania's musical tradition, the *"lab"* dance represents the South of the country.

in front the flower of their blood. Lule[14] Sofo—Lule, my son ... and the same thing continued. Can we consider such people as our liberators? Can we classify them as reasonable beings?

We are gathered here to commemorate the 11th of November, 1990. It was a memorable day, when Shkodër youth, without distinction of religion, brought me here, protected me, carried me in their arms right to the altar in order to celebrate the first Mass in the middle of the communist terror. This event lifted the fear that all Albanians felt, and marked a new era for our country, that of religious freedom, which is the foundation of all other liberties. If Christopher Columbus had not discovered America, there would have been another to take his place. But the merit comes back to the Genoese navigator who put his life in danger, navigating among unknown seas and oceans. Likewise, religious liberty would have come without the city of Shkodër, but the merit of this great event falls on this city and its youth. None of the fifty thousand people present at that Mass were sure that they would be able to return to their homes that day. Many of them were beaten, tortured, held in prison for several months before things changed. That is why to those who have the habit of deforming history, we say: "Bravery after the battle and wisdom after the reunion are not very useful."

November 11, 1990 is historically irreplaceable in terms of emotions. No one can erase this date which is already a part of history.

That ocean of people was filled with two contrary sensations: that of death and that of life. Each of them felt closer to those who rested in peace here in the cemetery. But when we began the Eucharistic Sacrifice, the most sublime act in religion, which announces the death and resurrection of Jesus, God and man at the same time, the sensation of life, of the resurrection, prevailed and triumphed over the sensation of death! In an ecstasy not seen for many years, everyone was out of themselves. Even the policemen and special forces forgot that they carried arms. It was the same on that day for the people of Shkodër, who departed for the Mass like they were departing for battle, taking out the arms from the place hidden in the wall and keeping them hidden under their clothing. On that day, no one did not feel Muslim, Catholic, or Orthodox. The fantasies of division had fled. Everyone felt they were children of the same God who had brought us together by his own will in order to commemorate the victory over the antichrist. Everyone had wet eyes. There were tears of pain and chagrin for the martyrs because

---

14   *"Lule"* signifies "flower" in Albanian.

there was not an Albanian family that did not have a martyr. But there were also tears of joy because in this country, where death had planted joy in the middle of the graves, we felt the powerful wind of the resurrection blow. Ah! If we could have always kept this unity and this love that made our hearts vibrate at the first Mass.

November 11, 1990 is historically irreplaceable even concerning audacity.

It was a day of terror and fear because many Shkodrans, in seeing a muezzin or a priest who had been able to escape persecution come towards them, changed their path in order to avoid greeting them because the religious were still enemy number one of the clan. Those were days of terror when our sons fell dead while seeking to get through the iron wall at the frontier. And after being massacred, their hands and feet were tied with the barbed wire of the frontier and then thrown onto trucks. They were toured around the city in order to terrorize the population. We saw them with our own eyes here, right in front of this cathedral! We saw their torturers enter into the houses to cynically ask their mothers, "Do you recognize him?" No, the mother could not recognize her own son because of how disfigured he was!

Participation at the Mass would have been at least twice as large if the communists had not terrorized the people with conferences in neighborhoods, businesses, and schools, and if they had not sent outside of Shkodër dozens of trucks filled with young people to pick wild pomegranates on Mount Tarabosh.

But hundreds of others were already there, ready to sacrifice their young age very close to the altar where the first Mass was celebrated after the persecutions. Therefore, I cannot not shout out today, five years later: "Brave youth. I am so proud of you because you brought joy to Shkodër!"

You, brave youth, you were the first to overturn the monuments to the false gods, Stalin and Enver, and in their place you put the real God, seeking to make Albanians softer through religion, Albanians who had become savage animals because of the terror.

Your glory will spread all the way to Tirana, dear youth of Shkodër. You indicated to the youth of Tirana that there was in Albania a much better civilization than Serb, Russian, or Chinese. You wanted to take all of Albania's youth by the hand to lead them onto the paths of Western civilization. Your voice, which was not at all the voice of Russian politicians, was heard in the four corners of the Earth where I, who am unworthy, was invited to speak of you. I will only mention the ceremony at the University of San Francisco. It was organized in 1991 to offer Shkodër the "honoris causa" diploma. The country's authorities never recognized this world role that, nevertheless, the world attributes to you because the liberty that the authorities of this country want is not the same as the one that you aspire to. The liberty to which you aspire is their definitive fall!

It is the liberty that only God can offer, the liberty that was hidden underground for fifty years, from where we often heard the rumble of an earthquake or groaning of a volcano that made the earth shake under the feet of the communist dictatorship. The crater had been situated at Fushë, Rrëmaji. From there, the lava spread throughout all the streets of Albania to cook all the tyrants, to defeat all the torturers, to warn the presumptuous, to raise the poor and the honest, and to put a smile on victims' faces.

November 11, 1990 was the ripened fruit under the rays of the prayers of the martyrs and souls of Purgatory, for whom we pray in particular nowadays.

You, the youth, you will reconstruct in three days the burned chapel of the cemetery, but do not forget that the ground where you place your feet is totally burned. We must rebuild souls, moral values, the sacred habits and customs of the Albanians who were stomped underfoot by a half-century of atheism. Do not leave your country, youth, because, far from the hearth, it is only the most servile work that awaits you, the work that the people of those countries do not deign to do. You will be the object of humiliations reserved for Stateless people. You will be the prey of the evil of that country and the deception of slavery.

Youth of Shkodër, martyred city, youth of democracy: Satan has not stopped, but we as well, we will not stop either! We must trouble his sleep, always in a peaceful way, deteriorate the panorama that pleases him, ruin his mood, pierce his conscience, until we can chase him once and for all out of our lands. It is only then that we will be able to enjoy the rights and freedoms that we had thought we had immediately obtained while we celebrate here, five years later!

TEN YEARS LATER: THE HOMILY FOR THE MASS ON NOVEMBER 11, 2000

This Mass was celebrated on the occasion of the tenth anniversary of the first Mass against the wish of the episcopacy, which suppressed this anniversary.

November 4, 1990 is one of the most important events that must occupy a place of honor in the Albanian pantheon, because it had a heavenly origin and was a spontaneous gathering that imposed itself in the hearts of the simple faithful. It is a triumph, a simple victory of God, who rewarded a people for their tears and sweat which were needlessly shed like nowhere else.

The fourth of November could never be repeated when it comes to audacity, nearly unbearable emotions, and a living faith. When we look back on it, our eyes fill with tears. These are tears of joy, which are the fruit of the triumph of God's Kingdom over the devil's. They are also tears of chagrin for all those who died for a European Albania.

The November 11th, 1990 celebration of the Holy Mass electrified us. We were all in ecstasy. We all felt equal, as brothers, as sons of the same God. We had forgotten all the weapons that we had hidden, some for attacking and some for defending ourselves. When we thought of that, we had the pleasure to serve only to "give the honor of arms" to the One who offered himself at the altar, who invited us to no longer use arms for barbarian actions, vengeance, or ignorance in order to start a new life.

November 4, 1990 is at the present in all of the world's encyclopedias, except in Albania—first of all because there is not an encyclopedia here, and also because, even if there were, Albania would not easily accept that freedom of religion is at the base of all the other liberties.

The first Mass was not the work of foreigners—Venetians, Turks, Austro-Hungarians, or Slavs—not the work of those who, here and there, throw a stone and look for a place to hide when it comes to major events in the nation's history.

On November 11, 1990, no one was implicated in this event aside from the simple Albanian people who poured in from the four corners to surround the altar of the first great Mass with the firm purpose either to die or to open all the churches and mosques and to invite God once again into Albania, into this Albania that had dared to chase Him out and dared to say that our territories are not the property of God.

The dominant class did the impossible by constructing a Society without God. It incited everyone to fight everyone. It played the principal role in the ferocity of souls and cultivated criminality, which shows itself more and more nowadays. It is enough to mention the result of this atheistic education. There are at present in Italian prisons more than five thousand Albanians and on the streets more than thirty thousand young Albanian women.

Today, after ten years, after so many events, most of them undesired, the first Mass remains in the national and international memory as a great event, pure like the source of its inspiration. Much more, the renewal of the Church, that is to say, the return of Jesus, remains the sole hope and the sole support for people who are profoundly disappointed in their most cherished dreams. Ten years ago, while simple people assembled by the thousands around the altar, even the political class took on a symbolic religious habit. It invited Mother Teresa and Pope John Paul II, in whom it showed that it had placed in the center of Tirana the athlete of Jesus, Gjergj (George) Kastrioti Skanderbeg. It was as if it wanted to say that it had been converted.

Therefore, this political class continued, with an unprecedented diligence, to make the whole world believe in this conversion. It also organized a scientific colloquium, "two thousand," blessed by the Pope. And people speak more and more of the opening of a Catholic University (at Tirana, naturally, and not at Shkodër, which every day gives its soul on its glorious ruins, without anyone giving it a helping hand). This political class therefore seeks to create a beautiful facade of Albania, like those in the great cities of the world, hiding edifices which are ready to collapse. This political class thought of this Catholic facade, because from that it can fool the Christian West, from where comes the principal support that keeps us living. It is a false facade because it is enough to open one sole window to see what is behind it all.

We can see an Albania deprived of electricity and water, fallen into the lowest kind of trafficking, without any public order, without education, without health services, and without agriculture. Everywhere we look, we see profound corruption and ever-growing poverty, a country that is not able to ensure its citizens their daily bread, which they earned from their sweat. We can also see how the Albanian people grow older day by day. Households only have old people who sob and cry, who keep their eyes always fixed on the mountains and seas which separate them from their sons and daughters who left if they were able to in order to work as real slaves in the West for a little bread for themselves and for the old ones who are at risk of dying alone in the obscure crevices of the brilliant facade. The number of young, desperate people who take the path of exile does not stop growing. They flee hell, stress, terror, and death, which reign in our country. At the same time, the number of old people does not stop growing, and their sadness rises, along with the risk of dying without burial because there is no one near them to do it.

We sent many young men and women overseas for their advanced studies. Many of them succeeded at their studies, but unfortunately, they found a place in the foreign countries, thereby enriching the brain of the world and impoverishing that of Albania. It is not their fault. The Albania of the other side of the facade declares that there is not any place for them because she does not need them while the country becomes poorer and poorer, with the lowest number of brains in all of Europe. That makes me think of the great Fishta: "In the darkness more than one person took a place that he did not merit.... In summer and in winter the poor horses look for nourishment on a dry prairie!"

Ten years ago, we had on our hands the iron handcuffs of communism. Ten years later, we still have handcuffs on. The iron handcuffs have been replaced by modern, cybernetic, American ones. Our Old Continent is reduced to a situation of slavery. It groans under the heel of American military bases, which we need to chase out if we want to have a future. Our Balkans, largely occupied by the same bases, which were constructed in the past ten years, will have a lesser future.

Ten years ago, we imagined that our situation would get better because we had seen the hypocrite Gorbachev on his knees in front of the Pope. He asked for pardon. We had seen and heard Bush announcing to the world that the Cold War had come to an end. We had thought that for us Albanians also the warm season had arrived. But the season that the two leaders of the two superpowers proposed to us was boiling. Hot war was their work: that which made Albania and the Balkans burn in those years, during which more than 300,000 people died, among whom were 10,000 children, who were cut down by death while they innocently played. We are not going to enumerate the other damage — more than two hundred edifices of religion transformed into ruins.

We have a self-declared Christian European Parliament which approves of the marriage of homosexuals and lesbians, thereby destroying the family founded by God from the time of Adam and Eve.

We live in the epoch of the antichrist, the time of the most dangerous attacks against values. That is why it is the work of each one of us to oppose this perversion organized by the political class.

The dominant global class disposes of gigantic economic reserves. If it wanted, it could build on earth the terrestrial paradise and get rid of poverty, misery, anxiety, and the worries of the whole planet. Another reason why that would be useful for Albanians is that the Government is not able to ensure our daily bread.

But this political class does not want the same thing as humanity. Impassioned by hegemony, the two superpowers make the bottom of hell even deeper, hastening the last day.

The general repetitions of this general catastrophe, as the people call it, took place in Albania in 1967, when the Government closed the churches and mosques and all of the religious were killed or deported.

The dominant international political class, due to the extraordinary military potential that has developed, is preparing the real day of the universal end of the world.

It [this class] needs to get into its head that at precisely the moment when it believes it has won, we will have the Second Coming of Jesus on Earth. He will chastise the persecutors and lawbreakers and compensate the good and the faithful, living or dead, who will once again reunite as they did on November 4 in this holy place. This will take place in the way we are doing things today: not by force, as if we were eating the forbidden fruit in the garden of long ago, because we are in our house, and it will be the same in the future. We are gathered here as brothers and sisters, as children of the same Father, to give thanksgiving to the great God and to beg Him that the ranks of the righteous of Jesus grow and that peace return to our tormented hearts among our working families in Albania and in the shaken world. So let it be!

25
Collapse of Idols

One beautiful Sunday, the residents of the City of the North filed towards the main area, which in Turkish is called *Milet Bahçe*.[1] On the garden's gate, whose name the State sought in vain to translate, as if to prove that the history of this city had fallen to one occupation after another, one yoke after another, a bronze Stalin emitted his severe look, as if he wanted to say: "I am Shkodër dominator!" On that Sunday, Shkodrans left their homes to condemn to death this type of man who had come from another part of the world to dominate them. Because they were incapable of challenging living dominators, as was required, they took it out on the men in metal. However, it is not easier to break metal than to break the bones of man!

My name began to circulate among the crowd. People had thought up the idea for a committee to seek me at my home to deliver a talk before the monument's execution. The residents said: "Go get him right away. He will know how to put a rope around the cannibal's neck." These and many other words spoken by these people were reported to me by the faithful who came to my home. In fact, this type of trust not only did not please me, but even alarmed me. As a priest, I have no role in slipping a rope around people's necks, whether the necks are statues, metal, or flesh.

Think about what they would have said if I had ventured to do such things and later spoke to the people from the altar with the words of Jesus: "Father, forgive them, for they know not what they do!" Would I have been convincing? Me, I am a man of the altar and not of the guillotine or execution post. That is why I did not accept any of the propositions that were made to me on that day. I was happy instead that the grace of God had allowed me to celebrate the Mass in public.

Without my presence, Stalin was toppled. I was informed that a few days later, a waiter from the cafe of Milet Bahçe was seen watering the hole which was left after this poisoned plant had been

---

1 *"Garden of Milet."*

uprooted. A Shkodran told him, "In the name of God who created you and pardons you, do not water it, because I fear that it will grow up again." It was said again that this Shkodran had been a true prophet.

26

Epilogue on Earth:
The Farce of Albanian Democracy

A half-century passed by for poor Albania with all of this lying and torture. The torture never bore fruit; the lies never produced bread. That is why the country was plunged into a profound misery, like the Red East. That is why the revolt intensified. Not us, dear reader, because the Albanians no longer had the smallest drop of blood. It started with our neighbors, friends and Marxist-Leninist sympathizers of yesteryear, with whom we had shared close ties and then fallen out a thousand times. Rebellions began and walls came down precisely in that region where the red cholera had begun and from which small Albania died little by little, with its fragile and sick body. At least that is what it looked like. While we built dreams when we were in prison, in the cells or while working in somber mineshafts, the Government had keenly understood that the moment had come to change roles. The cruel dictator left the political scene to cede place to a more refined director, *Ramiz Alia*[1], who, naturally, received instructions from another, more important and mysterious director. And to say that he once was a Shkodran!

Ramiz Alia went for a while down the path of glorious tradition. He calmly reasoned over the contemporary situation, always seeking to imitate the Kremlin. He thought of ending the tragedy that threatened to finish with the assassination of all the characters, even the director and the author. All of that needed to be transformed into a comical farce. We Albanians have proven for almost a century that we are as talented for farces as for tragedies. Enough of our blood has been shed in prisons. Apparently, goes the thinking, it now needs to be shed in the streets. It is not necessary to waste bullets. It is necessary to arm people so that they kill each other, or

---

1 *Ramiz Alia* — Born on October 18, 1925 in Shkodër, he was President of the Presidium of the Popular Assembly of the People's Socialist Republic of Albania from November 25, 1982 to February 20, 1991, President of the Presidential council of Albania from February 20 to April 30, 1991, and then President of the Republic of Albania from April 30, 1991 to April 3, 1992. He died in Tirana on October 7, 2011.

to open the borders so that they flee wherever they want to and leave us alone. These people who at present do not have a brain cell need to be convinced that ours is the only path. Whatever happens, they will be forced to follow. That is the Government's current thinking.

So the director thought that he would be able to write a new farce that would be played on the Albanian scene. It was not at all difficult for him to set it in action. He once again faithfully followed tradition. He took the text of a modern farce that was played in Moscow and started to adapt it to Albania. The great Noli, had not he done likewise? Then, the director dived with his imagination into the new scene. There, a farce was played in the middle of devastated mountains, of forests reduced to half, on the unexploited coasts, by lakes lost on the frontiers, in tired out cities, and among people paradoxically frightened to the point of becoming brave fools because of the terror that went down to the marrow. Those close to him reported what they had done to summon a citizen in order to award him the medal of bravery. But as they had not found the time to explain to him the reason, the poor citizen took the medal while trembling in fear.

The director, thus, sat at the same table where so many death warrants had been signed and so many orders given to puncture the eyes of certain people. From there, he began to translate the Russian farce into the Albanian language. The farce started with a popular revolt, organized and led by the director himself. Naturally, the participants were the poor chaps who believed that the revolt was real and the moment had come. The poor chaps were so tiny in number that, as always, their role was insignificant. Then came the plan for the creation of new parties. The comical situation could make one laugh himself to death. Yesterday's communists would make the big change, which would show up in their meetings. They would shout against themselves in order to defend themselves in order to appear more acceptable. However, one always needs to take precautions and not show too much zeal.

Then came the turn of the spies of the prison cells, which included Pjetër Arbnori, "the Mandela of Albania." He had suffered so much in prison. He and others with him, because they had left prison to participate in tribunals, could ascend to the altar and even to the summit of the tribune of Parliament. There was no evil in that. They already knew by heart their lesson. Then, in order to attract the spectators' attention, they organized a few semi-tragic scenes with broken glass, burned vehicles and buildings of the committee of the Communist Party, assassinations, destruction, and attacks against institutions (because, as this all came from communism, it was necessary to destroy everything). This accompanied break-ins at weapons depots and the resulting shots fired into the air day and night. Food was scarce, and everyone feared hunger. They even feared stepping outside the house. The notion of peace and security was lost, so no one even dared go into the street.

Lurking in this atmosphere was the farce of a novel conflict, which in turn threatened the unraveling of the economy. Fear spread that we could no longer do as before, and that the existing ridiculously tiny industry and its outmoded technology had to be destroyed. Everything was to be split into fragments in order to give the impression of a great change. Therefore, for a certain time, the principal actors had to hide themselves well in the backroom, waiting for the opportune moment to become the new masters of the situation. That would lead to everything falling back into the same hands which, for a certain time, had to remain invisible.

The emigrants would also be summoned to present themselves. It can never be forgotten that the tiny Albanian scene was only a minute part of the great international scene. If the actors were not authentic in their roles and were not pleasing to everyone, the scene could be modified at any moment. That is why it is necessary to always have the larger scene in view. Emigrants were the most obvious actors to take care of small accounts. Most of them were escapees, the sworn enemies of the powers. They would tell everything. Perfect. That is what needs to happen now in the act that is to be played. That would convince the whole world that here the entire drama of democracy was being played out instead of farce or tragedy. These emigrants would therefore empty everything out here and leave their words and currency. And after coming to see with their own eyes the giant changes between the country that they had left Albania for and the one in which they had the bad break to be born, they would leave in all haste to show Albania their achievements. They would swear in their souls to never again step foot in this country of which they had so often dreamed and that they had found completely changed. Perfect! They are welcome!

After having done the translation, the director goes looking for actors. Here he had a free field for creation. It was no longer translation work, but the adaptation to the time and country. That is why he said: "Let us change tactics. Until now we have sought to put a rabbit into the entrails of Albanians, and they have trembled in fear night and day. Let us put a dog in place of the rabbit — a dog that barks all the time but does not bite! Then they can bark as much as they want! While they bark, we have all the time to direct the entire farcical scene."

The director attentively scrutinized everyone capable of playing in their masterpiece — the main actors, the stand-ins, and the secondary roles. He called first of all to present on scene *Sali Berisha*[2], a nurse in cardiology. After all, the Albanian medical diploma is not recognized anywhere in the civilized world. He next proceeded to the preparation of public opinion. In doing so, he even exported the Voice of America radio broadcast which, in those times, was as reliable as the voice of God. It never occurred to us, idiots that we were, that even the great America could also sell itself for thirty pieces of silver. And to hear those newly arrived from America, who on the Albanian political scene had appeared to be the bravest among the brave, a professor, a doctor, a charismatic, an ardently anti-communist communist, a secretary of the Communist Party transformed into opponent of the Party. Everyone started to shout and physically fight with friends and sympathizers who had contrary convictions and took the side of Sali Berisha.

Then the producer brought in *Sabri Godo*[3], who was well-trained in the secret services, to direct the Republican Party. He summoned *Pjetër Arbnori*[4] as the most reliable representative of the political right. He had been tortured in prisons and could give incendiary talks, supported by other stormy characters. Then the Director decided to create a Green Party that closely resembles watermelon: green outside and red inside. He named Monsieur *Hoti* the President of

---

2 *Sali Berisha* — Born on October 15, 1944, he was an Albanian politician and President of the Republic from April 9, 1992 to July 24, 1997, and then Prime Minister from September 3, 2005 from September 15, 2013. He was a member of the Democratic Party of Albania and one of the principal Albanian politicians of the post-communist period.

3 *Sabri Godo* (1929–2011) — He was a writer and conservative politician who was often threatened throughout his life for his officially anti-communist ideas. Dom Simon seems somewhat unenthusiastic about this person.

4 *Pjetër Arbnori* (1935–2006) — He was a politician who spent twenty-eight years in the Albanian gulag, perhaps as a spy.

the Greens. Hoti never took off his hat, even when he appeared on television. People said, "He cannot stand that he is bald. That is why he never takes off his hat!" Then the Director tried things with the comedian *Zef Bushati*[5], whose family and given names were suitable for the Democratic Christian Party. It was a well-ordered Christian Democrat Party, regulated in the offices of the secret service, unlike that which the foolish Shkodrans wanted to create in their continuing belief in the existence of pure liberty and democracy in this world. From that belief the Director's fantasy followed its course, and like a sow it had twenty piglets — I want to say twenty political parties. In this way, the troupe of actors was soon ready.

Then the Director divided them in two: partisans of power and the opposition. Fatos Nano and his followers were no longer called communists, but socialists and representatives of the left. Sali Berisha and Pjetër Arbnori and theirs would no longer be called the terrible labels of "communists" and "prison spies," but the Democratic Right. Nothing remained then but to film as truthfully as possible the new farce in order to calm ever so slightly the soul of a people that no longer knew how to laugh.

Contrary to good technical practice, the Director decided to put even the understudies in the scene for this premiere. Almost no one was prepared for the roles that had to be played in the prisons after they had signed on for this on a somber day. The Director controlled all of them and could effortlessly replace them with the real actors, which is to say with those who had always been the masters. And if these latter no longer had the energy to play the modern farce, the Director had taken care to educate their children in the capitalist countries, and he kept them in reserve in order to put them into the newly-hatched scene.

In that way, Ramiz Alia brought together all the communists, the secret service agents, and spies and inserted them into the farce, into the new political reality. He handed out the script to everybody and urged them to learn it by heart as quickly as possible. Once the text had been learned, they had to start the repetitions. But careful! They had to be very faithful to the text. There was not much room for creativity. Creativity, during the directing, was up to the great

---

5   *Zef Bushati* — Born in 1953, he was a talented actor and director, and President of the Christian Democrat Party of Albania (2000–2002). He was founder and President (2011) of the Party of the Christian Democrat Alliance of Albania.

Director, who controlled all of the marionettes' strings. If they did not understand their roles as was necessary, they had to present themselves immediately before the Director. He knew how to get them to understand.

Thus began the first repetitions before the general repetition. The organization of the initial demonstration at Shkodër started. Stalin's bust was overturned. Enver Hoxha's bust in front of the prefectural building in Shkodër was decapitated. The Communist Party committee building in Shkoder was set on fire, some people were killed, and files were burned. Seeing these things, the Director rubbed his hands in glee. *It was enough to be a Shkodran because they had done everything!*[6] Ramiz Alia had also taken care of the decor where the spectacle would begin — in the city that, with its lit liberty torch, would do nothing other than definitively burn itself. That was how the Albanian political parties were created. The Albanians were dazzled to see, in the principal roles, the victims and the torturers, former secret service agents and former prisoners, close to one another. They saw how the waters of the *Bune* and the *Drin* became red — was it blood?[7]

Do not forget that the farce continues, but not the tragedy. The poor people, stunned by the rapid changes, thought that it was the blood that they had expected, the blood of those who had themselves shed so much blood. The people believed that to be the only way to wash away the long-standing crime. But not at all, dear reader! The rivers turned red from the membership cards of the Communist Party at the exact moment when the director oversaw the scene of the mass abandonment of the Party. This was a show for the pretty eyes of the outside world. What is the importance, dear reader, of a Party membership card when your head and heart are being gnawed at by worms?

Then it was the turn of the economy to be undone, which meant devastation and desertification. The underlings got into their small boats and paddled full-out, giving way to the real actors. In this mess, the poor people finally came to the precise place where the invisible director had wanted to lead them. At the time, he had chosen prison as the best place to direct the rest of the farce. Ramiz Alia had

---

6 Diction that rhymes in Albanian.
7 The *Buna* and the *Drin* are two rivers that flow through Albania. The Buna (Bojana) flows from Shkodër Lake to the Adriatic, between Albania and Montenegro for 41 kms. The Drin is the longest river in Albania (335 km).

condemned himself in order to seem more reliable. Confusion grew even more, because everyone came to believe the mess to have been the outcome of a lack of leadership, a situation in which no one was in charge and in which the pelota ball of the eternal work of Albania made and unmade itself.

Where was the State that permitted such total destruction? Few people realized that the State was indeed playing its proper role according to the instructions received from the Director. He was always at the heart of things when financial pyramids were investigated. He had pushed Albanians to sell their houses and all their goods by getting them to believe that money makes money. He knew, dear reader, that for the Albanians, good work is that which does not need to be done. So, the farce came to an end: those who had dreamed their whole lives of the fall of communism voted for him once again. This amounted to a renewed call for communism. Voters placed communism back on the scene and chased away all of the understudies and actors who were of no use during the transitional phase.

This proved to me what the dissidents who were captured at Shkodër in the first rebellions told me. The former torturers, who were quickly putting on new masks, said directly to the victims during the investigations: "It should never occur to Simon Jubani or any other Shkodran that we will ever share power with them. Power belongs to us and will continue to belong to us!" Such thankless people! It never even occurred to them that I would likewise never sit at the same table as they who wanted to assassinate my God. They should have understood that I have no need to become a minister because I am already one: I am a minister of God. I also think that many of them do not know that "minister" signifies "servant." Otherwise, they would not fight each other, as they do, to occupy a seat in the ministries that are really places of infamy, not service.

As for the underlings, they played their roles as needed and therefore supposedly deserve better compensation. They take freely from the humanitarian aid that is meant for the poor. Therefore, at the scene of the farce, close to dilapidated and half-destroyed small houses, new luxurious mansions have started to spring up. And those pressured until the breaking point were given another task, that of smuggler, still in the service of the same director. In this way, the communists succeeded in destroying everything. But one thing remained standing: the former communist nomenklatura. It continued to pull the strings of the country like it had always done. Thus, Albania more and more resembled a plow tied to a dead horse. The money that was earned in the West was recycled back there because everything that the poor Albanians had to buy came from overseas, from tomatoes to horseshoes. These products could all have been produced in Albania if the powerful of the world left us in peace to do our work.

Dear reader, the farce has not finished yet! I hope that it does not once again transform into tragedy. That depends entirely on the mysterious Director who, once more hidden behind the scenes, is having fun with wooden marionettes until the country is completely destroyed. It is like one of my American friends tells me: Many people thank the Director with all their heart. The Director could not have done this without their support. He could not have seen the world where, thank God, neither prisons, nor cells, nor the direction or directors entered the people's minds. An ovation, therefore!

Long live the Director and the new comedy, written on the skin of the Albanians. At the moment, he is playing with their souls, which would be completely empty if God had not come back among us. Who knew if he had been baptized as had several of his friends and sympathizers. They took over Caritas and the Church herself, both in Albania and overseas. Were not the nephews of *Mehmet Shehu* baptized in Rome? Had not the Church proclaimed that fact as the greatest triumph of God over evil? For they told us that the day of their baptism brought us the long-awaited day of happiness. Nevertheless, I am convinced that he did not succeed at understanding the essential thing: Our planet is not moved by these directors, however big or small they are, but by an eternal Director. The last act has not yet been played.

Yet the farce continues. The scene is always the same. Nothing has changed, not even their fear. They are afraid. They fear that a critic will appear, someone who knows their art of directing perfectly well and can destroy their show. They fear the spectators' jeers and their own banishment from the scene, precisely now that they are sure of their game, which was hatched with consummate art. That is also a part of the scene. Does anyone remain who considers the mouth not only as a simple organ suitable for eating, like for animals, but also for demanding rights, liberties, and inherent rights? Most of those who asserted the need for liberty rot in anonymous pits. But the Director does not really fear the living. He fears the bones of the dead. That is why he ordered that they be dug up and reburied with honors, so that they also could rest in peace. The dead could also be actors in the farce. The Government searched everywhere for burial places, from Zalli i Kirit to Zall Herr. They went everywhere to see the various funerals in churches, which included Masses, talks, veneration, and decorations. Skeletons were given insignia! The coming and going of coffins, carried by hand, increased to the point that we believed only the dead benefitted from this comedy.

Despite everything, a good part of these skeletons remain buried in unmarked and forgotten graves. There are many lost graves like those in *Skanderbeg, Bogdani*[8], and *Fishta*. No longer able to carry out research on this, the Director ordered monuments erected over empty graves. It was better because there was not any risk that a ghost would pop out of these graves to trouble the young democracy's sleep. Was it necessary to publish their books? Nothing better! One of the most talented actors told us that it was a good thing to have them published because it clarified the fact that these books had no value. Thus, the issue was closed once and for all!

The farce continues even as my life nears the grave. I will die satisfied to have given to Caesar what belongs to Caesar. I spoke wherever and whenever I wanted, even when it required me to enter the scene of the farce, thinking that I could contribute to changing the course of events. From the beginning, I understood them well. To say it with Jesus' language to the scribes and pharisees: "Race of vipers, hypocrites. Tombs white on the outside but filled with filth on the inside!"

I will die with the conviction that I have given to God what belongs to Him. I have consecrated all my energies, sufferings, and life to the triumph of the Kingdom of Jesus Christ on Earth to the best of my ability. I am happy to have consecrated my life until the end to Jesus, to the One who, in the allotted time, intervened in human activities and altered the course of human history. He cleared the way for the development of an incomparable spiritual and material culture in

---

8 *Pjetër Bogdani* (1630–1689)—A devout Roman Catholic Albanian who received a demanding education and Catholic training, he was ordained a priest in 1651. His studies in Rome led to doctorates in philosophy and theology. He was bishop of Shkodër in 1656 and then archbishop of Skopje in 1677. He fought the Turks and died of the plague while in the middle of a campaign against the Ottoman Empire.

relation to what all the philosophers and ideologues had brought to the world from the creation of the human race. I am happy with the idea of being a simple soldier of this grand army of theologians, philosophers, scientists, writers, and artists who, in believing in the same Christ, gave to world culture ninety percent of its wealth, of which it proudly continues to give to authentic people.

The bark of St. Peter is always in the middle of the sea with its nets cast into the water! No tragedy or farce in the world will be able to stop its navigation in the spiritual waters until the Last Judgment Day, for it is God himself who is at the helm!

27

Epilogue in Heaven: My God, Where Do I Go Now?

The terrible night finally passed. I returned home, laying in the coffin, placed in the exact same chapel where I was the second time, in this chapel surrounded by cypress trees and cynara. I was finally dead. This gave pleasure to those who considered me to be a speck of dust in the eye, but it deeply wounded all of my sympathizers. I had accomplished a life journey which had forced me to accept so many thorns, although flowers had also not lacked. After all, God had permitted me to see spring and even much more: to be the first to open the door for Him. My body lay there but, uncharacteristic for me, was unmoving.

Hundreds of people filed past. It seems to me that they call that "paying homage," which is to say, honoring the dead. But me, I needed no type of honor. I needed a blessing to make the path easier until the end. I pray for someone to say: "Lord, give him eternal rest." But no one thinks it is prayer that the soul needs first of all. Most of them whispered in each other's ears what I had done while alive. Some even snickered under their mustaches.

As usual and as an irony of fate, the country's highest and always-deceptive communist authorities took up the first rows. Do you really believe that they were there to mourn? How I would have loved to rise out of the coffin at that moment, but I could not because, following custom, my feet were attached with my shoelaces to prevent me from becoming a ghost. I can assure you that they were not wrong. A cold sweat once again covered my body as I vainly tried to shout out: "What? Do you think I am dead? No, my dear people! I wished to chat with the melodrama that is playing out around my coffin." But it was useless.

At present, suspended between heaven and earth, I still do not know my location or route. My satisfaction from having accomplished my terrestrial journey was perturbed by another, more complicated idea: I had to begin my last, eternal voyage as soon as my mortal body was lowered into the black earth. While waiting, the soul would contemplate, not painlessly, this bodily case inside of which had passed more than seventy years on the roads of this world. Like all cadavers, my body would begin to decompose and release the odor of carrion.

Body and soul were still linked by a fragile lace which would soon break like the string that holds the balloon in air. This ceremony seemed to me at the same time both tragic and comical, with the bishops and other religious who celebrated the Mass for my soul in the exact spot where I had myself stood to do the same thing so many times. Then was pronounced the sermon that I would have loved to have heard when I was alive. The priest did not stop presenting a Dom Simon Jubani who had nothing in common with the real one or with the one that remained of me, who was neither of this earth nor of heaven. Instead of emphasizing the fact that I had directed the Shkodrans to the altar at the first Mass after the period of persecutions, he did not stop saying that I had been raised as an orphan. I never came to see whether having been raised without a father was a merit or a shame.

I thought with regret: "We make many more enemies through heroic acts than when we are humiliated by bad actions." I was then seized by laughter. In a few moments, I would definitely detach myself from my body and would no longer have friends or enemies. I would no longer be an orphan. Stupidity and merit would go to another balance which never lies. Gosh golly! Throughout my whole life, I was always a reactionary, both with others and with myself.

Absolutes came to an end. The bell that we had dug up from the earth to announce the first Mass after the persecution rang nostalgically and even sadly. The ringing passed through the cypress trees, which were crying green tears. The moving sounds of *Dies irae* spread throughout the cemetery. The choir began to sing the chant of the dead, of eternity, of God's anger. A large tear fell down from my frozen face just before it was forever covered by the lid of the casket. I did not see anyone else cry. I remembered the curious but possibly true expression that was repeated each time a priest died: "We assemble together without knowing each other, we live without loving each other, and we die without being lamented." Whatever. I was crying for myself. I did that my whole life: I laughed for myself and with myself and cried for and with myself! Now came the last tear. Then came . . . Precisely what was to come began to preoccupy me, although my soul felt light, light, light. I had taken into my heart my Savior through my mouth just before it was permanently closed — this mouth with its teeth having been broken in the prisons for my witness to the Lord.

The long line of members of the clergy, with their violet ornaments worn in my honor, gathered behind the casket for the last time. Then the hammer banged down the nails of the cover, and I did not see myself again. I disappeared forever, as if I had never existed. Now, yes, I was definitely dead. Four men picked up the casket, followed by a crowd. They were directed towards the open pit between Rrëmaji's simple graves. I got angry: Had I not done enough to be buried in the cathedral, close to the bishops and the first Cardinal? But then laughter seized me. At that moment, the place of my burial was of no consequence. I even had to be content to have a chance to sleep the last sleep close to the great *doctor Shiroka*[1]. He would be the first to help me rise at the Last Judgment, even if I lacked a few important bones.

The noise of mourning could be heard in the cemetery, as it collided with the face of the dead. Shovels moved rapidly. While they buried me forever in this hole, the thought lived about what was waiting for them behind the door. This was human greed for life and everything life offers. Finally, a heap of earth covered my grave, on which someone pushed a simple wooden cross with the following inscription: "Peace: Here rests Dom Simon Jubani."

Does he rest? No, sir! It is an error! Rest remained far off. I sensed that I was flying up and up. Large clouds surrounded me. They moved like wool of white *Peshtarake*[2] sheep. I do not know from what corner of my memory came the phrase which I had learned by heart from a scholarly anthology. I think it was written by Luigj Gurakuqi. I will gladly see him in paradise, I thought. He and no one else! I had the same sensation as when I was flying in an airplane.

When I finally arrived, the rapidly moving clouds created a great door in front of me. It was the door of paradise that shone like gold under these unknown clouds. It was closed. There was no lock. I did not have any way to announce my arrival without shouting, as I had

---

1 *Dr Frederik Shiroka* — Born on 27 September 1907 and died on 15 December 1953. Albanian surgeon of great reputation graduated in Austria.
2 *Peshtarake* — A kind of sheep renowned for its high quality wool, of several colors dominated by brown.

done so often when I got nearer to houses in my Mirditë. I shouted: "Are you accepting newcomers, Master of the House?" I was again seized with laughter before becoming serious again. I did not want to make a bad impression on St. Peter. He opened the door at once. I briefly told him who I was. I did not have any problems with that, because the words spoken about me at the cemetery were still in my ears. "Ah, ah, ah," he said, "so it is you, the priest who did not rest a moment in peace? Therefore, given that you were a priest, you know that you cannot enter paradise without weighing everything that you did in the other life. Then we will see to which side the balance tilts."

St. Peter half opened the great majestic door and let me take only one step into the interior. I thought that, from then on, I would be dealing with St. Michael. I had preached so often on his eternal balance. Whether one would partake in the vision of God or not depended on this weighing. But, dear reader, what did poor old me see? I saw approaching me, balance in hand, no one other than *Enver Hoxha* in person. Clad totally in white, he wore a giant cross in the place where the principal angels carried it.

Panic seized me. I shouted, stuttering: "St. Mellon (without wanting to, I had spoken Mellon's name when I wanted to say St. Michael's). Do you know who this is? It is not an angel. It is the devil himself! The Devil! The Deeeeviiil!" rang out my voice, as someone whose soul was stretched in the sky's endless space. This ghostly voice scared me. He who approached me with the balance in his hands was the same fellow who had mutilated my body into a thousand pieces. Now he would mutilate my soul and throw me into the fire of hell for roasting. I expected no iota of pity from him and, naturally, no iota of justice.

St. Peter put his hands to his ears to muffle my crazy shouting. When I stopped, he said: "You, Albanian priest, present firstly the scale! You are very late! You are old-fashioned, very old-fashioned! You have become moldy! St. Michael was summoned by God for a very urgent task. It is this gentleman who will take care of you — St. Michael's replacement. And as for what you said, it is not your concern. He entered Paradise in conformity with the rules, according to all of the rules of the Holy Mother Catholic and Apostolic Church because, dear sir, two seconds before dying, he repented and turned against Marx, Engels, Lenin, and Stalin. He converted in his heart and spirit to the religion of Christ. Then, once among us, he has behaved in an exemplary manner. He has not allowed one single soul to enter Paradise. This above all concerns the souls of Albanians, which he knows very well to be full of vice. It is for this reason that St. Michael named him no more and no less as his replacement. In most cases, with St. Michael busied with Party reunions, it is he who weighs the souls. And I regret to tell you that, up to this day, he has sent all of your peers to hell. He informed us that they were involved in politics, which is a great sin for a religious, who must concern himself only with the problems of the soul. In Paradise, sir, it is not useful to busy oneself with politics because pluralism does not exist here. Here, the Father All-powerful, Creator of Heaven and Earth, He who sees everything, dominates. No one can lie to him! It is like that," shouted St. Peter, "There it is."

He looked directly into my eyes as if to say, "Stop, now, get up on the balance and let us finish because there are others waiting in front of the door, which will make a longer lineup than that of the butcher's during the time of your communism." I looked at the balance, then at he who held it, and finally at the door of Paradise half open. Suddenly, I started running as fast as I could. Once outside, with my legs shrouded in the white clouds, I said to myself, terrified: "What am I going to do now?"

I had not finished saying these words when I woke up, covered in sweat. Oh God, I was dreaming. And all of that was because of the previous day's meeting. It was a meeting that I had anticipated. It was a little after the reopening of the Church. Many missionaries and various personalities of the Church had started to come to Albania. Some had come to stay permanently to help us get back up on our feet, while others had come to heal the wounds of our souls a bit and to bring us up to date with the happenings in the rest of the Church because we were still, as they told us, in the time of the Old Testament. That did not worry me at all. As a man of the Church, I always felt that it was the time of the Testament: of the Old and the New. I did nothing but witness to and defend the Church even at the price of my blood. Moreover, I felt that I was of that time because the Gospel does not know other times or other events, even religious, that could surpass the Gospel, which was given for eternity.

Nevertheless, it is never bad to find fresh words and to rejuvenate oneself spiritually. Each right-thinking person must know how to read the signs of the time and follow their rhythm. Otherwise, as they say, there is nothing else to do but walk into a museum and stay there, frozen, near the bell-bottomed trousers and ancient sailboats. We gave our full consent to this rejuvenation because many felt unconnected to the current age, which could become ridiculous. Such folk could be placed in old jars and displayed as mummies in archeological museums.

Therefore, fully content and clothed in my white habit and tie, I took a seat in the first row, as was my due. The reader was a Jesuit. That was the best choice, given that I had been an old student of his. The room was full because, on the one hand, people had nothing better to do in their joblessness and because, on the other hand, many were eager to learn about the rest of the world at a time when Albania was not a part of it. Albanians wanted to know what had taken place in the Church while we had been in hell.

Perfect, the assembly started as needed. The reader informed us about Vatican II and recommended that we learn about it as soon as possible if we wanted to keep up with the Universal Church. He gave a brief exposé of the Council's principal documents, the Catholic Church's current situation around the world, John Paul II's papacy, and our future and that of the Church. The listeners sat there, frozen, unable to fully comprehend half of the words of the speaker. He spoke in Italian with a translator at his side. The latter did not really understand the religious terms that he was hearing for the first time. Even those who spoke Italian felt overwhelmed. The problem was that the speaker did not know his audience.

Finally, we came to a question period. The only thing that anyone retained was the question of redemption. This prompted the first question: "What do we have to do in order to be saved?" and the second: "What will happen to those who committed grave crimes, such as Enver Hoxha?" Regarding the first question, I did not need much of an explanation because I myself had talked about it so often to everyone who had asked me the same question. I based my response on the Gospel, naturally.

As for the second question, I thought that the Jesuit would respond succinctly to the poor guy who had posed this idiotic question: "Hell was created precisely for those who denied God!" But my dear reader, it was not like that at all. It is true that I was old-fashioned! "If he repented at the last moment," replied the Jesuit, "he could also be saved. It is possible that he is currently enjoying the happiness of Paradise!"

I started shaking, though God alone knew. Unfortunately, I was wearing my dentures, which I cannot stand, in order to avoid appearing too old. They began tightening to the point that I thought I would go crazy. I took them out and put them in my pocket. As soon as I felt that my mouth was no longer tied up, I raised my hand and immediately asked, "Father, you are telling us that it is possible that Enver Hoxha is waiting for us in Paradise. If he has gone to Paradise, where am I going? Because Dom Simon and Enver Hoxha cannot exist together in the same place. In other words, the Paradise of Enver Hoxha would be the hell of Simon Jubani. Do you see this toothless mouth? It was Enver Hoxha who took out all of these teeth. What will he take out if I am with him in Paradise? Because he only thinks of tearing things out. In this case, Paradise would be a place of condemnation and not of salvation for those who were drenched in blood because they did not constantly change their flag depending on the circumstances! Nooo, sir, kill me or pardon me, but I have nothing to do with this Paradise that you are describing to us, not today nor when I give up my soul!" The room burst into laughter. Naturally, the majority shared my opinion and approved my words with loud applause.

But I do not care about applause or ovations. I could not stand the idea that I would find myself beside the one who had peeled me alive. He really knew how to pretend. Is it possible that he was so talented that he could even fool the All-Powerful Father? Like he had done with all the Albanians? And if that were so, what could poor Father Simon do? Was not prison enough? Father Simon would have to go to hell, and do so by the fault of Enver Hoxha? So, my Jesuit professor, who surpasses even God in mercy and grief, will open the gates of Paradise for Enver Hoxha and close them to me and my comrades? Funny story! My God, what will become of me? "Have courage, Simon Jubani," I said to myself while I opened the door to my house which at that moment seemed like true paradise. "Courage, therefore. First, you are not yet dead. Second, God the All-Powerful cannot commit such errors. At the end of the day, we can explain ourselves because that is why He gave us a mouth!" Therefore, seeking to calm myself somehow, I fell straight onto my hard bed and dreamed as if I were dead! I dreamed what I have just told you.

What do I have to do now? This question pounded my temples, even after I had fully awoken and the nightmare had disappeared. Curiously, the words that St. Peter had said to Jesus came to my spirit: "I cannot leave you, Lord! You are the only one who has the words of eternal life!"

A LAST WORD

I tried to thread the pearls of Dom Simon's story on a string while at the same time doing the other work and reading that I always do. I had unintentionally come upon the original text, which addressed what the author aptly named the bad writing of "the farce of democracy."

Pieces of this original were published in media around the world. One of the most important acts took place in the July 31, 2001 issue of the conservative Italian newspaper, *Il Giornale*. It was an interview with the former Soviet Prime Minister Valentin Pavlov given to journalist Francesco Bigazzi in Moscow in 1991 at a time when several acts of the farce of democracy were being played out. But the interview was only published in 2001 because it took readers by the hand into the corridors of power. That was where the real dramas and true tragedies of the life of each one of us were played and continue to be played today while we remain forgotten in our homes.

We believe that no one is watching us and that nothing can happen to us because, we reason, we have not done anything. We forget the most crucial thing: The great danger never comes from our homes. The greatest danger comes from the black houses that are called white! These much larger and much more powerful houses than yours have grown precisely by devouring the small houses which are just like your cabin where you go to avoid bothering anyone. But you are mistaken, dear reader. Our small destinies are played out precisely through the great scenes. The article that follows and that I will cite testifies best to this. Even the title is significant: "Gorbachev was aware of the putsch that shook Moscow in August 1991." This echoed what we said: "Ramiz Alia was well aware of the events in Albania in 1991. He was even the organizer."

The parallels between events in the former Soviet Union and in Albania on a smaller scale — because events were organized according to country size — are so obvious that they took place without commentary. We can see plainly that what happened in Albania directly proceeded from events in Moscow. We can follow the reasoning in this interview and stay faithful to it while making a few necessary additions to support our opinion. It is not necessary to refer to the parallels that Dom Simon highlights when he speaks of the French Revolution because the events, so fresh in the memories of friends and enemies, permit us to discover that each scene in Russia gave the impression of a democratic farce. This farce continues in Albania.

Pavlov himself asked that his interview, given in prison, be published ten years later when history would prove him right and the whole world would perhaps see, too late, that he had spoken the truth. The Soviet Prime Minister stated, "There is no doubt, and many have said it from 1991, that the coup was conceived to eliminate the federal State, but that the final goal of the insurgents was to attribute to Gorbachev real power." That was indispensable for receiving western credit. Few people know that today. Nevertheless, it is a little strange that to achieve this objective, the first thing that the putschists did was to isolate the head of State and the Party, and to present him as ill — as almost mentally incapable of carrying out his functions. Many people suspected that Gorbachev was fully aware of the plot and wanted to disappear from the action, to stay in the corridors, and to leave everything in the hands of the putschists so that they would take on the most ordinary work in order to come back and totally retake full dictatorial powers in their hands. This was openly exposed by the putschists in a press conference organized on the occasion of the tenth anniversary of the tragic events. Above all, we currently have knowledge of the minutes from secret meetings that decreed the changes merely for the sake of survival.

Should someone answer for this in the name of justice for having created such a situation? The former Prime Minister was asked that question. No, he was of the opinion that at that moment a legal process would help no one and bring no concrete result. It would lead to a tense situation without any use. He deemed such a process completely undesirable.

It would be understandable for him to think in such terms because he too would join the ranks of the accused if ever a "Nuremberg Process" for communism took place, even if too late. It would be a different process from that of Nazism and be similar to that for cholera. In waiting for this day, events will develop in such a manner that the West, which never has enough money, will continue to open its medical bag to treat the bloating, which is weighed down by old age and eaten by ancient and new rheumatisms from the Red East. History testifies that the Western world, "yesteryear's prostitute," ceaselessly changes clients!

But let us return to the interview. "My situation is too complicated," the former Prime Minister said. "I do not know what else to add. These are things that did not depend on me, on which I can no longer make any commentaries."

His reluctance gives us the sense that the truth has not yet totally come out and that ten years are insufficient for unearthing dirty backroom games.

This prompts another question: "Do you think that Gorbachev was aware of or, even better, that he had the principal role in the preparation of the putsch?"

"I do not think so. I know. I am sure that he was completely aware that a putsch was being engineered, or to say it better still: the farce of the putsch," the former Prime Minister responded.

The journalist continued: "But you were in power. No one would dare stop you from continuing. Why then would they want to spark such an initiative?"

The former Prime Minister responded: "Everyone could see that the country was sliding towards fracturing, towards a total collapse, not only politically, but above all economically. It was therefore natural to have more discussions to discover the necessary path in order to avoid catastrophe. It was for this reason that we had the proclamation of the state of emergency. That was not done by chance. Such decisions are not improvised. They are weighed very carefully before being taken. You and me, we can meet in a cafe and decide how to pass the weekend, but that does not happen for decreeing a state of emergency. These decisions are studied and taken elsewhere and in a different manner.

If we analyze the two teams, Gorbachev and Yeltsin, we can affirm that what constitutes a value with one is an alternative with the other. Gorbachev wanted to make a good impression in each case. But one cannot be good and strong at the same time," the former Prime Minister added.

Our *Sali Berisha* came to my spirit. He wanted to show himself on good terms with everyone at the same time. People say that one day, when visiting an institution for the physically handicapped, he spoke in the official language to make everyone happy, though it differed from the language spoken in his birth area of Tropojë: "You need me, and I need you! You are the future of Albania!" I assure you that he was not wrong!

The former Soviet Prime Minister continued: "I do not at all like words like *putsch*, *coup d'Etat*, or *insurrection*, which are journalistic terms, without forgetting that these words—in adding to them the word *criminal*, to include those who participated in the farce of the coup d'Etat—were put into circulation by the President of the Republic himself. It is even stronger when we consider the fact that no investigation was ever carried out on this matter in order to understand the legal aspects of these events. In such conditions, it is totally illegitimate to want to impose your point of view on public opinion and on the international community. Above all for a President."

"In this period," the former Prime Minister continued, "given that I knew Gorbachev up close, it would have been best for me to think that he would be able to betray me. I should have learned from Shevardnadze's experience (Shevardnadze was foreign minister during perestroika), Iakovlev's experience (he was an ideologue of perestroika), and those of many others. I should have attached much more attention to this eventuality, knowing that he was capable of abandoning even those most faithful to him."

"Nevertheless, the real problem was that the Soviet Union was moving inevitably towards decomposition. It was the simple logic of events. The Soviet Union had to come undone because it had no force of existence. It was in fact reduced to this state. Despite the very critical situation, the Soviet Union succeeded in retaining stability by confronting all the attempts to make it blow up—interior and exterior, though clearly much more interior. Faced with such a state of affairs, with the country moving towards collapse, Gorbachev and the rapid changes that he would bring were needed because he could assure Western credit. It was not a matter of a little provisional aid, but a lot of long-term credit, without which the country could no longer stay afloat because economic reconstruction and modernization were needed. The West was ready to help Gorbachev. However, no one ever managed to solve these problems. Formal accords were ready, but the lines of credit were blocked because the world of money does not easily move things along. It does not give money unless absolutely sure that it will not loose it, but also not before calculating the benefits it will gain."

"That is why during the meetings, we often heard it said. 'We are ready but, excuse us, we would first like to know, Mr. Gorbachev, how much of your power is real? Is it reliable? Is the Soviet economy really able to guarantee our investments?' They believed that without

Gorbachev they would not get the credits. It was not a question of personal sympathies. In politics, personal sympathies play a role only to a certain point. But there was a difficult reality: the country needed credits and could only receive them through Gorbachev, and always with the guarantee that he would have real power in the future. The dilemma was the following: If Gorbachev left, there would not be any credits, but if things continued along the same path, economic restructuring and modernization would require much more time and enormous sums. The politician who opted for such a path would not stay in power for very long because the people could not wait forever even if, in our country, people loved fables!"

We will stop the interview here. It coincides with the Albanian reality of the last ten years of fairy tales and fables. Under the Hoxha regime, people often told the following: "Enver Hoxha wanted to hear some stories. He was told that there was an old gentleman in Mirditë, a very good storyteller. He was brought in. The mountaineer of Mirditë, in traditional attire, walked with his clogs on the thick carpets of the palace of the King. For him it was like trekking over the prairies of his region. Enver received him very gracefully because the storyteller was linked to the people like a fingernail to a finger. Enver said, 'Do you see this carpet on which you walk with your boots? We took it from Verlaci so that you, man of the people, could walk on it. Everything that we have here, you also have at Mirditë!' Then he showed the man a large color television and said to him: 'Look at the television. Do you see what the Party has done for you? Everything that we have here, you also have at Mirditë!' And in such a way, Enver showed him objects, one after the other, in proudly affirming that everything that the King had, the slave also owned. Finally, the old man of Mirditë could not hold it in any longer, cut him off, and said: 'Tell me, then, did you call me here so that I can tell you stories, or so that you can tell me some?'"

So that is how it is. Even Albanians love stories. For more than half a century, they have listened to stories but without being capable of confronting the unfortunate reality of who was destroying their everyday lives. Will the truth be revealed one day? Perhaps if people saw Ramiz Alia, Sali Berisha, and *Fatos Nano*[1] lining up in order

---

1 *Fatos Nano* — Born in 1952, he was a Marxist economist with a doctorate in political economy and an Albanian Statesman. He was head of the Government of the People's Socialist Republic of Albania three times. He left politics in 2005.

to confess to Dom Simon! Even in this case, the people would not trust it because, first of all, Dom Simon does not have the right to make a confession public. Then, after so many lies and crimes, one more lie in the confessional will not change the balance. After all, some believe only when God's name helps to acquire credits from the West. At this moment, they can say, as Berisha at the end of his meetings, "God is alive!"

Ana Luka

Political-religious Situation in Albania in 2020

The communist dictatorship collapsed abruptly in Albania in 1991, leaving the people in moral distress and the country in a very poor state economically and facing severe market laws. Turkey and Islam are struggling to rebuild the spider web of their influence. The old Chinese military bases have become American.

Albanians work mainly in agriculture. They opened a multitude of businesses in the cities. But there are hardly any industries that create jobs. New roads have been built, but not enough to cope with the explosion in car traffic. The political parties have changed their names, but they are still governed by the same politicians, refusing to let go of power. The richest Albanians rub shoulders with the poorest and there is hardly anyone in the middle.

"Religion and culture are the two differences between man and animal. 'Leave the people ten years without priests and they will return to the animal state,' said the Curé of Ars, Saint Jean-Marie Vianney. This is what happened in Albania. Today, most of the Albanians ignore God, have become uneducated, and think only of obtaining money dishonestly, and this at all levels of society" (Dom Simon Jubani).

Today corruption is very widespread here. Many people steal money from others and from the community. "Under Communism, these Albanians stole the money with one hand. Now that they have freedom, they steal with both hands. This is how they conceive of the concept of freedom" (Dom Simon Jubani)

The leaders are robbing international institutions and diverting the aid they receive from them for their profit. For example, the World Bank funded the rebuilding of Albanian roads, but for many years the work was not carried out. The money in State banks has been plundered by the rulers. But the international institutions have their share of responsibility in this disaster, for they did not control how the money which they had put in was spent.

Likewise, the rulers steal the people's money. Everyone remembers the emergence of pyramid banks in this country. When they collapse, all depositors are ruined. As everything under communism belonged to the State, the whole country is today plundered. Thus, in this country, a Mafia oligarchy has developed, which is richer than the State itself. Governing the country is not a service to make the Albanians happy, but it is a way for the rulers to get rich quick and dishonestly.

But many ordinary Albanians also steal public property. When communism fell, they stole the roof tiles from the old State farms (collective farms) to build their own houses. Likewise, they cut down trees for firewood. When the Government stole them on a large scale, the Albanians revolted and stole the Kalashnikovs from the State barracks. Today many Albanians have such weapons in their cellars.

Since these goods belonged to the State, Albanians believed that they belonged to everyone and therefore to each of them in particular. In Albania, stealing from the State seems normal to many Albanians. Every Albanian hates collective property today. It is individualism and resourcefulness that prevail.

The Albanian landscape is made ugly by the many factories of the former State combines, which are now closed and abandoned because they are unprofitable and not destroyed. Everything is broken, including the windows. The rail network is no longer in working order. The old roofless State farms are in ruins. Everything has to be rebuilt.

From the liberation of communism in 1991, the country covered itself with mosques, the construction of which was financed by oil money. Seeing them, the visitor can think of an Islamic invasion in this country. But they are empty. The country would remain 60% atheist. Many Albanians do not want to return to Islam, which means East, and therefore, for them, tyranny and oppression. According to the latest statistics, Islam, which represented 70% of Albanians when the Communist Government took power, today attracts only around 56% of the population. This proportion should however be put into perspective. True Muslims are probably far fewer. As in Russia, where many people call themselves "Orthodox and atheists," many Albanians define themselves as "Muslims and atheists." This means that for these people, the concept of religion is nothing more than a label, because they mix religion and nationality. And it would be more accurate to classify these "Muslim atheists" on the side of the atheists.

In 2005, the Catholic Church in Albania was restructured

with the reconstitution of five dioceses, almost all located in the North-West of the country (Shkodër-Pult, Lezhë, Sapë, Rrëshen and Tiranë-Durrës) and the Apostolic Administration of Southern Albania (Italo-Albanian rite). The bishops are still missionaries (Italian or Maltese). As early as 1991, many missionary priests, mainly from Italy and Kosovo, arrived to ensure the transition period until the arrival of indigenous priests. Churches and shrines everywhere have been rebuilt in every village and town, with the help of the brethren in the West. It is necessary to underline the exceptional contribution of Italy, at the same time in priests and religious as well as financial means. Every diocese of Italy, from the Northern Dolomites to Southern Italy, participated extensively. The influence of Italy is particularly strong today in the Catholic region of Northwestern Albania, where Italian is the most widely spoken foreign language, more than English. During communism, knowledge of this language was maintained by many Northern Albanians who listened to television programs from neighboring Italy through satellite dishes on their balconies. In addition, the diocesan seminary of Shkodër has been rebuilt with the help of German Catholics. A new generation of young priests is beginning to emerge, which will gradually assure Albania of purely Albanian priests. Finally, the two traditional religious orders of Albania, Franciscans and Jesuits, are undergoing a revival. The missionary work which awaits these young diocesan priests and these religious is very important. The Catholic religion continues to attract the people, because for them it is synonymous with the West and freedom. This is a little biased reasoning. There will be a lot of work to be done so that the coming of young Albanians to Catholicism corresponds to real vocations. According to some sources, Catholicism in Albania today represents around 16% of the population, as opposed to 10% when the Communists took power at the end of the Second World War and the years of State atheism that followed.

The Orthodox Church of Albania is reconstituting itself similarly, mainly in the South of the country, which is the region where it is most alive. A large Orthodox cathedral has been rebuilt in the center of Tirana, the capital city.

Communism has left its mark everywhere in Albania, especially in the mentalities of the leaders and the people, and they will take a long time to heal. To change them, a new generation of young and honest politicians will have to take power and this new Government will have to spend a lot of money to educate and train the masses in Albania in honesty. However, corruption must be uprooted from oneself first.

The problem of widespread corruption is the same in all countries that have suffered under the Communist yoke. But it is in Albania that it is highest compared to the small size of the country.

Albania is potentially rich, notably possessing significant resources of raw materials, including copper mines. In order to benefit the people from these riches, the Government will have to resist the temptation to sell them to foreign interests with long teeth, in particular those of Westerners (USA, Canada, Great Britain, European Union, Norway), Russia, Turkey or China and will have to keep them in the hands of Albanian interests.

After many years of isolation, Albania is opening up to the world. This openness arouses hope and fear. Today negotiations will begin shortly for Albania's accession to the European Union. On the security level, the reader should not be afraid of it. Dom Simon always said that the Albanians of Albania, unlike some of its neighbors (Kosovo or Bosnia), represent a peaceful people. In fact, political and violent Islam does not exist in Albania. No one in Albania would ever think of killing his compatriot because he does not share the same religion or thinks differently from him. If the concept of democracy means, among other things, respect for one's neighbor who does not think for himself, then democracy in Albania today is perhaps more real than in some countries of Western Europe. And the integration of just nearly 3 million Albanians is a far less risk than letting the country go into the hands of authoritarian regimes like Turkey, Saudi Arabia or China. Today, Albania, which already geographically and historically belongs to Europe, needs the European Union, just as the latter needs Albania. Welcome, Albania, to the Western world to which you belong since your birth, but for which you will have to fight every day against your vices!

Dominique Combette

The Church in Albania:

A CHURCH ALWAYS UNDER THE CROSS BUT NEVER DESTROYED[1]

I am very touched by the request that you have made of me to bear witness to the life of the Church in Albania during the many years that we have spent at the foot of the Cross. I myself was in prison for 26 years (1963–1989), and this period of my life, the most trying physically, morally and mentally, remains at the same time in my memory today as the happiest spiritually, so much did I experience the force of the presence of Christ in me during these years of nightmare.

Unlike the other satellite communist countries of the former Soviet Union (Poland, Hungary, former Czechoslovakia, former East Germany, etc.), where priests were able to exercise their ministry relatively, or unlike the former Yugoslavia of Tito, which experienced a milder persecution, Albania saw its Church properly decimated systematically: 6 bishops murdered out of 7, 170 priests killed out of 200, 170 men and women religious slaughtered out of 200. Likewise, all our Ecclesiastic properties have been razed, which includes our churches, monasteries, shrines, schools and Catholic institutions. Everything was savagely destroyed. Likewise, the Catholic intelligentsia has been eradicated. We have experienced a real "spiritual genocide." But in the face of this great distress, God's unlimited help has never been lacking.

The most important episode of the heroic resistance of our Church took place when Enver Hoxha, head of State, wanted to suppress the three religions that exist in Albania. Out of 3 million inhabitants, there were then 300,000 Catholics, 600,000 Orthodox and 2,100,000 Muslims. Our tyrant summoned the leaders of these three religions, on pain of death, to solemnly renounce their Faith before the people, declaring that God does not exist and that religion is the opium of the people. He thus wanted to make the world believe that the

---

1 Text from Dom Simon Jubani's lecture pronounced in France on November 4, 1996

religious leaders themselves had asked him to suppress their own religion, because they had become convinced that the future belonged to communism. Since Muslim and Orthodox religious leaders were married, they were therefore more vulnerable than us. They thus sacrificed their religious family to save their earthly family and they publicly renounced their faith. On the other hand, our religious leaders, thanks to their celibacy, which allowed them complete independence from political power, refused to obey.

This heroic attitude of the clergy encouraged the faithful to gather every day on the ruins of the shrines, to pray in full view of the Police, who continued to imprison, deport and sometimes even kill. We have seen the Lord and the Blessed Mother of God, the Virgin Mary, work miracles on the ruins of the churches. Muslims and Orthodox even came to join us, and we lived with them a de facto ecumenism.

Faced with this obviously supernatural force, the Communists went to cemeteries to break crosses, which by their presence recalled a sign of religion. The Albanian faithful gathered more beautifully on the ruins of their churches to pray aloud. Thus, the Communists arrived in force and numbers in our houses to confiscate our sacred books, our crucifixes on the walls, our statuettes and our rosaries in order to remove any religious sign from Albania. When they left, we would tell them: "Wait, you forgot a cross!" "Where is it?" "That one (and we made the sign of the cross). And you cannot take it away from us!" We continued to celebrate Christmas, Easter and other religious holidays in our homes.

It is in this very special context that my personal experience took place. Everyone remembers that from 1944 onwards, the former Soviet Union had set up its only military base in the Mediterranean in Albania. If at that time a third World War had broken out, the whole of Europe would have been reduced to ashes from Albania and by means of conventional and nuclear weapons installed in bases such as those of Vlorë, Pashaliman, Giadri.

In that year, 1944, I was 17 years old and intended to become a Jesuit. I entered the Shkodër seminary. This city, with its press, its schools, its socio-charitable institutions, is the center of the Catholic Church in Albania. Its influence has spread throughout our country through its political, economic and cultural history.

In 1946, all Catholic schools were abolished. Consequently, I had to leave for Tirana, the capital, to study medicine and work there as a radiologist at the military hospital. Mobilized after a year, I was returned to civilian life in January 1950, which allowed me to return to Shkodër, my hometown, to present myself to the Primate of Albania, Archbishop Ernest Çoba (subsequently shot by the Communists), with a view to becoming a priest. He replied that he urgently needed priests, as 23 of them had been put to death, while the other 20 were in prison, 40 parishes being vacant. However, he could not order me without the permission of the Government. The latter was pursuing a policy of systematic segregation and discrimination towards the Catholic Church. Catholic seminaries were abolished, while their counterparts, Muslim and Orthodox, were subsidized by the State.

The Archbishop therefore had to transmit my application to the service of worship, to the Prime Minister, and await his response. The authorization finally arrived . . . in 1957, 7 years later! We were 7 young people who persevered in our vocation. We met in secret to study a little theology and philosophy in preparation for ordination. I worked during the day as a radiologist at Shkodër hospital. Lucky enough to be a sportsman (which helped me a lot to physically endure the years in prison), I was a member of the Shkodër football team as well as the national team.

When State authorization came in 1957, you can guess my joy and that of the Catholics of Albania, who saw a new priest ordained in the midst of religious persecution. Communist propaganda had mocked my ordination, leaving only to hear that the Church had nothing more to propose as a priest than a football player . . . For my first homily, I therefore did my best to return to the original goal with the help of a sermon which I had learned by heart by the great French preacher Bourdaloue.

I was then appointed parish priest in the region of Mirditë, the cradle of Christianity in Albania. This region heroically resisted atheism, to the point that the French historian Castellane, in his history of contemporary Albania, wrote: "If Enver Hoxha spread the revolution throughout Albania, he had to ten more years to establish it in Mirditë. Like the Vendée during the French revolution, Mirditë resisted heroically."

Thousands of Catholics died during this persecution. I carried out my ministry in the midst of the population. My Archbishop told me that our Church being the "Church of Silence," we only had to administer the sacraments and not preach.

My brother Lazër Jubani was also a priest. He was persecuted and tortured for 36 years, thrown in prison, deported, and sentenced to forced labor before finally being poisoned with arsenic, discreetly deposited in his food. The poison had its effect. He died "slowly" and in indescribable suffering.

I celebrated Mass every day and also preached. It caused me to be threatened and insulted by the communists. Every Sunday, I received letters from the Police, inviting me not to celebrate and telling me that the people had more important concerns than Mass . . . I continued to celebrate, however, without being intimidated by these threats. One evening, a group of communists broke into my rectory, pistol in hand. I told them to wait . . . and that I was going to ring the bells . . . All the people came to see what was going on. In the meantime, my intrepid visitors had disappeared...

It was only a respite: in March 1963, 6 years after my ordination, I was arrested and sentenced to forced labor in a mine, this after 4 months of severe interrogations and special treatment . . . like the deprivation of mattresses in my cell. Likewise, my hands and feet were tied, I had no food but only water to drink. I reacted to this sentence by explaining that a political prisoner is exempt from forced labor and that therefore I refuse to work. The next two years were very difficult. My feet and fists were often shackled, my hands tied to a ring attached to the wall. I was fed on bread and water. I was beaten and my body was covered with bruises. I have been treated less well than an animal. . . .

In the mines, the work was so hard that prisoners deliberately broke their hands and feet or contracted infectious diseases to be released from work and go to the hospital.

As I persisted in my "very bad temper," I was dispatched to Burrel Prison. This prison, like those of Bedeni, Vlocishti, Maliqi, Valboba, Zalle Kirit, Zalli Herrit of sinister memory, has seen thousands of Albanians pass. They were tortured there, put to death or committed suicide themselves. Their only crime was to remain true to their Faith and to refuse to join Communism.

Burell Prison consisted of 8 × 4 meter cells, in which 36 prisoners were crammed. We were as comfortable as sardines in their box, with the difference that this same space served as a dining hall, dormitory, bathroom . . . and living room. We lived in complete promiscuity, in dirt, noise and foul odors. Continuously locked up, we thought of the enviable fate of the animals, which can leave the stable to graze in the open air and benefit from a little sun. . . . You can easily imagine that the poor prisoners would go mad, get hurt, indulge in all vices, homosexuality included. These conditions of detention, common to all prisons in Albania, were intended to annihilate us physically and morally, causing us to lose all personality and dignity. The permanent confinement was so painful that those who became insane were transferred to psychiatry, where they were kept lying down, tied to their beds.

It was continual prayer and that alone that enabled me to endure these sufferings. My prison had become . . . my parish. I celebrated Mass there, confessed, gave Communion, preached, catechized and even confirmed. I also read many books that, though banned, got into the prison through the "sheep." The "sheep" were the detainees who were particularly affected by our conversations. I was very attracted to the writings of Bossuet and the greats of French literature, who are totally unknown to France's youth today. I also read the History of Philosophy . . . hidden under the cover of a book by Mao Tse-Tung.

To maintain my "bad temper," I also wrote to Enver Hoxha, our tyrant, and to all members of his clan, openly denouncing their faults, acts of tyranny, gross violations of human rights. The style of my letters was reminiscent of certain passages from the Old Testament, for example the attitude of the prophet Nathan to King David . . . No doubt this style also lacked anointing . . . I was then condemned to life imprisonment, with the added bonus of frequent additional disciplinary penalties. Ramiz Alia, who succeeded Enver Hoxha in 1985, imposed on me 18 months of solitary confinement in total darkness to destroy me from within. Enver also put me in solitary confinement, hand and foot tied. I slept on the concrete floor for a long time. I can testify today that I came out of this evil hell safe and sound through a miracle from God, prayer, reading and another gift from God, my excellent physical constitution.

The last word of Christ on the cross was: "Father, forgive them, for they do not know what they are doing." Like him, we can only forgive our torturers. We do not want them dead; our prayer is that they convert, that they live and that we rebuild Albania ruined by Marxist ideology.

In 1985, our tyrant Enver Hoxha died. The tide then turned a bit. Then, in 1989, "perestroika" had an unexpected consequence for me: my release from Burell prison. Following the remission of sentences, I only had ... 25 years to accomplish.

At that time, half of the Communist leaders sought to exterminate the other half. There were in Burell prison, the Minister of Foreign Affairs Cesti Naja, the Minister of Commerce Kilo Ngjela, the Minister of Defense Beqir Balluku etc ... They lost all dignity, spending their time denouncing each other or even fighting. The Minister of the Interior was humiliated by the guards, who addressed him in front of everyone and shouted: "Minister, come here and clean the prison toilets ... "

The universal Catholic Church made the most brilliant contribution to the fall of communism, notably through prayer, bloodshed, tears, pilgrimage. The "glasnost" and the "perestroika" made visible the triumph of Christ over the antichrist; the triumph of Gospel Truth over the lie of Marxism, the triumph of Light over darkness, the triumph of the Kingdom of God over the kingdom of the devil, the triumph of Peace diplomacy over Cold War diplomacy.

Communism in Albania produced the climax, the height of social decomposition and ignorance. It reduced a whole people to misery. It destroyed political, religious and cultural life. Today, no one wants to remain living in an Albania without schools, without suitable roads, without hospitals and in total chaos. The youth themselves seek to abandon this country, whose ignorant and lazy leaders think only of themselves.

However, as during the persecution, our Church, although very much in the minority, still remains the symbol of religious and political freedom. Today it serves as a link between Albania and Europe.

I end this lecture with a brief account of an unexpected event that occurred on November 4, 1990. Having been asked to give a Christian burial to a deceased person, I was led to celebrate the first public Mass after almost 50 years of atheism. This ceremony took place in the old cemetery of Rrëmaji in Shkodër, which was the only place in the city where a chapel remained. I celebrated by appealing to my memory, because all our liturgical books had been burned. This Mass was held in front of 50,000 faithful, where Catholics, Orthodox and Muslims mingled. In the homily, I adapted a saying from our national hero Gjergj (George) Kastrioti Skanderbeg, saying, "I did not come to bring you religion, but I have found it in your hearts."

Following this celebration, a new Mass was announced for November 11, 1990. Considerable Police reinforcements had arrived to prevent it. Everyone, including the faithful, was armed and the atmosphere was explosive. The celebration began with a minute's silence for all the Albanians that the terror regime had wiped out . . . At any moment, I risked death . . . Another priest stood behind a tree to replace me if I had been murdered. Mass went off without incident, everyone forgetting their weapons and being gripped by the simplicity and depth of the event. The Rrëmaji cemetery has become the "cemetery of the Resurrection." Crosses have been replanted there everywhere. The power of God has manifested itself, playing with a climate of terror, to transform enemies who kill each other into a people of brothers. The impact of this rally in the country was such that it forced the Tirana clan to once again recognize rights and a beginning of freedom for the Albanian people. Since then, thanks to the Holy See and to missionaries from abroad, our Church is being reborn and putting into practice the human values trampled on by half a century of atheism.

Time is always working for the Church of Christ. Communism pretended to want to build the heart of man, the family and the Nation without God. It simply confirmed to the world the word of the psalmist: "If Yahweh does not build the house, the masons toil in vain; if Yahweh does not guard the city, in vain the guard watches." Prayer joined with the blood of the martyrs obtained from God that Albania be the first Muslim country to begin to convert, as many of our brothers in Islam testify today.

> "Christus vincit!
> Christus regnat!
> Christus imperat!"[2]

---

2   Latin expression meaning: "Christ is victorious, Christ reigns, Christ commands!"

The 38 Catholic Martyrs of Communism in Albania

BEATIFIED IN SHKODËR ON NOVEMBER 5, 2016

1 ARCHBISHOP AND 1 BISHOP

1. *Archbishop Vinçens Prennushi* (September 4, 1885–March 19, 1949), Archbishop of Durrës and Primate of Albania. Died in Durrës prison following his torture at the age of 64.

2. *Bishop Frano Gjini* (February 20, 1886–March 11, 1948), bishop of the diocese of Rrëshen. Shot at the age of 62.

20 LATIN RITE DIOCESAN PRIESTS

3. *Fr. Dedë Maçaj* (February 5, 1920–March 28, 1947), priest of the Archdiocese of Shkodër-Pult. Shot during his military service following a show trial, at the age of 27.

4. *Fr. Dedë Malaj* (November 16, 1917–May 12, 1959), priest of the Archdiocese of Shkodër-Pult. Shot at the age of 42.

5. *Fr. Anton Muzaj* (May 12, 1921–1948), priest of the Archdiocese of Shkodër-Pult. Died from an illness contracted during his torture at the age of 27.

6. *Fr. Alfons Tracki* (December 2, 1896–July 18, 1946), priest of the Archdiocese of Shkodër-Pult. Considered a spy because of his German nationality. Shot at the age of 50.

7. *Fr. Dedë Plani* (January 21, 1891–April 30, 1948), priest of the Archdiocese of Shkodër-Pult. Died under torture in Shkodër Prison at the age of 57.

8. *Fr. Jak Bushati* (August 8, 1890–February 12, 1949), priest of the Archdiocese of Shkodër-Pult. Died under torture in Lezhë Prison at the age of 59. His body rests in the cathedral of Shkodër.

---

1   More details and photos of the martyrs can be found on: https://kishakatolikeshkoder.com/it/martiri-di-comunismo (in Italian).

9. *Fr. Ejëll Deda* (February 22, 1917–May 12, 1948), priest of the Archdiocese of Shkodër-Pult. Died in the Shkodër Prison Infirmary at the age of 31.

10. *Fr. Lekë Sirdani* (March 1, 1891–July 29, 1948), priest of the Archdiocese of Shkodër-Pult. Died in sewers under torture in Koplik at the age of 57.

11. *Fr. Mikel Beltoja* (May 9, 1935–February 10, 1974), priest of the Archdiocese of Shkodër-Pult. Executed in Tirana Prison Yard at the age of 39.

12. *Fr. Ndre Zadeja* (November 3, 1891–March 25, 1945), priest of the Archdiocese of Shkodër-Pult. Shot in Shkodër Prison at the age of 54.

13. *Fr. Lazër Shantoja* (September 2, 1892–March 5, 1945), priest of the Archdiocese of Shkodër-Pult. Shot in Shkodër Prison at the age of 53.

14. *Fr. Pjetër Çuni* (July 9, 1914–July 29, 1948), priest of the Archdiocese of Shkodër-Pult. Died in sewers under torture in Koplik at the age of 34.

15. *Fr. Mark Xhani* (July 10, 1909–1947), priest of the Archdiocese of Shkodër-Pult. Died under torture in Shpal at the age of 38.

16. *Fr. Ndoc Suma* (July 31, 1887–April 22, 1958), priest of the Archdiocese of Shkodër-Pult. Sentenced to 30 years in prison and forced labor. Released for serious illness. Died in Pistull at the age of 71.

17. *Fr. Marin Shkurti* (October 1, 1933–April 1969), priest of the Archdiocese of Shkodër-Pult. Shot in Djac at the age of 36.

18. *Fr. Anton Zogaj* (July 26, 1908–December 31, 1946), priest of the Archdiocese of Tirana-Durrës. Shot in the Roman port of Durres at the age of 40.

19. *Fr. Shtjefën Kurti* (December 24, 1898–October 20, 1971), priest of the Archdiocese of Tiranë-Durrës. Shot in Gurëz at the age of 73.

20. *Fr. Jul Bonati* (May 24, 1874–November 5, 1951), priest of the Archdiocese of Tiranë-Durrës. Died in prison in Durres at the age of 77.

21. *Fr. Josef Marksen* (August 5, 1906–November 16, 1949), priest of the diocese of Lezhë. Died under torture in Lezhë prison at the age of 59.

22. *Fr Luigj Prendushi* (January 24, 1896–January 24, 1947), priest of the diocese of Sapë. Shot in Shelqet "in odium fidei" (for hatred of the faith) at the age of 51.

1 CATHOLIC PRIEST OF THE BYZANTINE RITE

23. *Fr. Josif Papamihali* (September 23, 1912–October 26, 1948), priest of the Albanian Greek-Catholic Church. Sentenced to 5 years in prison and forced labor. Buried alive in Maliq, in the swamp where he fell, exhausted by forced labor. He was 36 years old.

7 FRANCISCANS

24. *Fr. Gjon Shllaku* (July 27, 1907–March 4, 1946), priest of the Franciscan order. Shot in Shkodër at age 39. His body was left there with those of Fathers Giovanni Fausti, SJ, Danjel Dajani SJ, seminarian Mark Çuni, two young people Gjelosh Lulashi and Qerim Sadiku and others.

25. *Fr. Mati Prendushi* (October 2, 1881–March 11, 1948), priest of the Franciscan order. Shot in Shkodër Prison at the age of 67.

26. *Fr. Gasper Suma* (March 23, 1897–April 16, 1950), priest of the Franciscan order. Died of cancer at Shkodër Prison at the age of 53. His body rests in the Franciscan Church of Shkoder.

27. *Fr. Serafin Koda* (April 25, 1893–May 11, 1947), priest of the Franciscan order. Died from torture at the Franciscan monastery of Lezhë, turned into a prison, at the age of 54. His body rests in the Franciscan Church in Lezhë.

28. *Fr. Bernardin Palaj* (October 2, 1894–December 2, 1946), priest of the Franciscan order. He died in Shkodër Prison as a result of torture at the age of 52.

29. *Fr. Ciprijan Nikaj* (July 19, 1900–March 11, 1948), priest of the Franciscan order. Shot in Shkodër at the age of 48.

30. *Fr. Karl Serreqi* (February 26, 1911–April 4, 1954), priest of the Franciscan order. He died in prison as a result of his torture. Died of a heart attack in Burrel prison at the age of 43. Martyr of the secrecy of the confessional.

3 JESUITS

31. *Fr. Giovanni Fausti* (October 19, 1899–March 4, 1946), priest of the Society of Jesus. Shot in Shkodër Prison at the age of 47. His body was left there with those of Fathers Danjel Dajani, SJ, and Gjon Shllaku, OFM, seminarian Mark Çuni, two young people Gjelosh Lulashi and Qerim Sadiku and others.

32. *Fr. Danjel Dajani* (December 2, 1906–March 4, 1946), priest of the Society of Jesus. Shot in Shkodër Prison at the age of 40. His body was left there with those of Fathers Danjel Dajani, SJ, and Gjon Shllaku, OFM, seminarian Mark Çuni, two young people, Gjelosh Lulashi and Qerim Sadiku, and others.

33. *Br. Gjon Pantalija* (June 2, 1887–October 31, 1947), religious brother of the Society of Jesus. Died under torture in Shkodër at the age of 60.

I SEMINARIAN

34. *Mark Çuni* (September 30, 1919–March 4, 1946), seminarian of the Archdiocese of Shkodër-Pult. Shot in Shkoder at the age of 27. His body was left behind along with those of Fathers Danjel Dajani, SJ, Giovanni Fausti, SJ, Gjon Shllaku, OFM, two young people Gjelosh Lulashi and Qerim Sadiku, and others.

I POSTULANT TO A RELIGIOUS ORDER

35. *Marije Tuci* (April 12, 1928–October 24, 1950), postulant in the order of the Stigmatine Sisters (Franciscan family), of the Archdiocese of Shkodër-Pult. Died in Shkodër Hospital as a result of her torture, at the age of 22.

3 LAYMEN

36. *Gjelosh Lulashi* (September 2, 1925–March 4, 1946), layman of the Archdiocese of Shkodër-Pult. Shot in Shkodër at the age of 21. His body was left there with those of Fathers Danjel Dajani, SJ, Giovanni Fausti, SJ, Gjon Shllaku, OFM, seminarian Mark Çuni, young Qerim Sadiku and others.

37. *Qerim Sadiku* (November 18, 1919–March 4, 1946), layman of the Archdiocese of Shkodër-Pult. Shot in Shkodër at the age of 27. His body was left there with those of Fathers Danjel Dajani, SJ, Giovanni Fausti, SJ, Gjon Shllaku, OFM, seminarian Mark Çuni, young Gjelosh Lulashi and others.

38. *Fran Mirakaj* (1917–September 1946), layman of the Archdiocese of Shkodër-Pult. Shot in Shkodër at the age of 30. His body was left there with those of Fathers Danjel Dajani, SJ, Giovanni Fausti, SJ, Gjon Shllaku, OFM, seminarian Mark Çuni, two young people, Gjelosh Lulashi and Qerim Sadiku, and others.

IN THE COURSE OF BEATIFICATION

Must be added

Fr. Gjon Gazulli (diocesan priest of the Latin rite). Imprisoned in the Franciscan convent of Lezhë transformed into a prison. Died from torture in Lezhë, at the age of 54.

Fr. Luigj Paliq (Franciscan priest). Martyred near Gjakovë (Kosovo), at the age of 34, for refusing to become an Orthodox priest whose cause for beatification has not been completed (2020).

APPENDIX [C]
Maps and Additional Photos

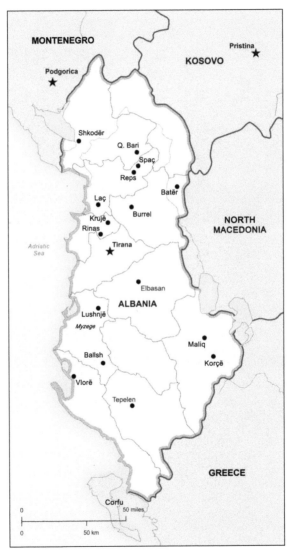

1. Prisons and camps in communist Albania

2. *Northern Albania*

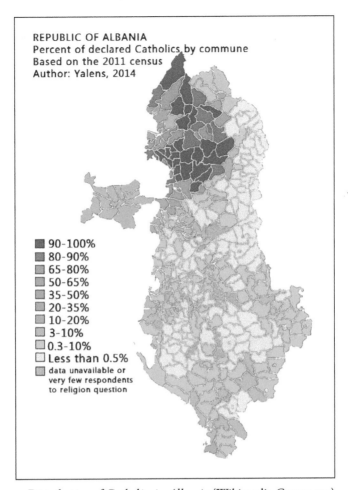

REPUBLIC OF ALBANIA
Percent of declared Catholics by commune
Based on the 2011 census
Author: Yalens, 2014

■ 90-100%
■ 80-90%
■ 65-80%
■ 50-65%
■ 35-50%
■ 20-35%
■ 10-20%
■ 3-10%
□ 0.3-10%
□ Less than 0.5%
▨ data unavailable or
   very few respondents
   to religion question

3. Distribution of Catholics in Albania (Wikimedia Commons)
Why are almost all Catholic Albanians in the North?
Before the 15th century all of Albania was Catholic. At this
date, the country was invaded by the Ottoman Turks from
the South. Frightened Southern Catholics took refuge in the
North or fled to Southern Italy. Those who have become
Muslims have become so by force and under the threat of
bayonets. Islam in Albania is not a freely chosen religion
but an imposed one. Muslims in Albania therefore retain a
background of Christian culture, which makes them immune
against politico-religious fundamentalism.

4. Dom Simon in France. (1995)

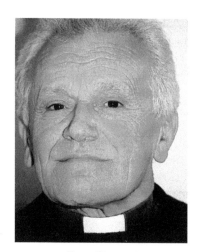

*5. Dom Simon in
France. (1996)*

*6. Dom Simon in
Albania. (1999)*

7. Dom Simon in front of his new jeep replacing the old one (2001).

8a. Dom Simon's jeep, nicknamed his white wolf, on the tracks leading to his parishes. At the wheel, Dominique Combette, author of the preface and postface of this book (2001).

8b. Dominique Combette following Dom Simon in his pastoral ministry with the old Toyota jeep (2001).

9. Dom Simon hearing confessions in a hangar in Milot in the absence of a church (1993). Photo: Famille Chrétienne

10. Dom Simon hearing confessions in the open air (1993). Photo: Famille Chrétienne

11. Dom Simon celebrating Mass in the open air due to the absence of a church (1993). Photo: Famille Chrétienne

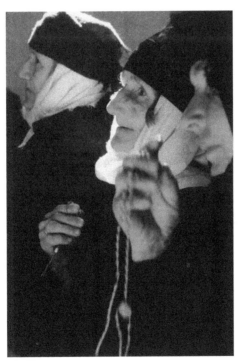

12. Dom Simon's faithful reciting the Rosary (1993.) Photo: Famille Chrétienne

13. Kalivaç (Mirditë), Dom Simon's mission center. Church and monastery rebuilt thanks to the support of the Catholic brothers from the West (1998).

14. The church in Kalivaç being rebuilt (1998).

15. Kaftalli—Mass outside in front of the school due to the lack of a church and to the refusal of the communist director of the school to celebrate inside (1999).

16. Mass in the open air due to lack of a church in Kaftalli (1999).

17. Kaftalli — Dom Simon handing over posters of Mary to his faithful (1999).

18. Ceremony to Mary in the open air due to the lack of a church in Kaftalli (1999).

19. Korthpulë—Parish church's reconstruction (1999).

20. Korthpulë—Parish church's reconstruction (1999).

21. Gomsiqe — Dom Simon with his faithful (2001).

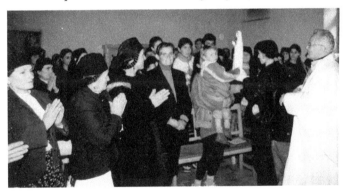

22. Dom Simon with his faithful in Gomsiqe (2001).

23. Vigu — Parish church's reconstruction (1999).

24. Ungrej — Rebuilt church (1999).

25. Spiten — Dom Simon in front of the rebuilt church (1998).

26. Shkodër — Tomb of Dom Simon in Rrëmaji cemetery's chapel (place of the first public mass on 4 November 1990).

27. Shkodër — Former Tomb of Dom Simon — Current grave of Dom Lazër Jubani and family.

"On this plain of Rrëmaji, Dom Simon Jubani, called, protected and carried to triumph by more than 50,000 believers of Shkodër, courageous people of the three religious denominations, in the midst of communist terror, which he challenged without compromise, celebrated on 4th and 11th of November 1990, the first public Masses and held the first programmatic speeches for the future after 24 years of silence. From the catacombs the Church heard the first signal of the bell which had been carefully hidden in the land of Rrusti's family. The sound of this bell heralded the end of the darkest era in the history of Albania. It was the national spiritual awakening and the starting point for all other freedoms. This event of international significance shifted the world's attention to Tirana with a particular focus on the heroic, martyr and democratic city of Shkodër. These Masses celebrated in this historic place were plebiscitary declarations of a people who love God and the spontaneous beginning of an ecumenical dialogue between the three confessions" (*Translation of the epitaph on the grave*).

28. Enver Hoxha (1908–1985) ca. 1971

29. Nexhmije Hoxha (1921–2020),
wife of Enver Hoxha (ca. 1944).

30. Vaso Pasha (1825–1892)

31. Tuk Jakova (1914–1959)

32. Ernest Koliqi (1903–1975)

33. Martin Camaj (1925–1992)

34. Father Gjergj Fishta OFM (1871–1940)

35. Fan Noli (1882–1965), ca. 1924

36. Fan Noli as bishop of the Orthodox Autocephalous Church of Albania (1939)

37. Ahmet Zogu (1895–1961)

38. Ismali Qemali (1844–1919)

39. Faik Bej Konica (1875–1942)

40. Ramiz Alia (1925–2011)

41. Hilmi Seiti (1922–1960)

42. Bardhok Biba (1920–1949)

43. Gjergj Kastrioti Skanderbeg (1405–1468)

44. *Mehmet Shehu (1913–1981)*

45. *Father Anton Harapi OFM (1888–1946)*

46. Father Gjon Shllaku OFM (1907–1946)

47. Dom Ndre Zadeja (1891–1945)

48. Prek Pjetër Cali (1872–1945)

49. Luigj Gurakuqi (1879–1925)

50. Sami Bey Frashëri (1850–1904)

51. The trial of four Catholic clergymen in Shkodër (April 27–29, 1977)

52. Father Zef Pllumi OFM (1904–2007)

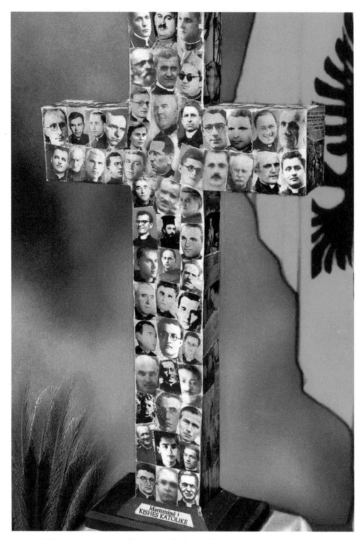

53. The 56 martyrs of the Catholic Church killed by the Atheist communist regime in Albania.

Joseph Bamberg studied medieval and intellectual history, theology, and education. His interests include medieval, Russian, and Church history, the imagination, virtue ethics, and Greek philosophy as spiritual exercise. He prepares students for university by teaching essay writing, advanced reading, literature, and history. His teaching specialty is exam preparation. He has been working on building a holistic vision of education, spiritual and psychological development, and aesthetics, and how this all expresses the truth.

CPSIA information can be obtained
at www.ICGtesting.com
Printed in the USA
LVHW072016140921
697832LV00018B/624/J